Chimes at Midnight

Rutgers Films in Print

Charles Affron, Mirella Jona Affron, and Robert Lyons, editors

Chimes at Midnight

Orson Welles,
director

Bridget Gellert Lyons,
editor

Rutgers University Press

New Brunswick and London

Chimes at midnight/Orson Welles, director; Bridget Gellert Lyons, editor.

    p. cm.—(Rutgers films in print; v. 11)

    "Welles' filmography": p.

    Bibliography: p.

    Contains an introd., continuity script of the film, an interview with Welles, reviews, and commentaries.

    ISBN 0-8135-1338-3

    ISBN 0-8135-1339-1 (pbk.)

    1. Falstaff, John, Sir (Fictitious character)—Drama. 2. Chimes at midnight (Motion picture) 3. Falstaff, John, Sir (Fictitious character) 4. Welles, Orson, 1915——Interviews. I. Welles, Orson, 1915– II. Lyons, Bridget Gellert. III. Chimes at midnight (Motion picture) IV. Series.

PN1997.C46437   1988

791.43'72—dc19   88-9420

                          CIP

British Cataloging-in-Publication information available

All photographs are reproduced courtesy of the Museum of Modern Art/Film Stills Archive.

Juan Cobos and Miguel Rubio, "Welles and Falstaff: An Interview," *Sight and Sound* 35 (Autumn 1966): 158–161, reprinted by permission. Interview with Keith Baxter (February 19, 1988) reprinted by permission of Keith Baxter. Bosley Crowther's review of *Chimes at Midnight* (March 20, 1967) copyright © 1967 by The New York Times Company, reprinted by permission. Judith's Crist's review in the *New York World Journal Tribune* (March 21, 1967) reprinted by permission of Judith Crist. John Russell Taylor's review (March 23, 1967) reprinted by permission of *The Times,* London. John Coleman's review in *The New Statesman* 73 (March 31, 1967) reprinted by permission of the Statesman and Nation Publishing Company (London). Review by Penelope Houston (March 31, 1967) in *The Spectator* reprinted by permission of The New York Times Syndicate (France). Pauline Kael, "Orson Welles: There Ain't No Way" (June 24, 1967) copyright © 1967 by The New Republic, Inc., reprinted by permission of *The New Republic.* "Welles au pouvoir" by Serge Daney and "L'Autre face" by Pierre Duboeuf, both from *Cahiers du Cinéma* 181 (Autumn 1966); translated by Bridget Lyons, reprinted by permission of *Cahiers du Cinéma.* Cesar Lombardi Barber, *Shakespeare's Festive Comedy: A Study of Dramatic Form and Its Relation to Social Custom,* copyright © 1959 by Princeton University Press. Dudley Andrew, *Film in the Aura of Art,* copyright © 1984 by Princeton University Press. Both are reprinted by permission of Princeton University Press. Michael Anderegg, "'Every Third Word a Lie': Rhetoric and History in Orson Welles's *Chimes at Midnight,*" *Film Quarterly* 40 (Spring 1987); copyright © 1987 by the Regents of the University of California, reprinted by permission.

**To Elliot Rubinstein
In Memoriam**

Acknowledgments

I am grateful to the general editors of the Films in Print series, who have given unstinting editorial help with this project; Charles and Mirella Affron further provided a print of the film and technical expertise for the frame enlargements. For assistance of various kinds I also want to thank the following scholars and friends: Paul Bertram, Terry Comito, Gilles Delavaud, Jeffrey Engel, Laura Kendrick, Raymond Leppard, Jonathan Rosenbaum, and Peter Westergaard. Leslie Mitchner and Christina Blake of the Rutgers University Press have been unfailingly gracious and supportive, and Marilyn Campbell a scrupulous copy editor.

My greatest debt is to Robert Lyons, who has given me more help than anybody has the right to expect from a series editor, or even from a husband.

Contents

x   Contents

Introduction

The Shakespearean Camera of Orson Welles

Bridget Gellert Lyons

For Orson Welles, *Chimes at Midnight* was the culmination of an involve-ment with Shakespeare that spanned his entire career as an actor, director, and critic. Despite his long and varied association with the theater, the only plays that he chose to adapt for film were Shakespeare's. He released three Shakespearean films (*Macbeth*, *Othello*, and *Chimes*), finished another that was never released, and drafted yet another.[1] But of all Welles's Shakespearean films, *Chimes* entailed the most thorough process of transformation, partly because it is a conflation of several plays rather than the representation of a single work, and partly because its gestation in Welles's imagination was extraordinarily long, dating back to his adaptation of Shakespeare's history plays for a high school production. That original project was transformed first in 1938 into *Five Kings*[2]

1. Welles discussed his completed film, *The Merchant of Venice*, of which the middle three reels were stolen, in an interview with Bill Krohn printed in *Cahiers du Cinéma*, n.s., no. 12 (1982): 47–48. See also Jonathan Rosenbaum, "The Invisible Orson Welles: A First Inventory," *Sight and Sound* 55 (Summer 1986), for an account of the unreleased *Merchant of Venice*, and the detailed plans for *King Lear*.
2. The "five kings" were to include Henry VI and Richard III, but Welles was able to stage only the first part, dealing principally with Henry IV and Henry V, when the work was performed in Boston. A typescript at the New York Public Library, Library of the Performing Arts at Lincoln Center, indicates that while Welles followed the Shakespearean scenes he used more exactly than he did in *Chimes*, he was even more indebted to Holinshed, whose chronicles were used for a continuing choral commentary. For a discussion of Welles's theatrical sources for *Chimes*, see Robert Hapgood, "'Chimes at Midnight' from Stage to Screen: The Art of Adaptation," *Shakespeare Survey* 39 (1987): 39–52.

(an undertaking so ambitious that, ironically, the need to finance it took Welles to Hollywood), then in 1960 into the stage production of *Chimes* in Ireland, and finally into the film, which was shot in Spain and first released in 1966.

Paradoxically, Welles's most assertive adaptation was inspired by the figure he considered Shakespeare's greatest creation, Falstaff. For Welles, the plays represented, especially in the banishment and death of Falstaff, "the death of Merrie England. . . . the age of chivalry, of simplicity, of Maytime and all that."[3] He thus elicited a nostalgic theme from Shakespeare's best-known historical cycle. This cycle had depicted, with considerable political specificity, the transition from the medieval period to a more modern one in the progression from Richard II, the last (if self-serving) medieval exponent of the divine right of kings, through the rivalries and dissensions consequent on Henry IV's illegitimate seizure of the throne, to the triumph of Henry V over the French at Agincourt in 1415.

Although Welles used all four plays of this historical tetralogy,[4] his main sources were the two parts of *Henry IV,* which juxtapose Falstaff—his championing of physical appetite (emblematized throughout by his fatness), his comic disdain for "honor" as a mere abstraction not worth the risk of life and limb, his parodies of those in authority—with the public figures of the high plot and their pretensions. But while Falstaff has always been the most memorable figure in the plays for most readers, it is Hal who is their hero. Throughout, his supple intelligence and versatility are as obvious in his speech as is his courage in his actions. Equally at home in the verse of the nobility and in the prose of the tavern, he is able to joke familiarly with Falstaff or Dame Quickly, to defend his honor before his father (whom he rescues during *Part I*'s climactic Battle of Shrewsbury), and to eulogize Hotspur, after defeating him, in moving and measured poetry. For a brief moment in history he recreates the lost chivalric ideals of honor, loyalty, and courtesy, while he is also adept in the postmedieval strategies of kingship so well understood by his father: the political effectiveness of theatrical self-display, the uses of popular (rather than merely baronial) support, and the need—never fully satisfied by Henry IV himself in his fruitless desire to go to the Holy Land—to assert an extrapolitical sanction for his rule.

3. Juan Cobos and Miguel Rubio, "Welles and Falstaff," *Sight and Sound* 35 (Autumn 1966):159. All statements by Welles or direct quotations from him, unless otherwise indicated, come from this interview, which is reprinted in this volume.
4. Welles also took some lines from *The Merry Wives of Windsor,* a comedy in which the character Falstaff figures but which is unrelated to the historical cycle.

Shakespeare makes Hal's future heroism clear by having him announce, at the end of the first scene where he appears, that he is not the tavern wastrel he appears to be, but that he will "redeem the time" and his own reputation when people least expect it, casting off his low-life companions (the chief of whom is Falstaff). The calculation in Hal's heroic transformation, and his seeming exploitation of the tavern as a learning experience, have alienated many readers, including Welles. As he noted, the emotional core of *Chimes* is the betrayal of friendship. In making Falstaff and his rejection by Hal central, Welles imbued the film with melancholy and nostalgia that are announced in its very title, taken not from the public or historical action but from Falstaff's and Shallow's reminiscences about their past: "We have heard the chimes at midnight." [5] The phrase, which is given further resonance by the repeated intoning of bells throughout the film, is associated for the audience with sadness and mortality more than with youthful carousal.

Falstaff's perspective, one that is tinged with melancholy, thus dominates *Chimes* from the start. Even before the film's credits come on, the camera follows Falstaff and Shallow, two small figures making their way, one with the aid of a cane, through a snowy landscape, in an extreme long shot that first seems to obliterate them in white space. The wintery scene is succeeded by a closeup of the two men, their faces lit by the fireplace flames inside Shallow's house, and it is here that Welles introduces part of the humorously maudlin "chimes-at-midnight" dialogue from *2 Henry IV*—to be repeated with variations once more before the film is over—in which the two old men recall (with what Falstaff takes to be mock grandiosity) their dead or aging acquaintances and the amorous and heroic feats of their past. Shallow looks at Falstaff during the conversation ("said I well, Sir John?"), but Falstaff's eyes are unfocused, introspective. As the credits come on with some rousing martial music, the film gives the impression of being the memory of the two old men by the fire.

The precredit sequence is only the first of many indications that *Chimes* will work as much by orchestrated thematic and imagistic contrasts as by logical and sequential dramatic progression. The same could be said of the imagery behind the scrolling of the credits. An army is shown moving across the screen through the countryside, but it is not a heroic one. Rather, the soldiers straggle across in disarray, carrying a variety of weapons, and the wind blows off the hat of one of

5. *Chimes* was first released in some countries under the title *Falstaff*, one which Welles later claimed to prefer for its simplicity (see the interview in *L'Avant-Scène* 291/292 [July 1–15, 1982]: 10). Both titles deemphasize the public, historical plot.

the men, who tries to retrieve it. In images that foreshadow the battle scenes later, nature and accident intervene to disrupt the postures of the conventionally glamorized army: orderly, uniform, imperturbable. When the men do take up symmetrical and stylized positions at the end of the credit sequence, it is in front of a series of gallows (gallows that recur after the Battle of Shrewsbury), an image of the brutality, rather than the heroism, of warfare.

For Welles, the artistic problem posed by *Chimes* was how to render in spatial and pictorial terms his particular vision of the parallels and contrasts that were achieved by Shakespeare in language.[6] The first part of *Henry IV* creates a particularly sharp juxtaposition between the stiff world of Henry's court with its pompous verse, and the freewheeling, earthy atmosphere of the tavern, Falstaff's world, where the prose dialogue is personal, racy, and refers openly to the intimate physical life of its participants. Welles differentiates vividly between these environments in spatial terms. Extended shots of King Henry show him in large and stone-walled cathedral-like spaces, elevated on his throne, his head, seemingly disembodied, lit with bars of light from a high window behind him, distanced from the courtiers beneath him and later from the dwarfed figure of his son. The soundtrack gives hollow echoes to the formal tremolo of John Gielgud's voice as he intones Shakespeare's verse—as opposite from the give-and-take of conversation as human speech can get—enforcing the sense of chilly isolation.

The tavern, by contrast, contains small spaces (Falstaff's sleeping quarters upstairs, or the space under the eaves from which Hal and Poins spy on his lovemaking with Doll, or the tunnel-like staircase), the large communal main hall with a gallery, and the yard with animals outside, from which the castle can be seen in the distance. It is thus connected with natural scenery (and it is noteworthy that while the castle can be seen from the tavern, the reverse is not true). Until the end when Falstaff is dead, the tavern spaces are crowded with people in motion; the high-angle shot of the sheriff's entrance with his dogs looking for the Gadshill robbers is an example of choreographic virtuosity, with the tavern whores disappearing to left and right, Hal moving around pillars and upstairs, and the sheriff marching diagonally across the screen with comic implacability. Hal particularly is often in motion in the tavern: going up and down stairs, leaping onto tables, or into bed to avoid the sheriff's inquiries, twirling whores onto

---

6. For excellent observations about the relationship of the spatial effects in *Chimes* to language see Terry Comito, "Notes on Panofsky, Cassirer, and the 'Medium of the Movies,'" *Philosophy and Literature* 4 (Summer 1980): 237–240.

the screen in dance-like groupings, or moving in balletic interactions with Poins and Falstaff.

It is also Hal, however, who at least twice finds the tavern too small for him, bumping his head against the low ceilings (shots 405 and 1108)—a telling indication that this is not his true environment. Hal enjoys the exuberance of the tavern, while maintaining his distance from it, too. When he pulls one of the tavern girls into bed with him in order to outwit the sheriff and protect Falstaff (humorously visible under a trap door), Hal is, as the audience knows but the sheriff does not, completely dressed, ready to leave the moment the danger is past. Like the tavern scene as a whole, the bed and the embraceable girl are props that he is able to use convincingly but which do not define him, and in his alliance with Falstaff he has reservations that are more visible to the film's viewer than to the inhabitants of either the tavern or the court.

This doomed friendship, whose limitations are made so visually explicit, dominates the film. While Shakespeare has Hal suggest at the end of the great tavern scene in *Part 1* (II.iv) that he will banish Falstaff, there is no further prediction of that conclusion later in the play. Welles emphasizes this motif by having four other scenes end in shots of Hal turning his back on Falstaff and walking or riding away, either toward the castle or his father's encampments. The final rejection of Falstaff by Hal thus becomes, as Welles stated, the climactic episode that everything else foreshadows.[7]

The banishment of Falstaff, cruel in Shakespeare, is even more so in the film because of Welles's vision of Falstaff as the innocent "completely good man."[8] Shakespeare's Falstaff becomes a somewhat less lovable figure in *Part 2*, where he is more crass about using other people for his own advantage. Most important, his age, appetites, and possible diseases become progressively more distasteful in *Part 2*, where his first words (spoken to his Page) are, "Sirrah, you giant, what says the doctor to my water?" (I.ii.1–2). The long tavern scene in that play (II.iv) is in sharp contrast to his hilarious parodies of the King and Hal at exactly that point in *Part 1*. Falstaff's language now refers more often to venereal disease and excrement ("Empty the jordan," etc.); his encounter with Doll Tearsheet

---

7. See Samuel Crowl, "The Long Goodbye: Welles and Falstaff," *Shakespeare Quarterly* 31 (Autumn 1980):369–380. Jack J. Jorgens points out how many partings there are in the film besides those involving the Prince and Falstaff (Falstaff and Doll, Hotspur and the Prince, etc.): *Shakespeare on Film* (Bloomington: Indiana University Press, 1977), p. 114.
8. The Cobos/Rubio interview with Welles expands on this point.

(who does not appear in *Part 1*) provokes conversation that is all about age, disease, death, and repentance; and when the Prince and Poins overhear the pair, they comment scornfully on the sordidness of desire in the overaged man and his whore: "Look whe'r the withered elder hath not his poll clawed like a parrot" (II.iv.265–266).

While Welles keeps these scenes in the film, they do not come with the shock of contrast that Shakespeare's second play conveys. The mood of *Part 2*, its insistence on the passage of time and on death, has been established in the film from the start, and later the closeups of Falstaff when, for example, he tells Doll that he is old, convey the poignancy rather than the ridiculousness or sordidness of the old lover.[9]

For Welles as for Shakespeare, furthermore, Falstaff's good humor is expressed by his buoyant theatricality, and Welles downplays those moments in Shakespeare where the playacting jars inappropriately with moments of seriousness outside the tavern. Falstaff is always at his best before an audience, and Welles insures that he generally has one, transposing even such soliloquies as the famous one on the virtues of sack (*2 Henry IV*, IV.iii.83–119) into entertainments for others (in this case, on the battlefield). In the tavern, he is of course at his most delightful: ostentatiously dipping his finger into his sack and licking it, rolling his eyes before denouncing his rival Poins (with a hint of a pause and meaningful inflection: "banish . . . Poins"), playing up to his audience, which is dissolved in laughter and applause, during the great scene where he parodies the King, and above all ready to forgive Hal's jokes and barbs against himself on the assumption—deeply erroneous, as even this scene shows—that all is play. It is Welles's theatricality that softens some of Shakespeare's scenes where Falstaff can seem least attractive, such as those where he impresses his ragged band of soldiers ("food for powder," as he calls them), and allows himself to be bribed by the more prosperous ones. In Welles's conscription scene in Shallow's house, the mugging and comic byplay indulged in by Falstaff as well the other characters serves as a distraction from the potentially disturbing implications of the action. Silence, holding a pig, becomes a comic stammerer, and Moldy and Feeble (the second not at all the insignificant figure Falstaff wants to make of him) are pushed out of the frame with a piece of stock vaudevillian business—the sounds of breakage offstage as they disappear.

Welles's emphasis on Falstaff's genial bombast, free of any ulterior purpose,

9. Contributing perhaps inadvertently to the pathos of the scenes with Doll is the miscast Jeanne Moreau's intensity in that role, commented on by several early reviewers.

makes him a pointed contrast to the chilly and unspontaneous King. This opposition between Hal's two "fathers" is enforced in a variety of ways in the film. In Welles's conflation of Shakespeare's texts, he has used all those passages (including one from *Richard II*) where Henry worries about his absent son, so that the King is rarely onscreen when he is not talking to or about Hal. Falstaff's role as a competing or parodic father becomes explicit in the tavern skit where he plays King Henry, hoisted with much effort onto his "throne" (a chair on top of a table), crowned with a saucepan, imitating Gielgud's voice as he scolds Hal, with mock solemnity, for his absence at court. Whereas Henry turns away from Hal or walks past him after their confrontations in court or on the battlefield (shots 421, 962), Falstaff looks silently and affectionately after Hal's departing figure in the leave-takings mentioned earlier—it is always Hal who departs first—until the culmination of this pattern in the final rejection scene.

Welles has often been criticized for making Shakespeare's language inaudible, partly through a filmic technique that features overlapping dialogue and partly through inadvertence—the poor synchronization of image and voice, particularly at the start of the film, which he did not have the resources to correct.[10] Instead, it may be more accurate to say that the downplaying of language is selective, especially in view of the King's resonant speeches. Falstaff's feelings (like the horror of war, depicted in the virtually wordless battle sequence) are often expressed in looks rather than words, either in comic grins and winks or in extended shots of his pensive face. "Do I owe you a thousand pound?" asks the Prince at one point, in an effort to catch Falstaff in one of his more outrageous claims. "A thousand pound, Hal? A million! Thy love is worth a million, thou owest me thy love." In Welles's reading of the lines, the last phrase is almost muttered to himself and accompanied by a significant pause and look; Falstaff's capacity to talk his way out of any verbal trap is less important than the claim of love to which Hal is unequal. When Hal rides off to war along the street on which the tavern (or bawdy house) is unexpectedly located, Falstaff, hearing the horse's hooves, leaves Doll to rush to the window and look after him; the suggestion, clearly, is that his emotional ties to Hal are the strongest he has.

Welles intensifies the impression of Falstaff's innocence and benevolence, then, not only through the contrasting portrayal of the King, but also by his emphasis on the complexity and calculation of the Prince, and of such subordi-

10. For an argument that the film's occasional inaudibility was intentional on Welles's part, see Michael Anderegg, " 'Every Third Word a Lie': Rhetoric and History in Orson Welles's *Chimes at Midnight*," *Film Quarterly* 40 (Spring 1987): 18–24; reprinted in this volume.

nate characters as Poins. While Falstaff plays games to entertain himself or his audiences, or for physical gratification, Poins's tricks and games in collusion with the Prince—the Gadshill robbery of the robbers, or the scene in which the two spy on Falstaff and Doll—are intended to expose or humiliate others, usually Falstaff. (The picking of the tavern reckoning from Falstaff's pocket is significantly transferred to Poins by Welles; the Prince does it in Shakespeare.) Poins, who characterizes himself as the Prince's "shadow," is made to seem Hal's real "ill angel" (the Lord Chief Justice's phrase about Falstaff) by repeatedly positioning himself near Hal (the first shots in the tavern after he has picked Falstaff's pocket are an example) and by habitually casting furtive glances at the Prince, keeping him within eyeshot. While he takes Falstaff's jokes against himself with excessive seriousness, he is not afflicted with the melancholy that gives most of the main characters in *Chimes*—King Henry, Hal, Falstaff—a serious psychological dimension. In a variety of ways, including the deletion or transference to Falstaff of some of Poins's more affectionate epithets to Hal ("sweet honey lord," shot 74, for example), Welles insures that of the two companions often framed with the Prince, Falstaff will be perceived as the truly good-natured one.

The most important way, however, in which Welles validates Falstaff's vision is by finding even less of value in the public world and its rhetoric than Shakespeare did. Thus Welles begins the film with Ralph Richardson's recital adapted from Holinshed's *Chronicles*—made to sound like an authoritative historical perspective on the drama to follow—to the effect that Henry possibly murdered his predecessor. This subject is only hinted at in the plays.[11] After the Battle of Shrewsbury in *Chimes,* Richardson again recites from the *Chronicles,* this time about the restoration of order; the gallows visible during this passage make it obvious that a brutal and repressive "order" is being described. In this context, Falstaff's disdain for the law hardly seems problematic.

Shakespeare's plays also suggest that the King and his rivals are more serious thieves than Falstaff. But even the Gadshill episode, humorous though it is, conveys disturbing undertones of the threat that lawlessness presents to the body politic. The prosperous trader-victims of the robbery at Gadshill, who are bound

---

11. At the end of *Richard II*, Shakespeare follows one of the possibilities offered by Holinshed to account for Richard's death: Pierce of Exton acts on what he takes to be Henry's wish and commits the murder, a deed that Henry then guiltily tries to disavow. Holinshed never says as directly as Welles has him do that Henry Bolingbroke ("some say") had Richard murdered. While most of the material in Richardson's voice-overs comes from Holinshed, Welles has edited and arranged the source passages very freely.

onstage in the play and cry out that they and their descendants are "undone forever," are figures with which a considerable section of the Elizabethan audience might have identified. Furthermore, the spectacle of the heir to the throne engaged in breaking the law that it would be his charge to uphold could not have been viewed without uneasiness by this audience. For this reason, Shakespeare's Hal makes it unjokingly explicit, for example, that he will pay back all the money stolen at the robbery "with advantage." In *Chimes,* however, the trader-victims are barely visible, and the entire Gadshill sequence consists of delightfully choreographed chases marked by the Prince's larkish behavior and constant laughter, making it clear that this Hal is involved, not in a robbery, but in a boyish prank.

Because the necessity for a secure and just public world is never developed as fully by Welles as it was by Shakespeare, Hal's conflict of allegiances is altered radically in *Chimes.* At the end of *2 Henry IV,* Hal's cruelty to Falstaff is balanced by his command over himself in elevating the very Lord Chief Justice who had the courage to punish him in his earlier, lawless days. Shakespeare's Lord Chief Justice, now proclaimed by the newly crowned king as his guide and "father of my youth," represents the best side of the law: its impartiality and indifference to privilege. The *Henriad* develops a morality-play structure in which Hal is torn between two pseudo-fathers, Falstaff and the Lord Chief Justice,[12] but Welles's film emphasizes only the contrast between the cold, austere Henry and the more robust (in all senses of the word) Falstaff. The Lord Chief Justice in *Chimes* has a small part as the tight-lipped, humorless figure Falstaff takes him to be, present (together with a bishop whom Welles seems to have added) only to deny Falstaff's claim to "youthfulness" as he goes to war, and to represent one of the self-satisfied and repressive authority figures charged with implementing Falstaff's banishment at the end. With the elimination of the Lord Chief Justice as one of Hal's alternate fathers, Welles has thus drawn the lines between King Henry and Falstaff even more clearly than they are in the plays, and even more to Falstaff's advantage.

Falstaff's vision of the emptiness of "honor" gains authority in *Chimes* also because of Welles's treatment of Hotspur, who is devoted to it. Welles intensifies all the suggestions in *1 Henry IV* that the charmingly impetuous Hotspur's obsession with military glory, which both his wife Lady Percy and Hal make fun of, is

12. This is a traditional interpretation, with considerable basis in the text. See J. Dover Wilson, *The Fortunes of Falstaff* (Cambridge: Cambridge University Press, 1945), pp. 17–25, 75; or E. M. W. Tillyard, *Shakespeare's History Plays* (New York: Macmillan, 1946), pp. 264–304.

absurd and unnatural. If the King's bloodlessness and isolation contrast with the physicality of the crowded tavern scenes, Hotspur presents a third possibility for Welles: the comic intrusion of the physical into the high-flown rhetoric of public valor. As James Naremore has pointed out, Welles depicts war as a perverse displacement of sexuality, and one example, explicit in Shakespeare's text, is Hotspur's preoccupation with battle while being embraced by his wife ("banished," as she puts it, from his bed), who tries to tease signs of affection from him as he prepares to go to war.[13] Welles underscores the comedy by making Hotspur read a letter from a fellow conspirator (*1 Henry IV*, II.iii.1–18) while taking a bath, and losing the letter in the water. Trumpets sound from the battlements of the castle and suits of armor can be seen, incongruously, in the background of the hall where the bathing takes place, while an amused Lady Percy looks on from the gallery, trying to get her husband's attention. One of the most self-consciously humorous shots in the film is that of Hotspur's buttocks, naked because the covering towel has fallen, while he shouts with extravagant gestures that his roan will be his throne; the multiple meanings of "throne," elevated and debased, are expressed in the comic discrepancy between his battle cry and his accidental exposure.

The insubstantiality of Hotspur's quest is rendered also by several shots in which he walks energetically in front of blank or patterned backgrounds, so that his energy seems fruitless: he is not going anywhere. The first scene in the King's castle provides such a patterned arras as Hotspur paces back and forth restlessly in front of it, fulminating about his recent interview with Henry. His own castle, with its sections of undifferentiated stone wall, provides other such settings as he walks rapidly away from his wife. Most strikingly, he is photographed before the battle from extreme low angles against a blank sky, which (sometimes with his black-clothed fellow conspirators, Vernon and Worcester) he dominates. As Naremore has suggested, the conspirators in this scene seem to be walking on air;[14] they are not grounded. But equally, the unclouded sky offers no distinguishing marks that might give Hotspur's dynamic walk a sense of direction. By contrast, his duel with Hal as well as the shots of his death take place next to trees that provide definition lacking both in his earlier scenes and at the end of the main battle with its pervasive mud. As several critics have pointed out, the final contrast between the flowering tree and the dying young man, robbed of his youth, is explicit and ironic. By focusing on the pathos and comedy of Hotspur's

13. James Naremore, *The Magic World of Orson Welles* (New York: Oxford University Press, 1978), p. 273.
14. Ibid., p. 276.

life Welles makes him confirm Falstaff's sense of the absurdity of honor, rather than representing a different perspective.

Most important in expressing a Falstaffian vision of public events, however, is Welles's representation of the Battle of Shrewsbury. This famous sequence overturns, in every possible way, filmic portrayals of battles as culminating expressions of patriotism and military courage, including (as Welles remarked) Laurence Olivier's magnificent Battle of Agincourt in *Henry V.* Olivier's film, which was perfectly attuned to express the mood of the time of its own making during the Second World War, celebrated the heroism of Henry V's outnumbered English forces, roused to acts of courage by the stirring example and exhortations of a king fighting for a just cause and identified strongly with the common soldier. Olivier suppressed or underplayed all of Shakespeare's negative suggestions about Henry V and his enterprise: that his foreign war was a device to distract his people from domestic discontents (see the advice of Henry IV to his son, *2 Henry IV,* IV.v.212–215), that he had to indulge in hair splitting legalisms in order to establish his rights in France (the exposition of this subject is turned into pure comedy), and that he was all too comfortable with bloodshed, killing his French prisoners. Rather, Olivier amplified the indications, also suggested by Shakespeare, that Henry became the perfect Christian king, modern not in his political manipulations but in his developed subjectivity and inner struggle about the fate of his men.[15] During the Battle of Agincourt, Olivier supplies the viewer with constant and unmistakable visual and verbal cues about the battle's progress and about which side is which, including battle cries, centered shots of the leaders, differences in costumes and banners (the simple red cross of St. George carrying, of course, a highly charged nationalistic and religious meaning for the English). At its climax, Henry faces the Constable of France in single combat as the soldiers on both sides watch; the battle thus affirms chivalric values as well as nationalistic ones. And throughout, William Walton's stirring music, containing references to the fifteenth-century "Agincourt Hymn" by Dunstable, supports the visual authenticity of the film as historical representation; it builds up with increasing intensity as the battle progresses to its victorious conclusion.

Olivier's layers of artifice in *Henry V,* one purpose of which was to establish the greater reality of the climactic battle, are in fact highly self-conscious and sophisticated.[16] But for Welles, artifice in that film connoted only falsehood, or as he memorably declared, people dressed in fancy costumes charging each other

15. Dudley Andrew, *Film in the Aura of Art* (Princeton: Princeton University Press, 1984), pp. 138–142.
16. Ibid., 133–138.

on a golf course. The virtuosity of his own battle sequence, the main part of which lasts only a little over five minutes but seems longer precisely because of its lack of narrative "plot" or emphasis on heroic character, has been justly praised; it reflects not only his personal horror of war, but also the changed perspective of the 1960s, when antiwar feeling and representations of all war as absurd were common. Welles universalized the theme by applying it to a distant historical period, and since actors appearing in medieval costumes usually evoke more romantic expectations, his techniques for rendering war as meaningless violence were radical and original. Although he may not have been strictly accurate in saying that each of the over two hundred shots into which he cut his long takes in the main battle sequence represented either a blow or a counterblow,[17] he succeeded in delineating a progression in which any vestiges of chivalric heroism—unreal to start with, like the excessive grandiosity of the low-angle shots of Hotspur and his confederates, or the rows of spears raised by invisible men of both armies—are gradually eliminated.

Paradoxically, Welles is clear in his structuring of a battle whose details become more and more inglorious, fragmented, and difficult to follow. There is an obvious spatial progression downward: first knights are hoisted onto their horses by cranes and pulleys (in a satirical recollection of Olivier's film, Falstaff falls off his hoist, toppling over the men who are trying to lift him), then mounted warriors with lances extended charge, then foot soldiers hack at each other, and finally men grapple in the mud, arms and legs intertwined and sometimes twitching spasmodically, engaged in movements that lack intention or effect beyond elementary violence and self-defense. Welles's characteristic cinematic style—decentered, fragmented, sometimes obscuring an image with an arm or a piece of clothing that blacks out the lens—is brilliantly used to portray the dehumanizing nature of the war. The music, too, that accompanies the battle reinforces a pattern. At the beginning, the martial music from the credit sequence is heard on the soundtrack, but it is followed by a chorus of angelic-sounding female voices, creating an ironic counterpoint to the war. Finally, the music is overwhelmed by the clang of weapons and the screams of men and horses.

But while this downward course of the battle is clear, Welles does everything possible to disorient the viewer about what might be called its horizontal dimension. The beginning of the battle, with its charge of horses from the right and left of the screen, briefly preserves the spatial decorum of conventional battle imag-

17. See Naremore's refutation (*Magic World,* p. 271) of Welles's claim that each shot in the battle scene was a blow or counterblow. As Naremore points out, this would have made for a monotonous sequence.

ery, and gestures of encouragement from the armored figure of Falstaff, distinctive because so comically small and fat, are presumably addressed to the King's troops. But even at the start, the markers that could distinguish between the two armies (costumes, banners, or comprehensible language—even the battle cries of "Percy" and "St. George" are largely inaudible) are muted or missing. As the battle progresses, the lines between the two armies become blurred entirely, and there is no language, only groans, thuds, neighing horses, and clanking weapons. When a group of soldiers shoots arrows across the screen (shot 663, for example), this does not represent a climactic moment, as it does for the English in *Henry V*; in fact we do not know who is shooting at whom. While Hal first appears in arms with the identifying fleur-de-lys of the Prince of Wales and is briefly seen again before his duel with Hotspur (one that takes place in the presence of Falstaff alone, who misrepresents it afterwards), neither the Prince nor the other leaders are shown during the main part of the battle. This is a war of anonymous soldiers, with the camera focusing occasionally and unexpectedly on the face of a man we have never seen before (see shots 769 or 789, for example). The figure of Falstaff, waving troops onward or hiding behind trees, is in fact the only one that can be consistently identified, and the battle ends with the camera panning over a desolate field full of corpses, confirming his vision of the meaninglessness of "honor."

The battle scene is perhaps the most obvious example of the ways in which Welles inserts his sensibility into Shakespeare's plays. Yet his adaptations were always based on his deep knowledge and respect for the original texts, which are so multifaceted that they allow for numerous valid interpretations. Both stances toward Shakespeare—freedom and deference—were already evident early in his career in his appropriately titled *Everybody's Shakespeare*:

> There are, for instance, a thousand Shylocks: grim patriarchs, loving fathers, cunning orientals, and even comics with long noses. . . . Remember that every single way of playing and staging Shakespeare—as long as the way is effective—is right.[18]

At the same time (and significantly with no sense of conflict) Welles upheld the value of the original: "Still I feel that one of the very wisest ways to play Shakespeare is the way he wrote it. . . . I believe he wrote it this way not because he didn't know better but because he knew best."[19]

18. Roger Hill and Orson Welles, eds., *The Mercury Shakespeare* (New York and London: Harper and Brothers, 1939), p. 22.
19. Ibid.

If, as Welles was still asserting many years later,[20] he felt no fundamental contradiction between his veneration of Shakespeare and his freedom as a filmic adapter, it is because his camera makes apparent the kinds of connections that are already in the plays. As has been suggested, the richness of Shakespeare's treatment of English history results in part from pervasive parallels and contrasts—those between the court and the tavern in the first two scenes of *1 Henry IV,* or among Hotspur, Hal, and Falstaff throughout that play are some of the more obvious—that create a spatial dynamic alongside a narrative or chronological one.[21] In *Chimes,* such thematic juxtapositions are intensified by rapid cutting from one scene to the next, not usually in the same order as in the original. Hotspur's wish, for example, that the "sword-and-buckler Prince of Wales" be "poisoned with a pot of ale" is moved in the film to precede rather than follow the first appearance of Hal (lifting a mug to his mouth) in the tavern—a direct realization, seemingly, of Hotspur's words. In the latter part of the film the King's sad thoughts about his inability to sleep and the miseries of his high office ("Uneasy lies the head that wears the crown") are directly followed by the Prince's expression of weariness to Poins (shifted from earlier in *Part 2*). Shortly after, Falstaff in the tavern with Doll reflects on his age and melancholy; the lines that make the thematic connection with the preceding scenes explicit (Falstaff's opening "I am as melancholy as a lugged bear") are transposed from *Part 1.* By the time the Prince continues his reflections to the cynical and disbelieving Poins (with whom he is spying on Falstaff and Doll) about his sadness over the King's illness and his own entrapment in his prodigal role, the pervasiveness of melancholy for the film's main characters has become even more pointed than in Shakespeare. Similarly, the last reprise of the "chimes at midnight" conversation in Shallow's house takes place just before the scene between Hal and the dying King; the words "dead" and "death" reverberate through the old men's reminiscences about their acquaintances ("'a drew a good bow, and dead!'").

Welles's juxtaposed scenes work by contrast as well as confirmation. An example, toward the end of the film, is Hal's assurance to the assembled noblemen, as he assumes the crown, that he will convert their tears after his father's death to joy, followed by the scene in Shallow's house where Silence and Shallow cavort

---

20. See, for example, Welles's interview with Cobos, Rubio, and J. A. Pruneda, *Cahiers du Cinéma* 165 (April 1965):20.
21. For a more extended description of Shakespeare's parallels and correspondences, see C. L. Barber, "Rule and Misrule in *Henry IV,"* in *Shakespeare's Festive Comedy* (Princeton: Princeton University Press, 1959), pp. 199–202; reprinted in this volume.

drunkenly, just prior to Pistol's entrance with the joyful news of Hal's becoming king. The two images could not be more different: the lords kneeling silently in a formal pattern, listening to Hal's oratorical pronouncement from an elevated distance as he raises the crown; Shallow and Silence out of control, tripping over Shallow's scarf as they do their jig, with Falstaff in the deep background, moving forward to dominate the screen when Pistol brings the news. But the scenes are linked ironically by the idea of joyfulness, and by the false expectations that each group has of Hal as king. Hal will be much more satisfactory to the lords than they expect, though the chilly court scene indicates the limitations of such "joy," while the hopeful Falstaff and Shallow move through the winter landscape to the coronation scene and Hal's rejection. The contrast is implicit in Shakespeare; Welles amplifies it visually.

It is not only through such juxtapositions that Welles achieves a Shakespearean effect, but also through the richness and complexity that crucial images in the film convey, and the film's consequent openness to multiple responses (not all of which, it should be said, cancel each other out). Like Shakespearean scholars who differ about the degree of value Falstaff is meant to carry, critics of the film have been in no agreement about the emotional impact of images in *Chimes*. For Welles's reader as for Shakespeare's, the interpretation of a text in which historical issues of authority are so implicated in psychological and familial ones necessarily evokes responses that are personally charged. Hal in particular has been the subject of varied interpretation: a devious Machiavellian who finally takes on the chilly demeanor of his father, or a complex young man torn between conflicting loyalties who, to his credit, grows up.[22] Analogously, Falstaff has been seen by some as a lovable and loving father-figure whose faults, as Welles declared, are minor and whose goodness fundamental; but at least one reviewer perceived him as distinctly unlovable,[23] and one scholar has made the shrewd observation that if Falstaff seems less than perfect, it is because Welles's camera is sometimes at odds with his stated intentions.[24] The camera's focus on the actors' mobile and expressive faces—especially Welles's own and that of Keith Baxter as Hal—

22. For an especially negative view of Hal, see Joseph McBride, *Orson Welles* (New York: Viking Press, 1972), pp. 150–158. For a positive one see Leland Poague, " 'Reading' the Prince: Shakespeare, Welles, and Some Aspects of *Chimes at Midnight," Iowa State Journal of Research* 56 (August 1981): 57–65.

23. Judith Christ in *New York World Journal Tribune* (March 21, 1967): 16; abridged in this volume.

24. Jorgens, *Shakespeare on Film*, p. 112. Jorgens's chapter 7 on *Chimes* is illuminating generally on Welles's "double perspective."

makes an important contribution to the film's multivalent meanings.[25] Thus while *Chimes* valorizes Falstaff and the tavern more emphatically than do the plays, the total effect is not simple or unequivocal.

The climactic coronation and rejection scene is a locus for this kind of complexity. Falstaff's interjection of himself into the coronation procession can be viewed, as Naremore and others do, as the action of an entirely innocent man, interrupting the inhumanely organized ceremonies of state with looks and language denoting pure affection ("God save thee, my sweet boy. . . . My Jove! I speak to thee, my heart").[26] But even in the film, which minimizes the element of calculation in Falstaff's action, his friendship with Hal is a potential source of power ("Blessed be they that have been my friends, and woe to my Lord Chief Justice!"). The formal procession with its banners, soldiers with staffs, and stately music attracts a cheering crowd; to the extent that everybody (including the viewer of the film) enjoys a parade, Falstaff's interruption, which for added shock value takes place in the cathedral, is a self-indulgent violation of a public ceremony that is not depicted as entirely sterile.

Hal's role in this scene is also complex. On the one hand, the display of public enthusiasm that greets his entrance marks a difference in the film from any scene in which his father participated, but the shots of the new king separated from the crowd by the soldiers' spears or seen from low angle against the cathedral background (as he is throughout the rejection speech) are reminiscent of his father's isolation. The beginning of the cruel and impersonal rejection of Falstaff ("I know thee not, old man") is spoken with the new King's back to him, the visual image contradicting the words themselves; Hal knows Falstaff so well, in fact, that he does not have to look in order to identify who is talking. His joke that the grave gapes thrice wider for Falstaff than for other men recalls the jocularity of the tavern, a familiarity that Hal quickly cuts off as soon as Falstaff responds. And the confrontation between the two men when they are facing each other is by no means a simple one to read. The extended closeups of Falstaff's face convey a mixture of affection and sorrow, a collusive insistence on intimacy, and even, perhaps, some pride in the "son" who has grown up to such public eminence. These are the last shots where he dominates the screen; after his defeat, he becomes a miniaturized figure against the huge arches and walls of the city.

---

25. Welles stated that *Chimes* was an actors' film in which he paid special attention to the faces, because for him it was the faces that expressed the universal human element in the Falstaff story. *Cahiers du Cinéma* 165 (April 1965):20.
26. Naremore, *Magic World*, p. 280.

In the film's final shots, Welles demonstrates with particular vividness first his respect for Shakespeare, and then the differences between his own medium and the playwright's. In the tavern yard, now uncharacteristically quiet and empty, Bardolph, the Page, and the Hostess sit motionless with Falstaff's coffin as Poins enters. While the Hostess speaks the long passage about Falstaff's death, the unmoving camera focuses on her in one of the rare moments in the film that privileges Shakespeare's text. The sight of the Hostess is no more important to the viewer at this point than what her clumsy yet expressive language evokes: a sense of her innocence and Falstaff's, or the image of his body getting colder as she feels it, his nose as sharp as a pen, his fingers fumbling with the sheets. The shot could have been taken from a stage performance, and it is worth remembering that when Welles staged *Five Kings* many years earlier, he gave prominence to the Chorus's famous plea at the beginning of *Henry V* that the audience let its imagination be inspired by the play's language.

The relationship of language to image is changed radically in the last shot of the film, however. While Richardson's voice intones Holinshed's words about the model new king's prudence and judiciousness, the camera follows Falstaff's coffin as it is pushed into the countryside, away from the tavern but not toward the walls of the castle. The image associates death with nature, and the extreme high angle from which it is shot gives it an authoritative perspective of its own. Most obviously, it refutes or qualifies what the voice of history is saying; the camera records a truth that has been left out of the official version of events. By disjoining voice and image at the end, Welles underscores an irony implicit earlier in the film, points a moral for a story that has become as much his own as Shakespeare's, and, not least, asserts the authority of his camera in interpreting the writer who, as Welles wrote in *Everybody's Shakespeare*, "said everything" and "speaks to everyone."

Orson Welles

A Biographical Sketch

Orson Welles was born in 1915 in Kenosha, Wisconsin, to prosperous parents who were able and disposed to encourage his early interest in the arts. His mother was a concert pianist and his father a manufacturer and inventor. The family soon moved to Chicago, where young Welles was recognized as a prodigy. His precocious bent was evident in magic exhibitions, puppet shows, and amateur theatricals he put on at home, and as a child he was employed as an extra by the Chicago Opera. His parents died early, his mother when he was nine and his father six years later; he was then unofficially adopted by a close family friend who had already been a surrogate father to him, Dr. Maurice Bernstein, whom Welles memorialized many years later in the character of Bernstein in *Citizen Kane*.

Welles was sent away to the unconventional Todd School in Woodstock, Illinois, when he was a sixth grader, and there his dramatic interests were encouraged by the son of the headmaster, the athletic coach, Roger ("Skippy") Hill, who would remain a lifelong friend. In addition to performing in and directing plays (several by Shakespeare, including an ambitious *Richard III* in his final year), Welles undertook to edit, with Hill, three Shakespearean plays for stage performance under the title *Everybody's Shakespeare* (later *The Mercury Shakespeare*).

After leaving school, Welles demonstrated his strong sense of independence by setting out alone at sixteen for North Africa and Europe, then by securing an acting job with the Gate Theatre in Dublin, where among other roles he played Mercutio in *Romeo and Juliet*. When he returned to the United States, he was successful in the same role in Guthrie McClintock and Katherine Cornell's touring company, but, never diffident about his gifts, he was disappointed to be assigned the lesser role of Tybalt when he made his Broadway debut with the company in 1934. The next year, when Welles was twenty, John Houseman brought him as a director into the Harlem branch of the government-funded Federal Theater. His first and most memorable production was an innovative *Macbeth,* set in the Caribbean and performed by an all-black cast. The association of Houseman and Welles with the Federal Theater came to an end after their production of Marc Blitzstein's "labor opera" *The Cradle Will Rock* caused a political furor. They then founded the Mercury Theatre, where Welles's first directorial venture was again Shakespearean—an anti-fascist *Julius Caesar* in modern dress with Welles in the role of Brutus. In 1939, Welles persuaded the Theater Guild to undertake *Five Kings,* his ambitious conflation of Shakespeare's history plays, intended to span two evenings. Only Part 1, in which Welles played Falstaff, was staged, and financial problems quickly closed the production. Welles never lost interest in the project and more than twenty years later he again played Falstaff when he staged *Chimes at Midnight* in Ireland in 1960.

During the 1930s, Welles, thanks to his mellifluous and expressive voice, had a highly successful career in radio as well as in the theater. His radio work, including such popular roles as Lamont Cranston in *The Shadow,* made him nationally known. As a result he was able to put on The Mercury Theater of the Air, in which members of his stage company performed truncated versions of some of its productions, such as *Julius Caesar,* as well as many other literary classics, with Welles serving as narrator, commentator, and actor. The radio show caused a well-publicized panic in 1938 when it broadcast H. G. Wells's *The War of the Worlds,* about an invasion of the Earth by Martians, in the form of a newscast that many listeners took to be real.

Because of his radio and theater successes, RKO lured Welles to Hollywood in 1939 with a contract granting him unprecedented control over the films he would make at the studio. His debut was remarkable, since *Citizen Kane* (1941), which Welles both directed and starred in, is arguably the finest film ever made in Hollywood. Though recent scholarship has shown how collaborative an effort *Kane* was between Welles, screenwriter Herman Mankiewicz, cinematographer Gregg Toland, and others as well, it was still a film dominated by Welles's imagination and unconventional expressive powers. Taking as its subject newspaper magnate William Randolph Hearst, who was portrayed as both megalomaniacal and deeply pathetic, the film had to contend with a boycott in Hearst's papers and was not a financial success. But twenty years later

Kane had become fully recognized as one of the most technically innovative films ever made, and some of its cinematic devices, such as wide-angle, deep focus photography and overlapping dialogue, would remain hallmarks of Welles's style. Equally, some of its themes, such as the personal cost of power and the nostalgic pull of a more innocent past, were repeated with variations in subsequent films.

Welles followed *Kane* with *The Magnificent Ambersons* (1942), his only film in which he does not appear. *Ambersons* portrayed, again with a strong element of nostalgia, a prosperous turn-of-the-century American family facing the transition to a more mechanized modern age. When Welles left for Brazil to work on a semidocumentary, *It's All True,* the editing of *Ambersons,* completed in his absence, made it into a more conventional work and, according to Welles, destroyed its artistic integrity. *Ambersons,* expensive and unpopular, was a financial disaster for RKO; Welles was recalled from Brazil to be dropped by the studio. From this point on, Welles had to struggle against a reputation in Hollywood for being intractable, extravagant, and, perhaps most damning of all, uncommercial.

Welles's one opportunity during the 1940s to reestablish his prominence within the studio system came with *The Lady from Shanghai* (1948). Columbia Pictures chose Welles in part because he had directed a reasonably conventional film, *The Stranger* (1946), efficiently and economically, in part because the film would star Rita Hayworth, who was at the time married to Welles. But *The Lady from Shanghai,* while a brilliantly stylized thriller, had a highly complicated and confusing plot, and its casting of the glamorous Hayworth as a scheming murderess proved deeply unsettling to film audiences. As a result, Welles's commercial dependability was more questionable than ever.

Welles's final Hollywood feature of the forties foreshadowed his subsequent career more than it concluded his studio years. *Macbeth* (1948), the first of his Shakespearean films, based on a stage production in Utah, was made hurriedly on a very low budget. Welles's inventiveness was often inspired by these difficult circumstances, but here, as in later films, poverty left its mark. The conception of Macbeth in league with primitive pre–Christian forces in a barely civilized Scotland was a strong and original one, but the film suffered from an amateurish cast, some technical lapses, and an often inaudible soundtrack (exacerbated by Welles's unwise decision to ask his actors to speak with Scottish burrs).

In 1948 Welles removed to Europe, where he spent the next nine years and, with interruptions, much of the rest of his life. He could easily find work as a film actor, and one of his notable successes was as Harry Lime in Carol Reed's film set in postwar Vienna, *The Third Man* (1949). Welles came to use his film acting as a way of helping to subsidize his independent films. Thus parts in costume dramas such as *The Prince of Foxes* (1949) or *The Black Rose* (1950), as well as more challenging roles, such as Harry Lime, Will Varner in Martin Ritt's *The Long Hot Summer* (1958), or Father Mapple in John Huston's *Moby Dick* (1966) helped to defray the costs of *Othello* (1952), *Mr. Arkadin* (1955; based on Welles's own novel), and *Chimes at Midnight* (1966). *Othello,* with Welles in the title role and his old employer from Dublin, Micháel MacLiammóir, as a sexually impotent Iago, was filmed under financial and logistical difficulties so severe that Welles, in his documentary *Filming Othello* (1978), treats them as high comedy. Although the filming was intermittent and the locations in Morocco and Italy were chosen principally for reasons of economy, Welles makes brilliant use of the exotic topography and architecture to create images that both translate and complement Shakespeare's verbal ones.

Welles returned to the United States in 1953 to star in Peter Brook's television *King Lear* (a role Welles was interested in all his life) and his own stage version of the play. His last Hollywood contract as a director—obtained almost inadvertently, since he was first signed only to act in the film—came with *Touch of Evil* (1958). Welles, playing the role of a dissipated and corrupt police captain, radically reshaped a script based on an obscure pulp detective novel and transformed a minor project into a film that won first prize at the 1958 Brussels World's Fair.

Welles's later years were taken up mainly with a seemingly endless number of unfinished or unreleased projects, including *The Merchant of Venice, King Lear,* and a modernized version of *Don Quixote*. He did complete several films in the sixties and seventies, including a version of Kafka's *The Trial* (1962), *The Immortal Story* (1968), and, most notably, *Chimes at Midnight* (1966). His last film to be released in his lifetime, *F for Fake* (1973), is a collage of existing documentary and new footage about art forgery, which is generally taken to express Welles's ambivalence about the artist as a creator of illusions.

Despite the meager output of the last years, Welles was a legendary figure when he died in 1985. The avuncular impresario of television commercials and talk shows was at the same time honored by both the American and British Film Institutes, decorated by the French government (1982), written about in major biographies and numerous critical studies, and idolized by many of the important younger American directors. Today, in the world of film making and film scholarship, Welles is a figure of truly Shakespearean dimensions.

Chimes at Midnight

Chimes at Midnight

Welles's script is based primarily on Shakespeare's *Henry IV Parts 1 and 2,* but he has also drawn on *Richard II, Henry V,* and *The Merry Wives of Windsor.* The details of this conflation sometimes offer specific indications of Welles's intentions; so I have indicated by a running marginal notation the Shakespearean sources of the script. Obviously, the marginal gloss cannot give the substance of the many passages Welles deleted, but it can show where (as in some of King Henry's speeches) Welles was most faithful to original passages, where he rearranged the internal dynamics of particular scenes, or where he clarified thematic emphases by introducing passages from other plays or short phrases he made up himself. To take one example: Welles wanted the bawdy-house aspect of the tavern to be obvious to the viewer from the start, although Shakespeare makes an explicit point of this only in *Henry IV, Part 2* and *Henry V.* Early in the film, therefore, when his "plot" is still that of *Part 1,* Welles begins to incorporate some of the language on this subject from the later plays (the Hostess's comically indignant remark about her honest gentlewomen who live by the prick of their needles comes, as the marginal gloss indicates, from *Henry V*).

Although most of the lines in the film can be found in Shakespeare, Welles occasionally interpolates some language of his own, usually in the form of short neutral phrases that clarify a particular point or simply help to get a character off the screen (e.g., "Goes the Prince with you?").

I have indicated these lines with the letter "W" in the margins. All line numbers of Shakespeare's plays come from the Signet Edition (New American Library), and I have used the following abbreviations for the glosses:

H1 = *Henry IV, Part 1*
H2 = *Henry IV, Part 2*
H5 = *Henry V*
R   = *Richard II*
MW = *The Merry Wives of Windsor*
W   = Welles

The continuity script has been taken from the soundtrack of the film. Thus extreme stylistic variants on the part of the actors have been noted; for example, Welles consistently pronounces "my" as "me" ("Who picked me pocket?"), and it is his pronunciation that is recorded. The same is true for marked inflectional changes—long pauses, for example, where they are not indicated in Shakespeare. In less extreme instances, however, I have used the spelling and the punctuation of the Shakespearean text.

Since Welles focuses on Falstaff, who is featured in prose scenes, there is a far smaller proportion of poetry in *Chimes* than in the plays. Passages of poetry when they do occur are indicated with capital letters at the beginnings of lines and single virgules at the ends (/). In accordance with the conventions established by this series, elliptical dots indicate that spoken sentences have been interrupted for cinematic description, or the introduction of a subsequent shot. Therefore I have used double virgules (//) to signify elisions from Shakespeare in the spoken text. I have indicated with footnotes those speeches that Welles gives to different characters than Shakespeare did.

Occasionally, I have had to be arbitrary in assigning speeches to minor characters. Welles, for example, uses the same actor to speak lines assigned to Westmoreland and to Warwick. As "Westmoreland" appears in the cast list, I have used that name for the actor throughout, indicating by asterisks those speeches given by Shakespeare to Warwick. The more important roles of Nym and Peto, on the other hand, are played by the same actor in different costumes, and I have therefore assigned the speeches to the two different characters.

The following conventional abbreviations have been used in the descriptions of the cinematography, with the understanding that they represent approximations:

ELS = Extreme long shot
LS   = Long shot
MLS = Medium long shot
MS   = Medium shot
CU   = Closeup
ECU = Extreme closeup

Credits and Cast

Director
Orson Welles

Executive Producer
Alessandro Tasca

Producers
Emiliano Piedra, Angel Escolano

Production Company
Internacional Films Española
(Madrid)/Alpine (Basel)

Screenplay
Orson Welles, adapted from plays
by William Shakespeare

Production Manager
Gustavo Quintana

Second Unit Director
Jesús Franco

Assistant Directors
Tony Fuentes, Juan Cobos

Director of Photography
Edmond Richard

Camera Operator
Adolphe Charlet

Second Unit Photographer
Alejandro Ulloa

Editor
Fritz Mueller

Art Directors
José Antonio de la Guerra,
Mariano Erdorza

Costumes
Orson Welles

Music
Angelo Francesco Lavagnino

Musical Director
Carlo Franci

Sound Recordist
Peter Parasheles

Locations
Barcelona, Madrid, and
other parts of Spain

Process
Black and White

U.S. Release Date
March 1967

(U.S. title: *Falstaff*)
(Spanish title: *Campanadas a
Medianoche*)

Length
119 minutes

Sir John Falstaff
Orson Welles

Prince Hal
Keith Baxter

King Henry IV
John Gielgud

Doll Tearsheet
Jeanne Moreau

Mistress Quickly [Hostess]
Margaret Rutherford

Henry Percy, called Hotspur
Norman Rodway

Kate Percy
Marina Vlady

Justice Shallow
Alan Webb

Silence
Walter Chiari

Pistol
Michael Aldridge

Poins
Tony Beckley

Worcester
Fernando Rey

Westmoreland
Andrew Faulds

Northumberland
José Nieto

Prince John
Jeremy Rowe

Page
Beatrice Welles

Bardolph
Paddy Bedford

also appearing
Charles Farrell
Fernando Hilbert
Andrés Mejuto
Julio Peña
Keith Pyott

Chimes was filmed in black and white in Spain from September 1964 through April 1965 (with an interruption from late December to February). Specific locations include Avila, Cardona, and the Casa de Campo park in Madrid, where the Gadshill and battle sequences were shot. For details of the film's production, see the interview with Keith Baxter in this volume.

The Continuity Script

1. ELS: *two figures silhouetted against a snowy field cross the frame from left to right. An outcropping of rock in left foreground and the trunk of a large tree in right foreground frame the figures. An unaccompanied recorder provides background music. They pass behind the tree.*

2. LS: *the two figures, one behind the other, approach the camera on the right. The tree now is at the left, and other trees form a background. The black-clothed figures and the dark trees and rocks are set off against the snow and the light sky. As they approach, the second figure, much larger than the first, can be seen to be walking with the aid of a cane.*

   JUSTICE SHALLOW: Jesus, the days that we have seen.
   FALSTAFF: He, he.
   SHALLOW: He, he. Do you remember, since we lay all night in the Windmill, in Saint George's Field? (*Shallow moves out of the shot frame right.*)
   FALSTAFF: No more of that, Master Shallow. (*Falstaff follows Shallow out of the shot.*)

   H2 III.
   ii.225

   199–204

3. LS: *Falstaff and Shallow enter a low-roofed building, supported by wooden posts. A brazier with a wood fire is in the right foreground.*

   SHALLOW: Ha, ha, ha, ha. 'Twas a merry night. (*A bell begins to toll in the background and continues intermittently through the scene.*) Is Jane Nightwork alive?
   FALSTAFF: She lives, Master Shallow.

4. ELS: *Falstaff and Shallow enter at the far end of a large barnlike room. Its timbered roof and beams are visible.*

   SHALLOW: Doth she hold her own well?
   FALSTAFF: Old, old, Master Shallow. (*The camera tracks back slowly as Falstaff and Shallow advance toward it diagonally from right to left, crossing the center of the room.*)
   SHALLOW: Oh, no, she must be old. She cannot choose but be old.

   209–215

Certain she's old, and had Robin Nightwork . . . (*Falstaff and Shallow are now in* MS, *having just passed under one of the large beams. Shallow, behind Falstaff, motions him forward.*)

5. *Falstaff's back is silhouetted in* MLS *at the left, against the light from a blazing fireplace, as he bends under a low beam and prepares to seat himself in front of the fire. He sits down on a bench, back to the camera, and Shallow, following, prepares to sit down next to him.*

SHALLOW: . . . by old Nightwork before I came to Clement's Inn.

6. *Falstaff at the left in* ECU, *Shallow at the right in* CU, *their faces reflecting strong light from the fire.*

218–222 SHALLOW: Jesus, the days that we have seen. // Ha, Sir John? Said I well?
FALSTAFF: We have heard the chimes at midnight, Master Robert Shallow.
SHALLOW: That we have, that we have, that we have. In faith, Sir John,
225 we have. // Jesus, the days that we have seen.

Fade out.

7. *The façades and roofs of Tudor buildings extend diagonally from the right foreground into the middle distance. At the left across the horizon, horsemen gallop toward the right. Bright sunlight. A strongly rhythmic martial theme, akin to the music of a morris dance, is heard on the soundtrack and continues through the credit sequence. In the upper right frame, across the sky, the following credits appear:* HARRY SALTZMAN PRESENTS (*Text fades.*) FALSTAFF (CHIMES AT MIDNIGHT).

8. *Façades and roofs of Tudor houses now at the bottom left; walls and turrets across the horizon at the right. Credit:* PRODUCED BY EMILIANO PIEDRA AND ANGEL ESCOLANO FOR INTERNACIONAL FILMS ESPAÑOLA, S.A. *Horsemen gallop left to right in the middle distance.*

9. *The turrets of a walled town now extend diagonally from the lower left to the horizon at the right. A bare tree stands in the foreground. A single*

horseman wearing a cape is seen from the back, crossing the frame from left to right. Credit: ADAPTED FROM PLAYS BY WILLIAM SHAKE-SPEARE.

10. *A bare, flat landscape in the lower foreground, dominated by bright sky filled with dramatic cloud formations. A long and straggling line of foot soldiers begins to appear from frame left, darkly silhouetted against clouds. As the soldiers cross the screen, the following credits appear above them:* THE CAST: / ORSON WELLES, JEANNE MOREAU, MARGARET RUTHERFORD / JOHN GIELGUD, MARINA VLADY, WALTER CHIARI / MICHAEL ALDRIDGE, JULIO PENEL, TONY BECKLEY, ANDRES MEJUTO, KEITH PYOTT, JEREMY ROWE / ALAN WEBB, FERNANDO REY, KEITH BAXTER, NORMAN ROD-WAY.

11. LS: *Two soldiers cross a stone parapet from left to right. In the right background is a wooden platform reached by a ladder. As in shot 10, the sky dominates. The wind blows off the hat of the second soldier, and he turns back to retrieve it. Credit:* JOSÉ NIETO, ANDREW PAULOS,

CHARLES FARRELL, FERNANDO HILBECK, PADDY BEDFORD, BEATRICE WELLES.

12. LS: *a group of soldiers stand facing the camera at various distances, legs apart but at attention. Behind them on the right are several crude gallows with bodies hanging from each. The sky again dominates, but it is heavily overcast. Credit:* NARRATION BASED ON HOLINSHED'S CHRONICLES SPOKEN BY RALPH RICHARDSON. *Several of the soldiers bend over to lay down their weapons.*

Dissolve.

13. *A cloudless sky at first creates the effect of an empty screen.*

NARRATOR (*voice-over*): King Richard II was murdered. (*A bell begins to toll.*) Some say at the command of the Duke Henry Bolingbroke. (*Camera tilts down to reveal a medieval castle set imposingly on a sheer rockface.*) In Pomfret Castle, on February the fourteenth, 1400.

Dissolve.

The Royal Castle

14. ELS: *King Henry IV is seated on his throne at frame left, in a cavernous stone hall. The light comes, cathedral-like, from two large windows, behind and to the right of the throne, illuminating the King's head against the dark background. Light also reflects from the helmets of armed soldiers standing at attention against the wall below the window at the right.*

NARRATOR: Before this, the Duke Henry had been crowned King, though the true heir to the realm was Edmund Mortimer, who was held prisoner by the Welsh rebels. The new King was not hasty to purchase his deliverance.

15. *Three noblemen stand together in* MLS, *apparently conversing, in the lower part of the assembly hall. In the background are soldiers with long spears, standing at attention against the great stone arches of the hall, which dominate the frame. As the narration proceeds, Northumberland,*

Hotspur, and Worcester cross from the right background to MS *in center foreground, where light from a high window momentarily illuminates each in turn. They exit at the left. The camera pans slightly left as they cross.*

NARRATOR: And to prove this, Mortimer's cousins, the Percys, came to the King unto Windsor. There came Northumberland, his son Henry Percy, called Hotspur, and Worcester, whose purpose was ever to procure malice, and set things in a broil.

16. *High angle* MS: *the King seen from behind and to the left as Worcester advances, then stops near the center, some distance below the King. Soldiers and courtiers crowd the background.*

KING: Shall our coffers, then, / Be emptied to redeem a traitor home? //   HI I.iii.84-93
WORCESTER: My liege . . .
KING: No, on the barren mountain let him starve! / For I shall never hold that man my friend / Whose tongue shall ask me for one penny cost / . . .

17. *Low angle* MCU: *Hotspur left of center frame. In the lower right, boldly lit like Hotspur, is the head of a courtier wearing a hat.*

KING (*off*): . . . To ransom home revolted Mortimer.
HOTSPUR: Revolted Mortimer? / (*He moves abruptly out of the shot at the left.*)

18. *Low angle* ELS: *King Henry seated on the throne at the left, his crowned head in profile, lit from the high window. Hotspur stands on the steps below at the right. Northumberland stands below Hotspur, back to the camera. Soldiers fill the background, and the heads of soldiers can be seen in the lower foreground.*

HOTSPUR: He never did fall off, my sovereign liege, / But by the chance of war.
KING: My blood hath been too cold and temperate, / Unapt to stir at   1-4
these indignities, / And you have found me, for accordingly / You tread upon my patience.

19. MLS: *Worcester on stairs. Behind him soldiers stand at attention.*

10-15

WORCESTER: Our house, my sovereign liege, little deserves / The
scourge of greatness to be used on it— / . . . (*The camera tracks with
Worcester as he advances to the throne, then reframes him in* MCU
profile at the extreme right with the King in MS *at the extreme left.
Between the figures, vivid light comes from the single large window
above.*) . . . And that same greatness, too, which our own hands /
Have helped to make so portly.
KING: Worcester, get thee gone, for I do see / Danger and disobedience
in thine eye.

20. MLS: *Northumberland in the left foreground, with Hotspur in* LS *at
center, both on the steps to the throne. The crowd extends along the wall
behind them.*

NORTHUMBERLAND: My lord—
116-122
KING (*off*): Henceforth, / Let me not hear you speak . . .

21. MS: *Worcester, seen over the right shoulder of the King, the back of
whose head and crown fill the left side of the frame.*

KING: . . . of Mortimer, // Or you shall hear in such a kind from me /
As will displease you.

*Worcester bows with a gesture of compliance and begins to turn away
from the throne.*

22. *Northumberland, with Hotspur, as in 20.*
W
NORTHUMBERLAND (*advancing a step toward the King*): My good
lord, hear me.
KING (*off*): My Lord Northumberland, / We license . . .

23. *Low angle* CU: *the King.*

KING: . . . your departure . . . (*His eyes move toward Hotspur.*) . . .
with your son.

24. *Northumberland, with Hotspur, as in 20. Northumberland bows, turns, and descends the steps. Hotspur takes a step toward the throne, then stops.*

25. *The King, as in 23.*

26. *High angle* LS: *Hotspur, seen from behind the King, whose back domi- nates the left foreground. Hotspur bows and turns away.*

27. *Low angle* ELS: *King Henry, as in 18. Northumberland and Hotspur, descending, move out of the shot at the right.*

28. *The assembly hall below the throne, as in 15. The camera pans slightly to the right as Northumberland crosses the frame from left to right, followed by Hotspur.*

29. *Low angle* MLS: *the King on his throne, at the left, lit by strong light from the large window in the upper center.*

30. *Low angle* LS: *Worcester in right foreground, is seen from the back of the assembly hall. He waits as Northumberland and then Hotspur move down the hall toward him. Northumberland passes behind him and exits frame right. Hotspur approaches him and speaks as he passes.*

    HOTSPUR: Speak of Mortimer? / . . .   128–130

31. MCU: *Worcester.*

    HOTSPUR (*in* MCU, *passing quickly in front of Worcester, and exiting at the right*): . . . Zounds, I will speak of him, . . . (*Off.*) . . . and let my soul / Want mercy if I do not join with him!
    WORCESTER (*turning first toward the throne as Hotspur speaks, then back to follow Hotspur's departure*): Hear you, cousin, a word.

32. LS: *Northumberland and Hotspur move away from the camera, into an anteroom of the assembly hall. As Worcester moves into the frame from left, Hotspur turns toward him and toward the camera. As they meet*

Worcester looks over his shoulder back toward the assembly hall, and Hotspur pulls Worcester's robe so that the two men face each other.

153–157 HOTSPUR (*excitedly*): Hark you, uncle, did not King Richard then / Proclaim my brother Edmund Mortimer / Heir to the crown?
NORTHUMBERLAND (*joining them*): He did, myself did hear it.
HOTSPUR: Nay, then I cannot blame his cousin king, / That wished him on the barren mountains starve.

As Hotspur speaks, he turns away and passes out of the frame at the right, with Worcester in pursuit. Northumberland looks back toward the assembly hall.

WORCESTER (*overlapping*): Good cousin . . .

33. *The camera pans to follow Hotspur as he emerges through an archway into another large open hall. It frames Hotspur in* LS *at the right. He turns toward the camera to address Worcester, in* MLS *in left foreground. As Hotspur speaks, Worcester again looks back in the direction of the assembly hall.*

168–174 HOTSPUR (*still agitated, shouting*): Shall it for shame be spoken in these days, / Or fill up chronicles in time to come, / That men of your nobility and power / Did gage them both in an unjust behalf / (As both of you, God pardon it, have done) / . . . (*Worcester moves to center, back to camera, and Northumberland enters, the side of his torso filling the left foreground.*) . . . To put down Richard, that sweet lovely rose, / And plant this thorn, this canker, . . . (*Moving out of the shot at the right.*) . . . Bolingbroke?
WORCESTER (*turning toward the camera, to look after Hotspur*): Peace, cousin.

34. *The camera tracks first from left to right, then from right to left to keep Hotspur, as he moves back and forth against a patterned arras, in* MCU *profile.*

199–206 HOTSPUR: By heavens, methinks it were an easy leap / To pluck bright honor from the pale-faced moon, / Or dive into the bottom of the

deep, / Where fathom line could never touch the ground, / And pluck
up drownèd honor by the locks. // (*As return track ends, Hotspur
passes Worcester and comes face to face with Northumberland.*) But
out upon this half-faced fellowship!

35. MCU: *Worcester.*

   WORCESTER: Farewell, kinsman, I'll talk to you / . . .   232–233

36. MS: *Worcester, right, and Hotspur, left, framing Northumberland in the
   background.*

   WORCESTER: . . . When you are better tempered to attend. (*As he
      speaks, he turns and exits, frame right.*)
   HOTSPUR: Why, look you, . . . (*Exits right.*)   237–255

37. *The camera at ground level shows the back of Hotspur's cloak in center
   foreground and the edge of Worcester's cloak stationary throughout the*

*shot in left foreground. As Hotspur moves away from the camera toward
the patterned arras behind, he appears in full* LS, *waving his arms
emotionally.*

HOTSPUR: . . . I am whipped and scourged with rods, / Nettled, and
stung with pismires, when I hear / Of this vile politician, Bolingbroke.
(*Reaching the arras, he turns and advances one or two steps toward
the camera.*) In Richard's time—what do you call the place? // where
I first bowed my knee / Unto this king . . .

38. *Low angle* MLS (*tilted to the left): Worcester, framed by an arch. Northumberland in the background moves closer to Worcester.*

HOTSPUR (*off*): . . . of smiles, this Bolingbroke—. . .

39. LS: *Hotspur, as at the end of 37.*

HOTSPUR: . . .'Sblood!—when you and he came back from Ravens-
purgh—
NORTHUMBERLAND (*off*): At Berkeley Castle.
HOTSPUR: Ah! You say true. / Why, what a candy deal of courtesy /
This fawning greyhound then did proffer me! / (*Imitating the King's
voice.*) "Look, gentle Harry Percy," and "kind cousin"— / Ah! the
devil take such cozeners! (*He turns back toward the arras.*)

40. *Worcester, as in 39. Northumberland moves forward slightly, becoming
more visible beside him. A bell begins to toll and continues until the end
of the scene.*

41. *Hotspur, as in 39.*

HOTSPUR (*turning back to the two other men*): God forgive me! / Good
uncle, tell your tale . . .

42. LS: *the hall, camera at ground level, with the three men in a diagonal
line. Northumberland stands back to camera in the left foreground,
Worcester in the middle distance at the center of the frame, and Hotspur,*

*facing them, in the far distance, toward the right. A high window throws
a dramatic shaft of light above them.*

HOTSPUR: . . . for I have done.
WORCESTER: Nay, if you have not, to it again. / We will stay your
leisure.
HOTSPUR: I've done, i' faith.
WORCESTER (*turning and advancing toward Northumberland*): You,   261–266
my lord, // Shall secretly into the bosom creep / Of that same noble
prelate well-beloved, / The Archbishop.
HOTSPUR (*moving toward the others*): York, is it not? // I smell it.
Upon my life, it will do well. // (*The three men are now together in*
MLS *at the left.*) And then the powers of Scotland and of York / To   274
join with Mortimer's.   277–278
WORCESTER: And so they shall. // Brother, farewell. No further go in   289–290
this / Than I by letter shall direct our course. (*Worcester exits, at the
right; Hotspur steps forward, and both he and Northumberland look to
the right after Worcester. Since the camera remains at ground level,
the two men dominate the screen.*)
NORTHUMBERLAND: Farewell, good brother. We shall thrive, I trust.   297
HOTSPUR: All studies here I solemnly defy / Save how to gall and pinch   226–231
this Bolingbroke; / And that same sword-and-buckler Prince of Wales,
/ But that I think his father loves him not / And would be glad he met
with some mischance, / I would have him poisoned with a pot of ale.

Tavern in Eastcheap

43. CU: *the Prince is seen from slightly below, his face concealed by the
bottom of a pot of ale as he drinks from it. The top of his head is at first
cut off by the frame. As he lowers his arm, wiping his mouth, his face
becomes fully visible. He gives a whistle. In the background bells can be
heard tolling. They continue intermittently throughout the scene, but they
are particularly prominent in these opening shots and the closing
(74–81) shots.*

44. LS: *the Prince stands in the cellar of the tavern, under a low-beamed
wooden ceiling. Immediately behind him, extending diagonally to the*

background, is a row of six large kegs. In the left foreground a young Page faces the Prince. The side of another keg can be seen behind the Page. The Prince tosses his empty pot of ale to the Page and then, laughing, crosses from left to right in front of the Page. The camera pans with the Prince, then holds with the Page as the Prince rapidly leaves at the left, then pans with the Page as he turns and moves left. The Page passes in front of more rows of kegs and then in front of the Prince, now surrounded by four laughing women in MCU, who hold him and attempt to block his way. As the Page leaves at the left, the camera stays with the Prince. He spins away from the women, laughing and kissing one as he goes, then backing out of a wooden door at the left as the camera continues to pan with him.

45. MS: *the Prince, seen from the side, climbs a short flight of stairs and passes through another wooden door. The camera pans to the left with him.*

46. *High angle* LS: *the Prince ascends a steeper flight of stairs. He now has a tankard in his left hand, taken, presumably, from one of the women. In the left foreground on a landing, an old man in* MS *sits staring blankly. The Prince, now in* MCU, *turns to him.*

W

PRINCE: Where's Falstaff? (*The Prince does not stop for an answer, but moves toward the right and begins to ascend another flight of stairs. As he does so, he is answered by Bardolph and Peto sitting on the stairs.*)

H1 II.iv.
529–530

* BARDOLPH: Fast asleep.

PETO: And snoring like a horse.

47. LS: *a dark narrow corridor, with a door in the background. The Prince enters and advances toward the camera.*

48. MCU: *Poins, first in profile and then turning toward the camera. He is holding a purse.*

* Peto

POINS: I picked his pocket. (*Snoring can now be heard.*)   w

49. MCU: *the Prince in profile.*

PRINCE (*whispering*): What hast thou found? (*The camera pans with*   533–534
    him as he passes in front of Poins, turns, and stops at Poins's right.)
POINS (*whispering*): Nothing but this, my lord. (*He holds up a piece of*
    paper, which the Prince takes from him. Camera reframes them for a
    moment in MCU.)

Both men turn to the right, with the camera panning slightly to follow
them, then holding as they move away. The shot now reveals a room
with low eaves, and an interior gable supported by posts. The Prince
turns almost immediately, to move left under an eave with an opening to
the outside. Poins goes farther down the room, then makes a half-turn
around a post in the background. Meanwhile, the Prince, at the far left
in MLS, *puts his tankard on the window ledge.*

50. MS: *the Prince sits down in right foreground, with the tankard clearly*
    visible on the ledge to the left. He takes the tankard, brings it down
    toward his lap, and is about to pour the contents on Falstaff's paper. The
    sound of snoring has become louder. As he is about to pour, a particu-
    larly loud snore accompanies the appearance of a white blurred object
    at bottom of screen—Falstaff's foot under a coverlet, we soon learn—
    that knocks the tankard out of the Prince's hand and over his shoulder.
    The Prince gasps, then laughs.

51. MS: *Poins at left, next to a post. He moves out of the shot at the right.*

FALSTAFF (*off*): How now, Hal?   HI I.ii.1–14

52. MCU: *the Prince.*

FALSTAFF (*off*): What time of day is it, lad? //
PRINCE: What the devil hast thou . . . (*The Prince dives forward, dis-*
    appearing into the lower foreground.)

53. *The back of the Prince's body blocks the screen as he turns forward and sideways, to land reclining at the right on his elbow next to Falstaff, lying under bedclothes. The camera, we are now aware, is positioned near the front of Falstaff's bed. Only Falstaff's head appears outside the covers, as the Prince leans toward him.*

   PRINCE: . . . to do with the time of day? (*Falstaff gradually raises himself in the bed, with the Prince leaning toward him to stay close to his ear. The camera pans with them.*) Unless hours were cups of sack, // clocks the tongues of bawds, dials the signs of leaping houses, and the blessed sun himself a fair hot wench in flame-colored taffeta, . . . (*Falstaff throws off the bedclothes and gets up to move toward the head of the bed. The camera pans with him, leaving the Prince out of the shot.*) . . . I see no reason why thou shouldst be so superfluous as to demand the time of the day.

   FALSTAFF (*now reframed in* MS, *standing at the head of the bed. He takes his purse, which has been hanging by a peg on the wall behind the bed*): Indeed you come near me now, Hal; for we that take purses go by the moon. (*Examines his purse; then, histrionically.*) How now, who picked me pocket? Hostess! Hostess! (*He turns into the doorway behind him.*)

54. *High angle* LS: *the Hostess ascends stairs at the left. A wall of the staircase fills the frame at the right. She seems agitated, as she moves toward the camera into* CU.

   HOSTESS: Sir John!

55. *Low angle* MLS: *Falstaff descending stairs. The camera looks at the staircase wall and Falstaff is seen only at the extreme left.*

H1 III.iii.
100– 101

   FALSTAFF: I fell asleep here and had me pocket picked!

56. MS: *the Prince stands in profile in a low, cramped space next to a doorway, laughing. He turns as the Hostess enters at the left, then turns again to follow her as she slips past him and enters the doorway.*

HOSTESS: Do you think . . .   56–57

57. *Low angle* MS: *Falstaff squeezes his bulk down a very narrow staircase seemingly hewn out of rock.*

HOSTESS (*off*): . . . I keep thieves in my house?

58. *Low angle* MCU: *the Hostess descending another staircase, this one with logged walls. She turns her head back toward the Prince, who can be seen behind her on the stairs. She stops, while the Prince continues to descend until he reaches her.*

HOSTESS: My Lord, I pray you hear me.   94

59. *High angle shot of a doorway and staircase with Falstaff standing in* LS *at the bottom of the stairs, framed by the doorway there. His back is to the camera, but he half turns to look back up the stairs.*

FALSTAFF: Go to. I know you well enough.   66–69

60. *The Hostess and the Prince, as in 58. The Hostess turns her head toward the camera and begins to move down the stairs.*

HOSTESS: I know you, Sir John.

61. *Falstaff, as in 59. He moves to the right, disappearing from the doorway.*

FALSTAFF: Go to.

62. *Low angle* MLS: *the Hostess in the doorway at the top of another staircase, with the Prince partly obscured but immediately behind her. She begins to descend.*

HOSTESS: You owe me money, Sir John. And now you pick a quarrel with me . . .

63. *The camera tracks with Falstaff in* ELS *as he crosses from left to right through the center of a long room. It is the main room of a tavern, filled with long tables and benches. Many people are seated randomly on the benches. The camera is positioned at the side of the room, and as it tracks, at one point it briefly passes behind a broad vertical post, which obscures the scene.*

HOSTESS (*off*): . . . to beguile me of it.

FALSTAFF: This house is turned bawdy house. (*As he speaks, he turns back to address the room.*)

64. MCU: *the Hostess, looking down and right. A young woman stands with her hands on her hips in the right background.*

HOSTESS (*indignantly*): Bawdy house?

FALSTAFF (*off*): Picked me pocket!

The Hostess turns and begins to move to the left.

65. *A corner of the tavern room, with a wooden balcony on which two women are standing. The Prince in* LS *leaps and runs from the left into the room as the camera pans with him. His laughter provokes general laughter in the room.*

66. MS: *the Hostess descends from the balcony. She stops in* MCU *to speak.*

HOSTESS: We cannot lodge and board a dozen or fourteen gentlewomen who live honestly by the prick of their needles, but it's thought we keep a bawdy house!

67. *The Prince, as in 65. More women have appeared, both on the balcony and in the room. The Prince, moving forward, leads the general laughter.*

68. *Low angle* MS: *Falstaff lowers himself into a chair.*

FALSTAFF: Shall I not take mine ease in mine inn, but I shall have my pocket picked?

101

H5 II.i.34–36

H1 III.iii.83–84

69. *The Hostess, as in 66. She resumes her descent.*

HOSTESS: You owe me money, Sir John.   68

70. *The camera pans with the Prince in* MLS *as he approaches Falstaff's chair from behind, then reframes with the Prince at the left and Falstaff in* MS *at the right.*

PRINCE (*Falstaff's paper concealed in his hand*): What didst thou lose,   103–106
    Jack?
FALSTAFF: Wilt thou believe me, Hal? (*The Page crosses from the right, serves Falstaff a tankard, and then moves behind the Prince and out of the shot at the left.*) Some forty pounds.
PRINCE: What?
FALSTAFF: And a gold seal ring of me grandfather's worth some forty   85
    mark. (*He drinks from the tankard.*)
PRINCE: You owe mine hostess money, Jack. (*He waves the paper in   W
    front of Falstaff's face and then pulls it away. The Prince then spins behind Falstaff's chair to its other side. The camera tracks back from the Prince, revealing Poins moving past a post and advancing toward Falstaff. The camera then tracks right and reframes the three men in* MLS, *with Poins behind Falstaff frame left and the Prince right of center. The Prince continues to speak as he moves.*) You lost the   W
    reckoning. (*Reading.*) Item: a capon, two shillings and tuppence; item: H1 II.iv.
    sauce, fourpence; item: sack . . . (*Clucks in mock disapproval.*), . . .   536–
    two gallons, five shillings and eightpence. (*The Prince hands the   542
    reckoning to Falstaff.*)
* POINS (*reading over Falstaff's shoulder*): Item: anchovies and sack
    after supper, two shillings sixpence . . . (*Takes the reckoning.*); . . .
    item: bread, ha'pence. (*He crosses in front of Falstaff to join the
    Prince.*)
PRINCE: Oh, monstrous! (*He and Poins move out of the shot at the
    right.*)
FALSTAFF: (*in a conciliatory tone*): Hostess, come! (*He extends his arm   H2 II.i.154–155
    to her as she enters at the left and stands before him. Bardolph and

* Peto

MW III.
v.3

Peto enter in the background and sit against the wall, eating.) Thou must not be in this humor with me. I forgive thee. (*He pulls her to him and kisses her cheek. He gives her his tankard and, getting up, slaps her on the rump affectionately.*) Fetch me a quart of sack.

71. LS: *the main room of the tavern. The benches are crowded with people laughing, drinking, and cheering.*

72. *Falstaff crosses in front of the Prince and stands next to him, both men in* MCU, *against a wall.*

H1 I.ii.95–99

H1 III.iii.15–18

FALSTAFF: Thou hast done much harm upon me, Hal—God forgive thee for it! Before I knew thee, Hal, I knew nothing; and now am I, if a man should speak truly, little better than one of the wicked. (*The Prince begins to laugh.*) I was as virtuously given as a gentleman need to be, virtuous enough: swore a little, diced not above seven times a week, went to a bawdy house not above once in a quarter . . . (*Pauses.*) . . . of an hour. (*The Prince begins to move away from the wall, passing in front of Falstaff.*)

73. *The main room of the tavern, as in 71.*

7–11

FALSTAFF (*off*): Villainous company . . .

74. *The camera pans right, following Falstaff as he leaves Poins, passes the Prince, and stops briefly in* LS *at the left of the door to the tavern yard. Laughing, the Prince follows, first in the foreground, then circling behind him.*

FALSTAFF: . . . hath been the spoil of me. If I have not forgotten what the inside of a church is made of, call me a peppercorn, a brewer's horse. (*The camera pans right as Falstaff advances toward it, and Poins enters at the right. It reframes the three men in* MS *with Poins and the Prince close to Falstaff on each side.*) Well, I'll repent.

5

* POINS: Where shall we take a purse tomorrow, Jack?

H1 I.ii.103–109

FALSTAFF: Zounds, where thou wilt, lad. I'll make one. //

* Prince

PRINCE: I see a good amendment of life in him—from praying to purse-taking.

FALSTAFF: 'Tis my vocation, Hal. (*The camera pans right to follow Falstaff as he moves a few steps away.*) 'Tis no sin for a man to labor in his vocation.

POINS (*reentering frame from left and drawing Falstaff and the Prince to either side of him in a tight* MCU): My lads, my lads, tomorrow morning early at Gad's Hill there are pilgrims going to Canterbury with rich offerings, and traders riding to London with fat purses.   128–131

FALSTAFF: Hal, wilt thou make one?   141–145

PRINCE: Who, I rob? I a thief? Not I, by my faith.

FALSTAFF: There's neither manhood, honesty, nor good fellowship in thee, nor com'st thou not of the royal blood, if thou darest not stand for ten shillings. (*As Falstaff finishes, he crosses in front of the other two men and circles around the Prince, who turns with him to face him. Poins is now out of the frame.*)

PRINCE: I'll tarry at home.   148–151

FALSTAFF: Huh! I'll be a traitor then, when thou art king. (*He moves out of the shot at the right.*)

PRINCE: (*with a derisive whinny*): I care not! (*As the Prince begins to move toward the right after Falstaff, Poins enters from the right, passes in front of the Prince, then catches his arm with one hand and puts the other on the Prince's shoulder.*)

164–166   POINS: Ride with us, my lord. (*Whispering.*) I have a jest, a jest I cannot execute alone.

Falstaff's laughter is heard offscreen. The Prince, reacting, begins to laugh. The camera pans with him as he moves right, and reframes him and Falstaff in MS *as they embrace.*

164   * FALSTAFF (*laughing*): Oh my sweet honey lord, ride with us tomorrow.
195   PRINCE (*laughing*): I'll go with thee.
      POINS (*crossing in front from the left to rejoin the others*): We can stuff
135–136   our purses full of crowns.

The camera pans right to follow the Prince from behind as he crosses in front of the others and dashes away toward an open door leading outdoors.

195–198   PRINCE: Well then, provide us all things necessary.

Poins and Falstaff follow the Prince, Poins reaching offscreen left to fling a young woman of the tavern toward the Prince.

POINS: Farewell, my lord.
PRINCE: And meet me . . . (*He kisses the woman and swings her back to Poins, who leaves at the right embracing her.*) . . . here in East-cheap. (*The Prince, on the far side of the open door, pushes open its aperture and sticks his head back through it.*) Farewell.
23–30   FALSTAFF: Hal, when thou . . .

75. *High angle* LS: *the Prince stands in a rectangular arched opening in a high wooden fence. Behind him can be seen a roadway with passing horsemen and, in the distance, the walls and battlements of a castle.*

* Poins

When Falstaff enters at the right, the Prince steps beyond the fence and turns toward him. Falstaff follows, until he too is outside the fence with his back to the camera.

FALSTAFF: . . . art king, let not us that are squires of the night's body be called thieves of the day's beauty. Let us be . . .

76. MS: *Falstaff, just outside of entrance, is seen over the Prince's shoulder. The Prince stands in the left foreground, his back to the camera.*

FALSTAFF: . . . Diana's foresters, gentlemen of the shade, minions of the moon, men of good government, . . . (*The Prince turns away from Falstaff and faces the camera.*) . . . being governed, as the sea is, by our noble and chaste mistress the moon, under whose countenance we steal.

PRINCE: (*now serious, and seeming to speak to himself. Behind him, Falstaff remains visible*): I know you all, and will awhile uphold / The unyoked humor of your idleness. / (*He looks up toward the sun; later in the speech he lowers his eyes again.*) Yet herein will I imitate the sun, / Who doth permit the base contagious clouds / To smother up his beauty from the world, / That, when he please again to be himself, / Being wanted, he may be more wond'red at. // If all the year were playing holiday, / To sport would be as tedious as to work; / But when they seldom come, they wished-for come. // So when this loose behavior I throw off, / And pay the debt I never promisèd, // . . . (*Turning back to look at Falstaff*) . . . My reformation, . . .

199–221

77. MS: *Falstaff left of center, at entrance to tavern yard. A donkey is tethered in the background, under the balcony, tended by a page.*

PRINCE (*off*): . . . glittering o'er my fault, / Shall show . . .

78. MCU: *the Prince, with road and castle walls in background.*

PRINCE: . . . more goodly and attract more eyes / Than that which hath no foil to set it off. / I'll so offend to make offense a skill / . . . (*He winks at Falstaff and begins to turn away. Bells toll through shot 81.*)

79. MLS: *Falstaff, seen from behind in the entry, with camera slightly elevated and tilted. Beyond him, the Prince walks away toward the castle.*

PRINCE: . . . Redeeming time when men think least I will.
FALSTAFF (*after a chuckle*): I prithee, sweet wag, shall there be gallows standing . . .

60–64

80. *Falstaff, as in 77.*

FALSTAFF: . . . in England when thou art king? // Do not thou, when thou art king, hang a thief.

81. *The Prince and Falstaff, as at end of 79, but the Prince, in* ELS, *has now turned back to face Falstaff.*

68–70

PRINCE (*shouting from a distance*): No, thou shalt have the hanging of the thieves, and so become a rare hangman. (*He turns and begins to run toward the castle, as Falstaff chuckles and waves to him.*)

Hotspur's Castle

82. *Low angle* CU: *a trumpeter playing his instrument at the right, with the walls of a castle in the left background. Blare of trumpets on the soundtrack.*

83. *Low angle* LS: *the camera tracks right as it follows a group of horsemen riding below the ramparts of the castle.*

84. *Low angle* LS: *a trumpeter at the edge of a crenelated tower, swiveling with his trumpet raised high in the air.*

85. *Low angle* ELS: *the trumpeter continues the same motion.*

86. MCU: *Hotspur, shoulders bare, reads a letter. Puffs of steam surrounding him indicate that he is in his bath. In the right background stands a suit of armor, and above it are racks of lances. Another suit of armor stands at screen left. Beyond it in the further background, an arch frames his wife, Lady Percy, looking down at Hotspur from a balcony.*

HOTSPUR (*reading*): "The purpose you undertake is dangerous." Kagh! H1 II.iii.6–19
  Why, that's certain! 'Tis dangerous to take a cold, to sleep, to drink!
LADY PERCY: Harry!
HOTSPUR: But I tell you this, my lord fool, . . . (*The camera pulls back to show him sitting in a wooden tub of water.*) . . . out of this nettle, danger, we pluck this flower, safety.

87. MCU: *Lady Percy, with the stone arch at right, looks out over three spearheads that form part of the balcony railing.*

LADY PERCY: Harry—

88. LS: *Hotspur, as at the end of 86.*

HOTSPUR (*reading again*): "The purpose you undertake is dangerous, the friends you have named uncertain, the time itself unsorted . . ."

Two attendants, each holding a bath towel, enter from the right and left of the frame. They envelop Hotspur with the towels as he rises from the tub.

89. *Lady Percy, as in 87. The camera pans with her as she moves left. She continues down and out of the shot, while the camera holds, in* CU, *on the visored helmet of a suit of armor.*

HOTSPUR (*off*): ". . . and the whole plot too light." Say you so?

90. MS: *Hotspur stands between the two attendants, who hold the bath towels around him. He steps out of the tub toward the camera; the attendant at the right of the shot crosses between Hotspur and the camera.*

HOTSPUR: I say unto you again, you are a shallow, cowardly hind, and you lie!

91. *Low angle* MS: *a trumpeter raises his trumpet into the air directly in front of the camera. In the far left background is a castle tower with other trumpeters, their instruments raised. The sound of the trumpets, muted in the previous sequence, now dominates the soundtrack.*

92. *Low angle* ELS: *a trumpeter playing and swiveling his trumpet at the top of a round castle tower.*

93. *Low angle* LS: *the same trumpeter on the tower as he continues to play.*

94. MS: *Hotspur, naked to the waist, is drying his lower body, below the frame. The two suits of armor are visible in the background.*

HOTSPUR: By the Lord, our plot is a good plot as ever was laid! Our friends true and constant: . . .

95. MLS: *Lady Percy enters a door at right of frame and walks into a courtyard.*

HOTSPUR (*off*): . . . a good plot, . . .

96. *High angle* LS: *Hotspur, a towel around his waist, seen from the side at left of frame. The tub occupies the lower foreground. One of the attendants kneels before him, putting on one of his stockings. Hotspur hops up and down to help the process. Lady Percy enters through a door in the background and walks rapidly toward Hotspur.*

> HOTSPUR: . . . good friends, and full of expectation. An excellent plot, very good friends.
> LADY PERCY (*to the attendant*): Leave us.

The attendant moves out of the shot at left.

> HOTSPUR: I must leave you, Kate. (*Hotspur retrieves the letter he was*   **36**
> *reading from the tub, where it has fallen. He makes a half circle around the tub, looking at the letter while Lady Percy follows close behind him.*) Oh, what a frosty-spirited rogue is this! "I could be well   **20, 2–6**
> content to be with you, in the respect of I love your house." He shows in this he loves his own barn better than he loves our house!

97. *Low angle* LS: *a trumpeter stands on a parapet at the top of a staircase, playing and swiveling his raised trumpet. Again, the soundtrack amplifies the fanfare that has been audible throughout the scene.*

98. MCU: *Hotspur, screen right, with Lady Percy in the left background.*

> HOTSPUR: What ho! // (*He rushes out of the shot at the left.*)   **66–72**

99. ELS: *Hotspur, still draped in towels, emerging through a set of doors into a courtyard, the back wall of which is striped with broad shadows.*

> HOTSPUR: Hath Butler brought those horses from the sheriff? //

A servant appears, seen partially, back to the camera, at the lower left.

> * SERVANT: What horse, my lord?

*Hotspur: What horse?

100. LS: *Hotspur stands before the shadowed wall and door.*

     HOTSPUR: A roan, a crop-ear, is it not?

101. MS: *Lady Percy, hands on hips, stands next to the tub at frame right. She smiles and looks down.*

     SERVANT (*off*): It is, my lord.

102. *Hotspur, as in 100. He turns away so that his back is to the camera and raises his arm excitedly.*

     HOTSPUR: That roan shall be my throne! (*His towel falls to his feet, leaving him naked. He quickly stoops to retrieve it.*)

103. MS: *four trumpeters. They move their trumpets until the trumpets' bells fill the screen.*

104. ELS: *Hotspur, as at the end of 99, with the servant visible in the left foreground. Draping his towels around himself, Hotspur runs off at the right.*

105. MCU: *Lady Percy, in front of the tub, laughs as she moves quickly out of shot to the right.*

106. MLS: *several horsemen enter a castle gate. The camera pans to the right with them as they turn into the shadowed area immediately below the wall of a building. Above, in sunlight, Hotspur, still barechested, leans out of a window.*

W   HOTSPUR: How now, what news?

107. MLS: *Worcester, from a slightly high angle. He has reined in his horse, as have four other horsemen behind him. In the background is a low wall and, beyond it, a long vista of the countryside. Worcester displays a letter.*

H1 IV.i.14–18   * WORCESTER: From your father.

     * Messenger

108. *Low angle* MLS: *Hotspur in the window.*

    HOTSPUR (*hastily putting on his jacket*): Letters from him? Why comes he not himself?

109. MLS: *Worcester and the others, as in 107, their horses reined but milling.*

    *WORCESTER: It seems that he is grievous sick.

110. MLS: *the horsemen seen from behind, as at end of 106. Hotspur, in the window, continues to dress himself.*

    HOTSPUR: Zounds! How has he the leisure to be sick / In such a justling time? Hah!

111. *Low angle* MLS: *Hotspur at the window from inside the castle room. Lady Percy moves into the shot from the left and joins him.*

    HOTSPUR: You will see now in very sincerity . . .   **HI II.iii.**
                                                              30–34

112. *Low angle* LS: *Hotspur and Lady Percy lean out the window.*

    HOTSPUR: . . . of fear and cold heart will he to the King and lay open all our proceedings. // (*Turns to leave the window.*)

113. *Hotspur and Lady Percy, as in 111. Hotspur, still only partly dressed, moves close to camera crossing to the left, as Lady Percy turns to follow him.*

    HOTSPUR: Well, hang him. Let him tell the King.

114. *Low angle* LS: *a single trumpeter stands on a parapet at the top of a staircase, as in 97. Again, the soundtrack amplifies the fanfare.*

115. *Low angle* MLS: *a trumpeter playing as he swivels, with a castle wall in far background.*

*Messenger

116. *Low angle* LS: *two trumpeters playing, with the crenelated top of a battlement visible in front of them.*

117. *Low angle* LS: *three trumpeters playing, again with the top of a battlement visible in front.*

118. *As in 114, but now four trumpeters are on the parapet playing.*

119. *Low angle* MLS: *Hotspur sits on a stone bench below an open door, preparing to put on his boots. Lady Percy approaches him from behind.*

120. MCU: *Hotspur and Lady Percy. She is at the left, behind him, leaning over his shoulder and kissing his cheek, with her arms around his chest.*

38–55   LADY PERCY (*softly*): For what offense have I this fortnight been / A banished woman from my husband's bed? //

Hotspur looks restless.

121. MLS: *Hotspur and Lady Percy. He half turns away from Lady Percy, back toward the door.*

W   HOTSPUR: What, ho!
W   VOICE (*off*): My lord?
LADY PERCY (*moving around Hotspur to kneel in front of him and truss his leather jacket*): In thy faint slumbers I by thee have watched, / And heard thee murmur tales of iron wars, / . . .

122. MCU: *Lady Percy at the left, seen over Hotspur's shoulder. Behind her, a fire burns in the hearth.*

LADY PERCY: . . . Speak terms of manage to thy bounding steed, / Cry "Courage! To the field!" . . .

123. *Reverse shot of 122, Lady Percy trussing the jacket, Hotspur moving impatiently.*

LADY PERCY: . . . And thou hast talked / Of . . .

124. CU: *Lady Percy, seen over the edge of Hotspur's shoulder.*

LADY PERCY: . . . sallies and retires, of trenches, tents, / Of palisadoes, . . .

125. *Hotspur, as in 123.*

LADY PERCY: . . . frontiers, parapets, / . . .

126. *Lady Percy, as in 124.*

LADY PERCY: . . . of basilisks, of cannon, culverin, / Of prisoners' ransom, . . .

127. *Low angle* MLS: *Hotspur and Lady Percy, with the doorway to a court-yard in the background. Hotspur gets up abruptly while she speaks, and moves out of the shot at the right.*

LADY PERCY: . . . and of soldiers sla—// Hear you, my lord!   75–118

128. *The camera holds on a wall as Hotspur, in* MS, *descends the stairs and crosses the frame from left to right. The camera then tracks right with Lady Percy in* MS *as she follows him.*

LADY PERCY: My lord!
HOTSPUR (*off*): What sayest thou, my lady?

The camera holds in front of an archway to a deep recessed space. Lady Percy turns into the archway and, moving away from the camera, disappears into the shadows of the space. Hotspur then emerges out of the shadows and turns to his left at the archway. He is now carrying a cloak along with his boots and is closely followed by Lady Percy. The camera then tracks with both of them in MS *as they run along the side of the wall and move out of the frame at the right.*

LADY PERCY: What is it carries you away?
HOTSPUR: Why, my horse, my love, my horse!

LADY PERCY (*trying to hold him back by his jacket*): Out, you mad-headed ape! // I'll know your business, Harry. //

129. LS: *Hotspur and Lady Percy move away from the camera through an archway into another courtyard. Hotspur tosses a boot to one servant, his cloak to another, and starts to sit on a campstool. Servants and Lady Percy converge around him.*

LADY PERCY: If you go—
HOTSPUR: So far afoot, I shall be weary, love. //

130. *A cascade of Lady Percy's hair momentarily passes in front of the camera, after which Hotspur is revealed in* MCU, *his body angled so that his head is sharply tilted to the right.*

LADY PERCY: Faith, I'll break thy little finger, Harry . . .

Hotspur grimaces in pain.

131. MS: *Lady Percy, left of frame. Hotspur's arm is visible, extended upward in front of her, as she grips his hand and pulls back one of his fingers.*

LADY PERCY: . . . if thou wilt not tell me all things true.

132. CU: *Hotspur, his face contorted, in the lower right of the frame. His arm extends upward on the left.*

HOTSPUR: Away, away, you trifler. Ow!

133. LS: *Hotspur and Lady Percy from ground level. Hotspur rises from the stool, freeing himself from Lady Percy's grip and pushing away the two servants who have put on his boots.*

HOTSPUR: Love? I love thee not; / I care not for thee, Kate. This is no world / To play with mammets and to tilt with lips. / (*A servant enters from the right and puts Hotspur's cape over his shoulders.*) We must have bloody noses and cracked crowns. // (*He turns to leave, moving toward the camera.*)

134. *Low angle* ELS: *a round tower with four trumpeters playing.*

135. *Camera pans with Lady Percy in* MCU *as she approaches and crosses in front of Hotspur from right to left.*

    HOTSPUR: Gods me, my horse! //

    The camera reframes Lady Hotspur in MCU *as she faces him and puts her arms around his neck.*

    LADY PERCY: Do you not love me? Do you not indeed? // (*Bringing her face very close to his*) Nay, tell me if you speak in jest or no.
    HOTSPUR: Come, wilt thou see me ride? / And when I am a-horseback, I will swear / I love thee infinitely. (*He pushes past her toward the left.*)

136. *Low angle* LS: *three trumpeters on a battlement playing.*

137. *The camera pans with Lady Percy as she moves toward the left and reaches the other side of the archway, where Hotspur is standing. The camera reframes the two in* MLS.

    HOTSPUR: But hark you, Kate; // I know you wise, but yet no further wise / Than Harry Percy's wife. (*Hotspur takes a step back, stumbles against the bottom step of the staircase behind him, and falls backward onto the stairs. Lady Percy begins to laugh.*)

138. MS: *Hotspur sitting where he fell.*

    HOTSPUR: Constant—you are, / But yet a woman; . . .

    Lady Percy's body moves into the frame as she advances toward Hotspur.

139. MCU: *Hotspur and Lady Percy, in profile, embrace. She smiles down at him.*

    HOTSPUR: . . . And for secrecy, / No lady closer—for I well believe /

Thou wilt not utter what thou dost not know, / And so far will I trust
thee, gentle Kate—
LADY PERCY: How? So far?
HOTSPUR: Not an inch further. (*They kiss.*)

140. *Four trumpeters, as in 118.*

141. MLS: *Hotspur waves good-bye to his wife as he moves toward the left.
Lady Percy moves into the shot on the right.*

142. *Low angle* MCU: *a trumpeter playing, with castle walls in the background and several other trumpeters on the parapets.*

143. *Low angle* ELS: *the trumpeters on the parapets.*

144. LS: *camera tilts slightly upward at horsemen riding away through the
castle gate. Lady Percy enters the shot from the left, running after them.
She stops at the gate, passed there by a final horseman.*

HOTSPUR (*off*): But hark you, Kate: / Whither I go, thither shall you
go too. //

145. *A horse passes the camera at very close range; Lady Percy is then revealed in* MLS, *standing by the gate.*

HOTSPUR (*off*): Will this content you, Kate?
LADY PERCY (*moving forward into* MS): It must of force.

146. LS: *Lady Percy in the gateway, back to the camera, looking after the departing horsemen.*

Gadshill, outside London

147. MS: *Low angle of Falstaff, with the camera tilted slightly to the right.
The Prince is squatting in front of him struggling with the white friar's
robe Falstaff is wearing as a disguise. He tries laboriously to pull the
front of the robe up and over Falstaff's belly. Trees in the background
indicate they are in a forest.*

PRINCE: How long is it, Jack, since thou saw'st thine own knee?

FALSTAFF: Mine own knee? When I was about thy years, Hal, I was not an eagle's talon in the waist. (*A man dressed as a friar crosses the background from right to left leading a horse. Falstaff's robe is now in place, and he holds in front of him the cowl he will wear. The Prince removes Falstaff's hat and begins to put on his own robe.*) A plague of sighing and grief, it blows a man up like a bladder.

HI II.iv.
328–333

148. LS: *Bardolph and Peto, partially dressed in their friars' robes, advance toward the camera through the trees. A third man follows them.*

BARDOLPH: There's money of the king's coming.

HI II.ii.
53-54

149. *Falstaff and the Prince, as at end of 147.*

*PETO (*off*): 'Tis going to the King's exchequer.

150. LS: *Bardolph and the other two robbers, now stationary.*

HI I.ii.135

† PETO: We may do it as secure as sleep.

BARDOLPH (*looking to screen left*): Ssh. They come.

W

151. *Falstaff and Hal, as in 149.*

PRINCE: You four shall front them there. // (*He points ahead of him, and continues putting on his robe.*)

HI II.ii.
59-64

‡ FALSTAFF: We four! How many be there of them? (*He puts on his cowl.*)

§ PETO: (*off*): Aah, some eight or ten.

FALSTAFF: Zounds, will they not rob us? (*The Prince laughs; he and Falstaff both turn away from the camera.*)

152. LS: *a stand of trees. The forest resembles a park with tall trees widely spaced and no underbrush. The robed and cowled figure of Poins emerges in* ELS *from behind a tree, whistles, and beckons.*

* Bardolph   ‡ Peto
† Poins   § Gadshill

153. MS: *Falstaff, among the trees, begins to move to frame right.*

29

FALSTAFF: Give me my horse, my masters.

154. MLS: *Falstaff, back to the camera, moves toward the Prince, who has his arm around one of the trees. Poins also moves toward the Prince from the rear.*

77

FALSTAFF: Every man to his business. (*He turns to face the camera.*)

60-61

PRINCE (*holding Falstaff from behind by his robe*): If they scape from your encounter, they shall light on ours.

1

POINS (*whispering*): Shelter, shelter.

25-26

FALSTAFF (*moving forward out of shot at left*): Hmm . . .

155. LS: *Falstaff moves away from the camera through the forest.*

FALSTAFF: . . . eight yards of uneven ground is three score and ten mile afoot with me.

156. LS: *the Prince and Poins in the same location as in 154.*

1-2

POINS: I've removed Falstaff's horse. (*They both laugh, and begin to run away from the camera through the forest.*)

157. LS: *Falstaff, in an open space among the trees, turns about uncertainly.*

12-13

FALSTAFF: If I go four foot further afoot, I shall break me wind. . . .

158. ELS: *Poins and the Prince, seen deep in the stand of trees, run from screen right to left, laughing.*

21-22

FALSTAFF (*off*): I'll starve ere I'll rob . . .

159. MLS: *Falstaff, at left of screen, advances toward the camera. A large tree trunk fills the right foreground. Falstaff now carries a sword in his left hand.*

FALSTAFF: . . . a foot further.

PRINCE (*off*): Peace, you fat . . .   31

160. ELS: *the Prince in the forest gesticulates to Falstaff and then does a fall on his side.*

PRINCE: . . . guts! // What a brawling dost thou keep! // Lie down!   6

161. *Falstaff, as in 159, but now stationary.*

FALSTAFF: Lie down?   w

162. MLS: *the Prince lies on the ground among the leaves.*

PRINCE (*pointing to the ground*): Lay thine ear close to the ground, and   32–35
list if thou canst hear the tread of travelers.

163. *Low angle* MS: *Falstaff, looking down.*

FALSTAFF: Have you any levers to lift me up again, being down?

164. *The Prince, as in 162. He rolls over on his back laughing. Poins enters the shot from the left background.*

POINS: They come, they come!   w

The Prince begins to get up.

FALSTAFF (*off*): I prithee . . .   40–44

165. *Falstaff, as in 163.*

FALSTAFF: . . . good Prince Hal, help me to my horse . . .

166. MLS: *the Prince gets up, as at end of 164, with Poins behind him.*

FALSTAFF (*off*): . . . good king's son.
PRINCE (*tossing leaves at Falstaff*): Shall I be your ostler?

167. *Falstaff, as in 163.*

> FALSTAFF (*as a shower of leaves falls over him*): Go hang thyself in thine own heir-apparent garters. (*He moves off right.*)

168. MLS: *the Prince and Poins, now cowled as well as robed, at the left, with the forest behind them. Laughing conspiratorially, they begin to run forward.*

169. ELS: *Falstaff leads Bardolph, Peto, and the third robber through the forest.*

W

> FALSTAFF (*beckoning them forward*): Now lads, come.

A lyrical folk theme begins on the soundtrack.

170. ELS: *a group of travelers, barely visible among the trees.*

78-80

> VOICE OF A TRAVELER: Come, neighbor, the boy shall lead our horses; . . .

171. LS: *the travelers' caravan moves away from the camera through the forest. In the far background, the four disguised friars of shot 169 can barely be seen.*

> VOICE OF A TRAVELER: . . . we'll walk afoot while and ease our legs.

172. ELS: *the four white-robed friars, framed by trees, walk in single file at left of screen. They mumble an imitation of a monkish chant. Falstaff, leading the file, looks back at the others.*

173. MS: *three of the friars, Falstaff, Bardolph, and Peto, hands clasped in prayer, continue to mumble their chant.*

174. LS: *the caravan strung out, single file, through the woods.*

175. *The four monks, as in 172. Falstaff pulls his cowl lower over his face. Their chanting continues.*

176. LS: *the Prince and Poins in the forest, with two tree trunks framing them in the center of the screen. They run forward, still laughing.*

177. ELS: *the four friars seen through the trees. As the caravan reaches them, all four draw their swords and cry out. The caravan begins to disperse toward the right of the screen. A general hubbub ensues, and the friars can be heard shouting* "Down with them" *and* "Cut the villains' throats." *The music shifts to a similar but more sprightly version of the martial theme used in the credit sequence. It persists through this and the subsequent chase scene (196–209).*

178. LS: *the backs of travelers fleeing through a stand of trees, pursued by the friars entering frame left.*

179. LS: *dense foliage. A horse and traveler pass directly in front of the*

camera in the foreground. After they pass, two of the friars can be seen coming down an incline in pursuit.

180. LS: *the friars, travelers, and horses, all seen from the back, run through the woods.*

181. LS: *the Prince amid the trees.*

PRINCE (*turning to left of frame*): Where are our disguises?

Poins hurriedly enters the shot from the left, hands the Prince a black cloak, and puts a black hat on the Prince's head. He leaves frame left as the Prince begins to sweep the cape around his shoulders.

182. MLS: *the Prince continues to pull his black cloak around himself until he is completely muffled by it.*

183. ELS: *the travelers, from behind, scattered, flee through the trees.*

184. MS: *the Prince, muffled to the eyes, tosses aside part of his white friar's costume. He moves toward frame right.*

185. LS: *the Prince enters frame from left, followed by Poins, both now wearing dark hats and cloaks.*

186. ELS: *the travelers, from behind, even more distant in the woods and more scattered than in 183.*

187. MLS: *Falstaff, in the center of the frame, among the trees, laughs and motions to his companions.*

FALSTAFF: Come, . . .

188. ELS: *Falstaff, from behind, beckons. His three companions move toward him through the woods.*

FALSTAFF: . . . come.

189. *The Prince and Poins, as in 185. The Prince is now brandishing a club.*

190. LS: *Falstaff leads the other three friars single file through the forest, from right to left of screen. He is the only one of the four who does not have his sword drawn at this point.*

191. *High angle* MLS: *the Prince and Poins, hatted and muffled, advance toward the camera and screen left.*

192. ELS: *the four friars from behind, now moving abreast through a clearing to reach four donkeys in the far background. The Prince and Poins enter the foreground from the right, both carrying clubs.*

193. MS: *Falstaff and Bardolph stand behind a laden donkey barely visible in the lower foreground. Falstaff holds a sword and two bags. Bardolph raises another bag.*

> FALSTAFF: Come, my masters, let us share. // (*He takes Bardolph's bag.*)   98–102

194. LS: *the Prince and Poins peer from behind a large tree trunk in the center of the frame.*

> FALSTAFF (*off*): And the Prince and Poins be not two arrant cowards there's no equity stirring. There's no more valor in that Poins . . .

195. *Falstaff and Bardolph, as at the end of 193.*

> FALSTAFF: . . . than in a wild duck. (*Falstaff and Bardolph react as they hear loud shouts and cries offscreen of* "Your money.")

196. LS: *the Prince and Poins leap from behind the tree shown in 194.*

197. MS: *Falstaff stands behind two of the pack animals. He raises his sword, turns away from the camera, and begins to run away. The Prince enters the frame at the right chasing him.*

198. LS: *the Prince and Poins, seen through foliage in the foreground, move from right to left past the pack animals, in pursuit of the white-robed friars.*

199. *The camera tracks to follow the friars, with the Prince and Poins at their heels, in* ELS *as they run through the forest. Falstaff circles around a tree, pursued by the Prince, while the others continue toward the left of the frame.*

200. *The camera tracks left to follow Falstaff in* LS, *as he passes behind the tree with the Prince, holding a club, at his back. Waving his sword above his head, Falstaff pivots completely around in a circle, even as he runs away from the Prince toward the camera. He then does another complete pivot in front of the next tree as he moves to the left of the frame, now in* MS.

201. *The camera tracks left to follow the entire group in* ELS. *They are seen through the trees running from the right to the left of the shot.*

202. LS: *Falstaff's accomplices are chased by Poins, with a clump of trees in right foreground. They move out of the shot to the left.*

203. *The camera tracks left to follow the friars in* ELS *as they are chased through the trees, moving toward the left. In the nearer distance, the Prince swings at the running Falstaff with his club.*

204. LS: *the camera tracks left with Falstaff and the Prince as the Prince swings his club, giving Falstaff a glancing blow on his back. Falstaff howls "Jesus" and keeps running toward left of frame.*

205. LS: *the three accomplices seen from behind as they run along a path in the forest. Falstaff enters the frame from lower right, following them. He is carrying three moneybags.*

206. LS: *the Prince and Poins come to a stop next to one another among the trees. Poins has already taken off his cloak and hat and the Prince's cloak now hangs loose, showing his friar's robe.*

PRINCE: The thieves are scattered. // (*They both laugh.*)   105-110

207. LS: *the friars, as at end of 205. Falstaff, slightly behind the others,
     drops the moneybags as he runs. The laughter of the Prince and Poins
     can be heard on the soundtrack.*

208. LS: *the Prince and Poins, as at end of 206. They move forward toward
     the camera.*

     * POINS: Each takes his fellow for an officer.
     PRINCE: Away, good Ned . . . (*They move out of the shot at left.*)

209. *The path in the woods, with the camera positioned as in 207. The Prince
     and Poins enter from the bottom of frame right, seen from the rear, and
     move into LS on the path. They both have now discarded their black
     cloaks and hats and are dressed in their friars' robes. They stop and
     pick up the three bags that Falstaff has dropped.*

     PRINCE: . . . Falstaff sweats to death and lards the lean earth as he
        walks along. (*The Prince puts his arm around Poins's shoulder,
        and, laughing, they continue to walk away from the camera along the
        path.*)
     POINS: How the fat rogue roared!   111
     PRINCE: Were't not for laughing, I should pity him.   110

The Royal Castle

210. *As a tall door opens, the camera pans left with King Henry as he passes
     through, and then holds on him in MCU as he stops. He is accompanied
     by his younger son, John of Lancaster.*

     KING (*turning toward the camera*): Can no man tell me of my unthrifty   R V.iii.1-2
        son?

211. LS: *a crowd of courtiers stands along the walls of a high hall. There
     is silence.*

*Prince

212. ELS: *the King is framed by two large pillars in the foreground. As he moves forward, he is obscured by the pillar in the left of the frame.*

KING: 'Tis full three months since I did see him last.

213. MLS: *The Earl of Westmoreland moves forward, to stand in front of the crowd of courtiers seen in 211.*

W

H2 III.i.36–39

WESTMORELAND: My liege!

KING (*off*): Have you read o'er the letters that I sent you? (*The King, seen from the back, enters the right foreground.*)

* WESTMORELAND: I have, my liege.

KING: Then you perceive the body of our kingdom, / How foul it is, what rank diseases grow—

95–96

H1 I.i.62–63

† WESTMORELAND: They say young Percy and Lord Worcester / Are fifty thousand strong. (*He gestures to the left.*) Here is Sir Walter Blunt, my lord, new lighted from his horse.

The King begins to move to the left, where Westmoreland is pointing.

214. MLS: *Blunt at the left. A bare wall and a large pillar occupy the rest of the screen.*

W

BLUNT: My liege. Northumberland lies sick. But a great power of English and of Scots . . . (*King Henry enters the frame at right.*) . . . follow young Henry Percy.

77–89

KING (*turning slightly away from Blunt*): Yea, there thou mak'st me sad, . . . (*Turns toward the camera and away from Blunt.*) . . . and mak'st me sin / In envy that my Lord Northumberland / Should be the father to so blest a son: . . .

215. MLS: *Westmoreland, with courtiers behind him.*

KING (*off*): . . . A son that is the theme of honor's tongue, // . . .

* Warwick
† King Henry

216. *Low angle* LS: *the King advances down a long and broad passageway toward the camera, followed by John of Lancaster and other attendants.*

> KING: . . . Whilst I, in looking on the praise of him, / See riot and dishonor stain the brow / Of my young Harry. (*He stops in* MLS.) O that it could be proved / That some night-tripping fairy had exchanged / In cradle clothes our children where they lay. // Then would I have his Harry, and he mine. (*He turns toward the attendants standing behind him.*) Where is the Prince of Wales?   w
>
> ATTENDANT: We do not know, my lord.   w
>
> KING: I would to God, my lords, he could be found. // (*He resumes his* R V.iii.4–12 *walk down the passageway, the camera tracking back to keep the King in low angle* MLS.) Inquire at London, 'mongst the taverns there, / For there, they say, he daily doth frequent / With unrestrainèd loose companions, / Even such, they say, as stand in narrow lanes / And beat our watch and rob our passengers, / Which he, young wanton and effeminate boy, / Takes on the point of honor to support / So dissolute a crew. (*By the end of the speech, the King has moved into a darkened area of the passageway, so that only his face is visible.*)

A Street; The Tavern in Eastcheap

217. LS: *the Prince and Poins, still dressed in their friars' robes, on horseback, gallop up a street with houses in the background. They move toward the camera and out of the shot at the left.*

218. LS: *the two horsemen seen from the rear, gallop up the street.*

219. *The camera moves with the Prince as he rides into the tavern yard and begins to dismount, in* LS, *at the far end of the yard. During the shot, Poins, on horseback, crosses from right to left in the foreground.*

220. LS: *the Prince dismounts, partially obscured by a beam in the foreground. He ties up his horse as Poins runs toward him from the background.*

> PRINCE (*laughing*): Got with much ease.   H1 II.ii.105

221. *The camera tracks left with the Prince and Poins in* LS *as they burst through the door and run through the kitchen of the tavern. As they run, the Prince swings to the near side of a long table, picks up a bucket and pulls off its lid, and continues running down the room. Poins, also on the run and carrying the bags of money, tosses one underhand to Hal, who catches it in the bucket. The camera continues its track to follow them until they finally throw themselves down on a stone recess at the base of a far wall.*

H1 I.ii.189–193   * PRINCE (*during the run across the room*): The virtue of this jest will be the incomprehensible lies this same fat rogue will tell us now: how thirty at least he fought with; what wards, what blows, what extremities he endured.

222. MLS: *Falstaff, still dressed in his friar's robe, his sword drawn, stands among the tavern kegs, a large keg in the foreground. Falstaff shakes his fist. Groans are heard on the soundtrack.*

223. *High angle* MS: *Poins (in foreground) and the Prince seated. The Prince cradles the bucket in his arms. They turn their heads away from the camera as they hear the groans and Falstaff's voice.*

H1 II.iv.114–116   FALSTAFF (*off*): A plague on all . . .

224. *Falstaff, as in 222.*

FALSTAFF: . . . cowards.

In front of the large keg, Bardolph and the third robber cross the screen from left to right in MCU. *They groan loudly.*

225. MS: *the Prince and Poins, seated cattycornered at the intersection of a wall. They turn to look at each other as the groaning continues.*

226. LS: *Falstaff and his accomplices emerge from under the balcony into the*

*Poins

large main room of the tavern. They are hobbling and groaning. Several women stand on the balcony and look down at them.

227. *Low angle* LS: *the Prince and Poins seated, enjoying the scene.*

228. LS: *Falstaff, holding his sword, moves toward the camera across the main room. His three accomplices have collapsed near a post and table in the foreground.*

> FALSTAFF: A plague on all cowards still say I. And a vengeance too. (*He approaches the table and, now in* MS, *picks up a tankard.*) Give me a cup of sack. (*He lifts the tankard to his mouth.*)

229. MCU: *the Prince and Poins.*

> *PRINCE: How now Jack, where hast thou been? (*He puts aside the bucket he has been holding.*)   113

230. MS: *Falstaff, as at end of 228.*

> FALSTAFF (*spitting out some of the sack he is drinking*): A plague on all cowards. (*He throws his sword down on the table.*)

231. *The Prince and Poins, as in 229.*

> FALSTAFF (*off*): Go thy ways, old Jack, . . .   127–277

The Prince turns and winks at Poins.

232. *Falstaff, as in 230, with the tankard in his right hand. He picks up a pitcher of sack with his left.*

> FALSTAFF: . . . die when thou wilt; if manhood, good manhood, be not forgot upon the face of the earth, then I'm a shotten herring. There lives not three good men unhanged in England; and one of them is fat, and grows old. (*He raises his tankard.*)

*Poins

233. *The Prince and Poins, as in 229.*

> FALSTAFF (*off*): God help the while!
> PRINCE: How now, woolsack?

234. *Falstaff, as in 230. He refills his tankard from the pitcher.*

> FALSTAFF: A king's son! (*He begins to move toward the camera.*) If I
> do not beat thee . . .

235. *Low angle* MCU: *the Prince and Poins.*

> FALSTAFF (*off*): . . . out of thy kingdom with a dagger of lath . . .

236. *The camera tracks with Falstaff moving forward in* MCU, *as at end of 234.*

> FALSTAFF: . . . and drive all thy subjects afore thee like a flock of wild
> geese, I'll never wear hair on my face more. You Prince of Wales?

237. *The Prince and Poins, as in 229.*

> PRINCE: Why, you whoreson round man . . .

238. MCU: *Falstaff sits down at the opposite end of the table from where he
> stood earlier in the scene. The Prince and Poins are visible in the far
> background at the right.*

> PRINCE (*off*): . . . you fat guts . . .

239. *The Prince and Poins, as in 229.*

> PRINCE: . . . what's the matter?

240. *Falstaff, as at the end of 238.*

> FALSTAFF (*turning to shout at them, over his shoulder*): Are you not a
> coward? Answer that. (*Turns to camera.*)—And Poins there?

241. *The Prince and Poins, as in 229.*

    POINS: Call me coward? (*He jumps up.*)

242. MS: *Falstaff at the table. Poins rushes from background to stand, at the right, at Falstaff's shoulder.*

    POINS: You fat paunch!
    FALSTAFF: I call thee coward? I'll see thee damned ere I call thee
        coward, but I would give a thousand pound if I could run as fast as
        thou canst. //
    PRINCE (*rushing from his seat to stand over Falstaff's shoulder, at the
        left; the camera moves forward to reframe the three men in* MCU):
        What's the matter?
    FALSTAFF: What's the matter? There be four of us here have ta'en a
        thousand pound this morning.
    POINS: A thousand pound? Where is it?   W
    PRINCE (*moving between Falstaff and Poins*): Where is it, Jack?
    FALSTAFF: Where is it? Taken from us, it is. A hundred upon poor
        four of us.
    PRINCE: What, a hundred, man?
    FALSTAFF: I was at half-sword with a dozen of them two hours to-
        gether. I have scaped by a miracle. I am eight times thrust through the
        doublet . . . (*Gestures to different parts of his robe.*), . . . four
        through the hose; my buckler cut through and through; my sword
        hacked like a handsaw.—Ecce signum. // (*He points in front of him.*)
        Let them speak. //

From behind Falstaff's chair, the Prince moves out of the shot to the left.

243. MLS: *Bardolph and Peto huddle together near a post just beyond the end
    of the table opposite where Falstaff sits. They rise, Bardolph holding a
    sword with its hilt upward, Peto holding a shield. The Prince moves into
    the shot from the right.*

    * BARDOLPH: We four set upon some dozen—

*Gadshill

244. MS: *Falstaff with Poins standing next to him, his hands on his hips.*

FALSTAFF: Sixteen, at least.

245. MLS: *the Prince, Bardolph, and Peto. The Prince has now turned to face the camera. As Bardolph speaks, the Prince moves forward into* MS *to sit at the table at the opposite end from Falstaff.*

*BARDOLPH: And bound them. // And as we were sharing, some six or seven fresh men set upon us. //
PRINCE: What, fought you with them all?

246. *Falstaff with Poins as in 244.*

FALSTAFF: All? I know not what you call all, but if I fought not with fifty of them, I am a bunch of radish. If there were not fifty upon poor old Jack, then am I no two-legged creature.

247. LS: *the Prince sits at the end of the table, with Bardolph and Peto in the left background. Part of the table can be seen in the lower foreground, with tankards and scraps of food scattered on it.*

PRINCE (*with mock concern*): Pray God you have not murdered some of them.

248. *Falstaff and Poins, as in 244.*

FALSTAFF: Nay, that's past praying for. I have peppered two of them. Two I am sure I've paid for . . .

249. *The Prince, as in 247.*

FALSTAFF (*off*): . . . two rogues in buckram cloaks.

250. *Falstaff and Poins, as in 244.*

*Gadshill

FALSTAFF (*leaning forward into* MCU): I tell thee what, Hal—I tell thee a lie, spit in my face, call me horse! // (*He points emphatically toward the camera.*) Thus I bore me point. Four rogues in buckram cloaks let drive at me.

POINS (*leaning over Falstaff's shoulder*): Four?

w

251. *The Prince, as in 247.*

PRINCE: Four? Thou saidst but two even now.

252. MCU: *Falstaff, with Poins, as at the end of 250.*

FALSTAFF: Four, Hal, I told thee four. // These four came all afront and mainly thrust at me. I made me no more ado but took all seven of their points in me target, thus. (*He raises his arm as if holding a shield.*)

253. *The camera moves with the Prince in* MS *as he gets up from the table and begins to move toward Falstaff.*

PRINCE: Seven?

254. MS: *Falstaff, still gesturing. Poins moves behind him to the left as the Prince enters at the right. They both look down on Falstaff from either side of his chair.*

PRINCE (*at first off*): Why there were but four even now.
FALSTAFF: Er, in buckram?
POINS: Ay, four, in buckram cloaks.
FALSTAFF (*shaking his fist*): Seven, by these hilts, or I am a villain else.

The camera moves with the Prince as he crosses in front of Falstaff, pushing Poins with him. Falstaff is now left out of the shot. The camera reframes Poins and the Prince in MCU *with their heads conspiratorially close together.*

PRINCE: Let him alone. We shall have more anon.

255. *Low angle* MS: *Falstaff at the left, seen from the side and rear. He has turned sideways in his chair toward the camera. His three accomplices stand at the far end of the table. The balcony, the far wall of the tavern hall, and the beamed ceiling are all visible in the background.*

FALSTAFF: Dost thou hear me, Hal?

256. *Low angle* MS: *the Prince and Poins.*

PRINCE (*folding his arms*): Ay, and mark thee too, Jack.

257. *Falstaff, as in 255. As he speaks, some women begin to gather on the balcony.*

FALSTAFF: Do so, for it is worth the list'ning to. These nine in buckram . . .

258. *The Prince and Poins, as in 256.*

FALSTAFF (*off*): . . . that I told thee of—. . .
* POINS (*out of the side of his mouth*): Two more already. //

259. *Falstaff, as in 255.*

FALSTAFF: . . . began to give me ground; I followed me close, came in, foot and hand, and with a thought, seven of the eleven I paid.

260. *The Prince and Poins, as in 256.*

PRINCE (*his hand concealing his mouth*): O monstrous! Eleven buckram men grown out of two.

261. *Falstaff, as in 255.*

FALSTAFF: But, as the devil would have it, three misbegotten knaves in

* Prince

Kendal green came at me back and let drive at me; for it was so dark, Hal, that thou couldst not see thy hand.

262. MCU: *the Prince and Poins.*

PRINCE: These lies are like their father . . .

263. CU: *Falstaff.*

PRINCE (*off*): . . . that begets them.

264. MCU: *the Prince and Poins. The Prince begins to move to the right toward Falstaff, and the camera moves with him to keep him in* MCU.

PRINCE: Why thou clay-brained guts, thou knotty-pated fool, . . .

The camera now includes Falstaff in MCU *in the right foreground, looking up at the Prince.*

265. CU: *Falstaff in lower left foreground, with the Prince's face partially visible in profile in the upper right.*

PRINCE: . . . thou whoreson obscene greasy tallow-catch—
FALSTAFF: What, art thou mad? Is not the truth the truth?
PRINCE: Why, how couldst thou know these men in Kendal green when it was so dark thou couldst not see thy hand? Come, tell us your reason. What sayest thou to this?

Poins crosses behind them. The camera moves right to follow him and reframes him at the right in CU *with Falstaff.*

POINS: Come, your reason, Jack, your reason.

The camera moves with Falstaff, keeping him in CU *from below, as he rises and moves to the left.*

FALSTAFF: Upon compulsion? Zounds, and I were at the strappado or all the racks in the world, I would not tell you on compulsion. // (*As Falstaff finishes speaking, he faces the Prince, who has appeared at the right of the shot.*)

266. *The camera pans right to follow the Prince as he waves his arm in disgust, moves away from Falstaff, and then in* LS *turns to point at him.*

PRINCE: I'll be no longer guilty of this sin. This . . .

267. MCU: *Falstaff turns to look toward the Prince.*

PRINCE (*off*): . . . sanguine coward, . . .

268. LS: *the Prince, as at the end of 266. The camera moves with him as he crosses in front of Falstaff and stands in the left of the frame face to face with him.*

PRINCE: . . . this horseback-breaker, this huge hill of flesh—
FALSTAFF: 'Sblood, you starveling, you eel-skin, you dried neat's tongue, you stockfish—O for breath to utter what is like to thee!— You tailor's yardstick, you sheath, you bowcase, you vile standing . . .

269. MCU: *the Prince and Falstaff, with Falstaff in profile at the right of the frame.*

FALSTAFF: . . . tuck!
PRINCE: Well, breathe awhile . . . (*The Prince disappears briefly behind Falstaff, as he moves from one side of him to the other.*) . . . and then to it again. (*The camera pans with the Prince as he moves away from Falstaff to the far end of the table, picking up a sword from the table as he goes. He casually brandishes the sword toward Falstaff's three accomplices in the background. They retreat a step.*) Yet hear me speak but this. // We two saw you four set on four. (*He turns to face the camera in* LS *with the sword held in front of him and pointed at Falstaff.*) Mark now how a plain tale shall put you down. //

270. LS: *Falstaff slowly seats himself at the end of the table. Poins stands beside him.*

PRINCE (*off*): And, Falstaff, . . .

271. LS: *the Prince, as at the end of 269. The camera moves with him as, still pointing the sword, he approaches Falstaff. Putting the sword to one side, he passes behind Poins and Falstaff and moves to the far corner, where he and Poins had previously been sitting. He picks up the bucket into which he and Poins had put the stolen money, and gives it to Poins, who has moved into the shot from the right. He and Poins, now facing the camera, move toward either side of Falstaff.*

PRINCE: . . . you carried yourself away as nimbly, with as quick dexterity, and roared for mercy, and still run and roared, as ever I heard bullcalf. What a slave to hack thy sword . . .

272. *Low angle* MS: *Poins leans forward, raising the bucket and overturning it.*

PRINCE (*off*): . . . and say it was in fight! What trick, . . .

273. MS: *Falstaff, with the Prince behind his shoulder at the right, as coins fall and clatter on the table. Poins moves into the shot at the left of the frame. The Prince pivots forward, so that both he and Poins now look intently into Falstaff's face at close range.*

PRINCE: . . . what device, what starting hole canst thou now find out to hide thee from this open and apparent shame?
POINS: Come, Jack, let's hear. What trick hast thou now?
FALSTAFF (*after a pause, during which he looks at each of them*): By the Lord, lads, I knew ye as well as he that made ye. Was it for me to kill the heir apparent? Should I turn upon the true prince? Thou knowest I am as valiant as Hercules, but beware instinct. The lion will not touch the true prince. I was now a coward upon instinct. // (*He pulls the Prince, who is laughing delightedly, close to him, and then puts his other arm around Poins.*) By the Lord, lads, I'm glad you have the money.
HOSTESS (*off*): My lord the prince!   285–297

All three men turn to look toward the right.

274. LS: *the Hostess rushes into the tavern from a door in the background. The camera moves with her as she goes rapidly past a long table toward the foreground. Through the door, the street can be seen, with horsemen riding by.*

   HOSTESS: There's a nobleman of the court at the door who would speak with you.

275. MLS: *the Prince, with Falstaff and Poins, seen from behind at the near end of the table. The Prince gets up quickly, turns, and moves toward the camera and down a step, stopping in* MCU *at left of frame.*

   PRINCE: How now, my lady hostess?

276. *Low angle* MCU: *the Hostess.*

   HOSTESS: He says he comes from your father.
   PRINCE (*off*): Give him as much as will make him . . .

277. MCU: *the Prince, as at end of 275.*

   PRINCE: . . . a royal man, and send him back again to my mother.

   Poins moves forward to stand immediately behind the Prince.

278. MCU: *the Hostess giggles.*

279. *Low angle* MS: *Falstaff seen from the side. He has turned in his chair to face the camera.*

   FALSTAFF: What manner of man is he?

280. MS: *the Hostess, leaning forward. Some of the women can be seen standing in the background to her right.*

   HOSTESS (*still amused*): An old man.

281. *Falstaff, as in 279.*

    FALSTAFF: What does gravity out of his bed at midnight?

282. *Low angle* MS: *Poins stands just behind and above the Prince.*

    *POINS: Shall I give him his answer?
    PRINCE (*turning to face Poins*): Prithee do, Ned.

    *Poins moves out of shot at the left. The camera tilts up slightly and
    moves back to show Falstaff advancing in the center of the frame. He
    throws his arm around the Prince's shoulder as the camera holds them in
    *MS. *Below them the three accomplices of the robbery have entered from
    the background at the left and now stand in front of Falstaff in the lower
    foreground, their backs to the camera.*

    FALSTAFF: Clap to the doors. Watch tonight, pray tomorrow. Gallants,   277–281
      lads, boys! Hearts of gold! What, . . .

283. LS: *Poins, about to go out of the door leading to the street.*

    FALSTAFF (*off*): . . . shall we be merry?

284. *Low angle* MS: *Falstaff and the Prince, framed by the figures of the
    accomplices, partially visible in the foreground.*

    FALSTAFF: Shall we have a play extempore?
    PRINCE: A play?   W
    FALSTAFF: Thou wilt be horribly chid when thou comest to thy father   373–379
      in the morning. An thou lovest me, practice an answer.
    PRINCE: Do thou stand for my father. //
    FALSTAFF: Content. (*They both begin to turn away from the camera, as
      the Prince reaches to take Falstaff's hat from his head.*)

*Falstaff

285. MCU: *the Prince in the lower foreground puts on Falstaff's hat.*

     FALSTAFF (*off*): This chair shall be . . .

286. *Low angle* MLS: *Falstaff, with the Prince at the left behind him. A chair, seen from the side, is in the foreground. Falstaff takes the large seat cushion from the chair and puts it on his head.*

     FALSTAFF: . . . me state, this cushion my crown.

     Falstaff moves majestically out of the shot at the right. The three accomplices have entered from the background and they with the Prince pick up the chair. The camera moves right showing them, seen only partially and from below, carrying the chair. The camera continues to move with the Prince as he lets go of the chair and moves away. Throughout this and the following shots sounds of laughter and lively music are heard on the soundtrack.

287. *The camera pans with the Prince in* MS *as he moves into the low-ceilinged area of the room below the balcony and, taking off his friar's robe and Falstaff's hat, runs along by the side of the wall. Ahead of him there is a glimpse of women coming into the room through a door and, as the camera tilts upward away from the Prince, of others running along the balcony above.*

288. *Low angle* LS: *the balcony. A woman, wearing only a sheet, runs from frame right to left.*

289. *Low angle* LS: *Falstaff crosses from left to right in the foreground. As he moves out of the shot, Bardolph can now be seen pushing back a table on top of which the chair has been placed. The Prince, now in his own clothes, crosses at a run in front of the table toward the left.*

290. *The camera tracks left with three women in* MLS *running along the balcony. They are seen from the side, from beyond the balcony railing. They reach a staircase where other women are descending toward the tavern hall.*

291. *High angle* LS: *the back of the balcony, looking down into the tavern hall.*

292. *The camera tracks right following Bardolph, Peto, and the third accomplice in* MLS *as they dance across the hall. Peto wears a necklace of garlic, while the others carry kitchen implements with which they beat time. The camera continues to track right with Peto, as he dances past the Prince, who is watching in the background.*

293. *The camera tracks left with Poins in* MS *as he runs into the room. He has taken off his friar's robe and carries it in his hand. When he reaches the Prince, the camera reframes them in low angle* MLS.

    * POINS: Here was Sir Thomas Bracy from your father. There's villainous news abroad.   334–337

294. *Low angle* MS: *Falstaff, the cushion on his head very conspicuous.*

    * POINS (*off*): That same mad fellow of the North—
    FALSTAFF: Percy?   W
    PRINCE (*off*): He that . . .   103–106

295. MCU: *the Prince and Poins.*

    PRINCE: . . . kills me some six or seven dozen of Scots at a breakfast, . . . (*The camera tracks backward to keep the Prince in* MCU *as he moves forward away from Poins and stops with Falstaff just behind him.*) . . . washes his hands, and says to his wife, "Fie upon this quiet life! I want work."
    FALSTAFF: Hal, could the world pick you out such an enemy again as   368–372
that fiend Percy, the Hotspur of the North? (*Winks.*) Does not thy blood thrill at it? (*Whispers confidentially.*) Art not thou horribly afeared?
    PRINCE: Not a whit, i'faith. (*He turns and knocks the cushion off Falstaff's head.*) I lack some of thy instinct. (*He grabs a low crossbeam behind Falstaff and begins to swing himself under it.*)

*Falstaff

296. LS: *the Prince moves toward the camera as he swings out from the beam. Behind him, Falstaff has turned his back, and Peto, Bardolph, and the third accomplice watch from the far right. The camera moves back and down quickly to show a woman in a white cap and dark cloak, seen from behind. The Prince runs up to her, pulling off her cloak and kissing her on the lips.*

297. MCU: *Falstaff now wears a metal saucepan with a long handle on his head.*

384–386 FALSTAFF: Give me a cup of sack . . .

298. *Extreme low angle* MLS: *three women lean over the railing of the balcony, laughing.*

FALSTAFF (*off*): . . . to make me eyes look red, . . .

299. *Low angle* MS: *Falstaff, pivoting toward the camera. He holds a cup of sack in his hand.*

FALSTAFF: . . . that it may be thought I have wept; for I must speak in a passion.

300. MLS: *the Hostess, chuckling.*

301. *Low angle* CU: *the edge of Falstaff's robe, filling the left of the frame. As Falstaff moves out of frame, the face of the Page, grinning, appears at the lower right.*

302. ELS (*from ground level*): *Falstaff slowly walks from right to left on the table. Behind him, the Page holds up the back of Falstaff's friar's robe as if it were a royal train. Women fill the balcony in the left background, and the entire scene is crowded and animated. In the foreground, some dogs bark and play with each other.*

303. LS (*from slightly above*): *the Hostess sits at the end of one of the benches, preparing herself for the show.*

304. *Low angle* LS: *Falstaff, seen from behind, as Poins, the Page, and the Prince all try to hoist him onto the chair that has been placed on top of the table. They give three heaves in the attempt to lift him.*

305. *High angle* MLS: *Falstaff, seen from the side of the chair, as he is being pushed upward. He grasps the arms of the chair and begins to turn himself so that he can sit.*

306. *Low angle* LS: *Falstaff collapsing into the chair. The three who have been lifting him recoil backwards. The crowd applauds and cheers.*

307. *Low angle* LS *(camera tilted to the left): women are crowded along the balcony, laughing and applauding. Two more women are seen hanging out of a dormer window high in the wall that projects above the balcony.*

308. *Low angle* MS: *Falstaff, enthroned in his chair, saucepan on head. The Prince is in the right foreground looking up at him. Falstaff dips his finger into a tankard set on the arm of his chair, and raises the finger toward his mouth with mock delicacy.*

309. CU: *Falstaff tastes the sack on his finger.*

   FALSTAFF (*imitating the voice of King Henry*): Harry—   397–481

310. *Falstaff, as in 308. The Prince takes off his hat and bows.*

311. MS: *the Hostess, looking toward the entertainment expectantly.*

312. *Falstaff, as in 308.*

   FALSTAFF: I do not only marvel where thou spendest thy time, but also how thou art accompanied.

313. *The Hostess, as in 311.*

   HOSTESS (*rocking and laughing*): He doth it just like one of these har-   395
   lotry players, as ever I see!

314. *Falstaff, as in 308. The Prince, laughing, turns toward the Hostess and then turns back to Falstaff.*

> FALSTAFF: Peace, good pint pot. Peace, good tickle-brain. (*He now resumes his role as king*) That thou art my son, I have partly thy mother's word, partly mine own opinion, but chiefly a villainous trick of thine eye and a foolish hanging . . .

315. *High angle* MLS: *the Prince, with the back of Falstaff's head and shoulder in the left foreground. Several women sitting on benches can be seen in the background.*

> FALSTAFF (*off*): . . . of thy nether lip that does warrant me.

> *The Prince makes a face, pushing out his lower lip. There is much laughter.*

check

316. *Falstaff, as in 308.*

> FALSTAFF: If then thou be a son to me, here lies the point: . . . (*He makes a quick pointing gesture.*) . . . why, being son to me, art thou so pointed at? //

317. *Low angle* MS: *three women (one partly out of the frame) lean over the balcony railing and laugh.*

> FALSTAFF (*off*): There is . . .

318. *Falstaff, as in 308.*

> FALSTAFF: . . . a thing, Harry, which thou hast heard of, by the name of pitch. Pitch doth defile; so doth the company thou keepest. // (*The Prince hides his head and cries in mock shame.*) And yet . . .

319. CU: *Falstaff.*

> FALSTAFF: . . . there is a virtuous man whom I have often noted in thy company, but I know not his name.

320. *Falstaff, as in 308. He has now settled back in his chair, with his hands folded over his belly, and the Prince is no longer hiding his head.*

> PRINCE: What manner of man, and it like your Majesty?
> FALSTAFF: A goodly portly man i'faith, and a corpulent; . . .

321. *Falstaff, as in 319.*

> FALSTAFF: . . . of a cheerful look, a pleasing eye, and a most noble carriage; and, as I think, his age . . .

322. *Falstaff, as in 308.*

> FALSTAFF: . . . some fifty . . . (*The Prince hoots.*) . . . or, by'r Lady, inclining to threescore; and now I remember me, his name—

323. *The Prince, as in 315.*

w   PRINCE: Falstaff!

324. MLS: *the Hostess is seated in the left foreground: several other women*
     sit on benches behind her. They are all laughing and applauding.

     FALSTAFF (*off*): If that man should be lewdly given, he deceiveth me;
     for, Harry . . .

325. *Falstaff, as in 308.*

     FALSTAFF (*wagging his finger for emphasis*): . . . I see virtue in
     his looks.

326. *The Hostess, as in 324.*

     FALSTAFF (*off*): Him keep with, . . .

327. *Falstaff, as in 308.*

     FALSTAFF: . . . the rest . . . (*He makes a gesture of dismissal with his*
     hand.) . . . banish. //

328. *The Prince, as in 318. Women seated in the background applaud. The*
     Prince moves left until, almost entirely concealed by Falstaff, he reaches
     to pull him out of his seat.

     PRINCE: Dost thou speak like a king? Do thou stand for me.

329. LS: *the Prince and Falstaff stand in front of the table as the Prince,*
     after pulling Falstaff away from the chair, reaches to grasp Falstaff's
     friar's robe.

330. *Low angle* LS: *the Prince and Falstaff, framed by two women and the*
     Page who sit on a bench in the foreground. Poins and Bardolph stand to
     the right. The Prince pulls off Falstaff's robe, grabs his saucepan hat,
     and begins to climb up on the table. Poins dashes forward toward the
     Page and reaches for his hat.

PRINCE: I'll play my father.
FALSTAFF: Depose me? //

331. MCU: *the Page, as his hat is lifted off his head, raises his hands to his head and laughs. A laughing woman is sitting behind him.*

332. MCU: *Falstaff puts on the Page's hat. On the platform behind and above him, the Prince stands with his dark cloak wrapped around him, the saucepan-crown now on his head. A low crossbeam in the middle of the frame separates the two men. The Prince sits down on the "throne" as Falstaff turns toward him.*

PRINCE: Here I am set.

333. *The Hostess, as in 324.*

FALSTAFF (*off*): And here I stand.

334. MCU: *Falstaff, at the left, turns toward the Prince, who is sitting sideways behind him on the right.*

PRINCE (*imitating the King's voice*): Now, Harry, whence come you?
FALSTAFF: My noble lord, from Eastcheap.

335. MCU: *the Prince from the side, his hand covering his eyes in mock despair.*

PRINCE: The complaints I hear of thee are grievous.

336. *Falstaff, as in 334.*

FALSTAFF: 'Sblood, my lord, they are false. (*He turns to the camera and the tavern audience, and winks.*) Nay, I'll tickle ye for a young prince. //

337. MCU: *a woman in the right foreground, with the Page at the left of the screen and other women standing and sitting in the background. All are laughing and applauding, and the Page cries "Falstaff!"*

PRINCE (*off*): There is a devil haunts thee in the likeness of an old fat man; . . .

338. *Falstaff, as in 334. The Prince now turns forward in his seat and points at Falstaff, who stands in profile to him.*

PRINCE: . . . a tun of man is thy companion. Why dost thou converse with that trunk of humors, that bolting-hutch of beastliness, . . .

339. *The Hostess, as in 324. She laughs and nods.*

PRINCE (*off*): . . . that swoll'n parcel of dropsies, that huge bombard of sack, that stuffed . . .

340. *Falstaff, as in 334. He looks up at the Prince and then turns partly away from him.*

PRINCE: . . . cloakbag, that roasted Manningtree ox . . .

341. *The camera moves with the Prince to keep him in* MCU *as he rises up out of his chair, then holds him in a low angle* MCU *as he continues to speak.*

PRINCE (*growing more and more declamatory*): . . . that reverend vice, that gray iniquity, that father ruffian, that . . .

342. *Women on the balcony, as in 307. They are laughing and waving their hands.*

PRINCE (*off*): . . . vanity in years?

343. *Falstaff, as in 334. He turns away, toward the camera, as the Prince, now standing and gesturing, speaks. Falstaff opens his mouth as if to say something, then closes it again.*

PRINCE: Wherein is he good, but to taste sack and drink it? Wherein neat and cleanly, but to carve a capon and eat it? Wherein cunning, but in craft? Wherein crafty, but in villainy?

344. *The Hostess, as in 324. She claps her hands in delight.*

PRINCE (*off*): Wherein villainous, but in all things?

345. *The Prince, as in 341.*

PRINCE: Wherein worthy, but in nothing?

346. *The Hostess, as in 324. She stamps her foot and joins the general merriment.*

347. *Falstaff, as in 334. He is facing toward the camera, with his back to the Prince.*

FALSTAFF (*taking a long breath*): I would your Grace would take me with you. Whom means your grace?
PRINCE: That villainous abominable misleader of youth, . . .

348. *Young woman and Page, as in 337.*
YOUNG WOMAN AND PAGE (*in unison*): Falstaff!   W

Behind them, others laugh and cheer.

349. *Falstaff, as in 334.*

PRINCE: . . . that old white-bearded Satan.
FALSTAFF: My lord, the man I know.
PRINCE: I know thou dost.
FALSTAFF: But to say I know . . .

350. *The Hostess, as in 324. She and the other women are laughing.*

FALSTAFF: . . . more harm in him than I know . . .

The sound of knocking at a door causes the Hostess to turn her head.

351. *Extreme high angle* MS: *Falstaff from above the Prince. As he speaks, Falstaff turns and looks up at the Prince.*

FALSTAFF: . . . in myself is to say more than I know. That he is old,
the more's the pity, his white hairs do witness it; but that he is, saving
your reverence, an old Satan, that I . . . (*Turns back to the tavern
audience.*)

352. *The Hostess, as in 324.*

FALSTAFF (*off*): . . . utterly deny! (*The knocking is repeated, and the
Hostess gets up from the bench and moves toward the left.*) If sack and
sugar be a fault . . .

353. MCU: *Falstaff, with the Prince standing directly behind him.*

FALSTAFF (*taking off the Page's cap that he has been wearing and
throwing it to the floor for emphasis*): . . . then God help the wicked!

354. *The camera pans with the Hostess in* LS *running to the door.*

FALSTAFF (*off*): If to be old . . .

355. ELS: *the Hostess moves away from the camera toward the door to the
street. The tavern audience is in the foreground.*

FALSTAFF (*off*): . . . and merry be a sin, then many an old host that I
know is damned. (*Falstaff enters the shot in the right foreground. The
camera tilts up and holds him in a low angle* MS.) And if to be fat is
to be hated, then Pharaoh's lean kine are to be loved. No, my good
lord: banish Peto, banish Bardolph, banish . . . (*He pauses meaning-
fully.*) . . . Poins . . . (*The camera moves back to keep Falstaff in* MS
as he slowly advances.) . . . but for sweet Jack Falstaff, kind Jack
Falstaff, true Jack Falstaff, valiant Jack Falstaff . . .

356. LS: *women on the balcony, as in 342. They wave and laugh.*

357. *Low angle* MS: *Falstaff, as at the end of 355. The camera holds as
Falstaff advances into* MCU.

FALSTAFF: . . . and therefore more valiant being, as he is, old Jack
Falstaff, banish not him thy Harry's company, banish not him thy
Harry's company, banish plump Jack, and banish all the world!

358. LS: *women on the balcony applaud. The Prince jumps into the shot,
apparently from the table, at the right. He stands in* MCU *at the center
of the shot.*

PRINCE: I do. (*He begins to move forward.*)

359. *Low angle* MCU: *Falstaff, with the Prince moving into the frame profiled
in* MCU *at the right.*

PRINCE (*with quiet intensity*): I will.

360. LS: *four women sit against a wall of the tavern hall near the outer door. The Hostess enters running from the right.*

486–489   HOSTESS (*agitated*): O Jesu, my lord, my lord!

361. *Low angle* MS: *the Prince at right, with Falstaff seen from behind dominating the left foreground.*

PRINCE (*moving forward*): What's the matter?

362. LS: *the Hostess in the middle of the tavern hall, with the door to the street open in the background.*

HOSTESS: The sheriff and all the watch are at the door!

363. *The Prince, as in 361. He takes the saucepan-crown from his head.*

484–485   FALSTAFF: Play out the play, . . .

364. *Falstaff with the Prince, as in 359. In the lower foreground, the Prince can be seen discarding the saucepan and the cloak.*

FALSTAFF: . . . play out the play. I have much to say in behalf of that Falstaff.

365. *The Prince, as in 361, but now entirely out of his "play" costume. He stands erect and looks directly at Falstaff. Behind the Prince in the background women run along the balcony and there is a general commotion.*

366. *The tavern hall, as in 362. The Hostess is running out of the shot at right, followed by young women who run toward the camera and scatter in various directions.*

367. LS: *Falstaff and the Prince stand in front of the "throne"; Falstaff holds the Prince by both arms. The camera tracks briefly, passing behind a post and then reframing the two men. The Prince turns away from him*

and jumps up on the table. Women run past them from right to left, both in the foreground and background.

368. *High angle* MS: *the Prince, framed by two beams, leaps from the table between the beams and toward the camera. The camera, now level with the Prince, pans with him as he swings around one of the posts and runs down a balcony corridor.*

369. *High angle* LS: *Bardolph runs under the overhang of the balcony, followed by Peto.*

370. *The camera pans to follow the Prince in* LS *from the side and rear, as he races down the balcony corridor and disappears around a corner. At the corner, women are running up the stairs to the balcony from the main hall.*

371. LS: *a woman moves toward the camera and out of frame right. Behind her are large kegs. When she leaves the shot, one of the friars can be seen running toward the left in the background.*

372. *High angle* LS: *women cross the tavern hall, seen from a corner of the balcony. A woman running on the balcony passes directly in front of the camera.*

373. *High angle* MLS: *Peto, seen from the rear, crawls through the space under a wooden staircase and emerges on the other side. Bardolph passes immediately in front of the camera, and the camera then tilts upward to follow him as he begins to climb the stairs.*

374. *High angle* LS: *the Sheriff and soldiers, seen from the balcony entering the tavern hall at the left rear. A woman looks down at them from the balcony, part of her head, seen from behind, taking up the left side of the frame. She and another woman cross to the right directly in front of the camera.*

375. LS (*ground level shot, from under a table*): *dogs run by, followed by the legs of the Sheriff and his men.*

376. *The camera pans with the Sheriff and his men in* LS *as they move into the center of the hall.*

377. LS: *the Prince, at first obscured by figures in the foreground, runs away from the camera toward Poins, who is near a door at the left through which several women are escaping.*

378. *The camera, first darkened by figures immediately in front of it, pans left to show the same space as in 377. Falstaff stands in* LS *in the center of the frame, with the Prince near Poins in the background. Falstaff turns himself in a complete circle as two women cross from right to left between him and the camera.*

379. *In an adjoining room of the tavern, two women cross from left to right immediately in front of the camera. After they pass, the camera shows the Prince in* ELS *pulling a woman by the arm through the door. The first two women run into the center of the room close to the Prince.*

380. LS: *the Prince, seen from the rear, still holds the woman by the arm. He tosses her forward through the air into a bed by the wall and then leaps into the bed with her. Then he reaches down to pull the covers over them as the other two women run by the camera in the foreground.*

381. *The camera focuses on the bedclothes, then tilts up slightly to frame the Prince in* MS *as he raises himself in the bed.*

501–524   PRINCE: Go hide thee, Jack. Now, my masters, for a true face and a good conscience.

382. MS: *Falstaff, with only his face showing through a half-open trap door, held up by his head, in the middle of the floor.*

FALSTAFF: Both of which I have had, but their date is out; therefore I'll hide me. (*Falstaff lowers his head, and the trap door closes with a thud.*)

383. LS: *the Sheriff enters a doorway to the Prince's room. He stands in the doorway, his soldiers and two gentlemen clustering behind him.*

384. LS: *the Prince in the bed, seen from the side. The bedclothes are wrapped tightly around him, and only an outline of the woman is visible under the blanket.*

385. LS: *the Sheriff, as in 383, but now advancing alone toward the camera. He stops in* MLS *near a post.*

386. LS: *the Prince, now seen from an angle nearer the foot of the bed.*

PRINCE: Now . . .

387. *Low angle* MCU: *two of the soldiers gawking, with other men in the background.*

PRINCE (*off*): . . . master sheriff, what is your will with me?

388. MLS: *the Sheriff, as at the end of 385.*

SHERIFF (*uneasily clearing his throat*): Pardon me, my lord. A hue and cry // Hath followed certain men into this house.

389. *The Prince, as in 386.*

PRINCE: What men?

390. *The Sheriff, as in 388.*

SHERIFF: One of them is well known, my gracious lord—/

One of the gawking soldiers of 384 scurries into the room.

391. MCU: *Falstaff, with only his hat and eyes visible under the barely opened trap door.*

SHERIFF (*off*): a gross fat man.

392. MLS: *the Sheriff, as in 388, with the solider now crouched next to him.*

SOLDIER: As fat as butter!
PRINCE (*off*): The man . . .

393. *The Prince, as in 386.*

PRINCE: . . . I do assure you, is not here. //

The woman in bed with him raises her head.

394. *Falstaff, as in 391. He quickly drops his head and the trap door closes.*

395. LS: *the Prince, as at the end of 393. The woman now cuddles up next to him, her arm around his neck.*

PRINCE: And so let me entreat you leave the house.

396. *The Sheriff, as in 392. The soldier now scurries back to the doorway where the other men are standing.*

SHERIFF (*with some disdain*): I will, my lord. (*He turns away.*)

397. *The Prince, as in 384. He laughs and looks after the Sheriff as the woman smiles and nuzzles him. Bells begin to peal on the soundtrack and continue to the end of shot 408.*

398. *The sheriff, as in 383. He now stands sideways in the doorway.*

SHERIFF: There are two gentlemen / Have in this robbery lost three hundred marks.

Two gentlemen, apparently the victims of the robbery, are standing next to the sheriff. One nods.

399. *The Prince, as in 395. The woman presses her cheek against his.*

PRINCE: If he has robbed these men, / He shall be answerable; . . .

400. *The Sheriff, as in 383.*

PRINCE (*off*): . . . and so farewell.

SHERIFF: Good night, my noble lord. (*He bows and leaves, his men following him.*)

401. MS: *the Prince pulls the bedcovers away, revealing that he is fully clothed. He gets up without looking back at the woman, and moves out of the shot at the right.*

402. LS (*from the ground level*): *the Sheriff and his men descend the stairs and, with several dogs, cross the tavern hall.*

403. LS: *the Prince moves away from the camera toward the door of the room where he has been in bed. To the right the trap door is opening and Falstaff is emerging from his hiding place.*

PRINCE (*over his shoulder to Poins, who enters the frame from the right, following the Prince*): I'll to the court in the morning. We must all to the wars.   545–546

404. LS: *the Sheriff with his men behind him, at the extreme left of the frame, moves toward the camera as they pass through the main hall of the tavern, now entirely empty. The Sheriff stops and turns as his men pass by him.*

SHERIFF: Good night, my noble lord.   524–526

405. MS: *the Prince under a low-ceilinged section of the balcony. He bumps his head, rubs it, and then moves forward, turning toward the railing.*

PRINCE: I think it be good morrow, is it not? (*The camera continues to pan away from the Prince's face and down his arm, looking through the balcony toward the floor of the main hall.*)

SHERIFF (*off*): Indeed, my lord . . . (*The pan now includes the Sheriff and his men in the distance at the lower left.*)

406. MS: *The Sheriff in right foreground, with two of the gentlemen behind him.*

SHERIFF: . . . I think it be two o'clock. (*He gives the Prince a per-functory bow.*)

407. *Extreme low angle* LS: *the Prince at the railing of the balcony, with the camera tilted to the left.*

408. *The Sheriff, as in 406. He bows perfunctorily again—even derisively— and turns to leave.*

409. *The camera pans left with Falstaff in* LS *as he, along with several others from the tavern, walks along the balcony corridor. As they walk, they pass the Prince, who now stands in the foreground with his back to the camera.*

W

H1 III.iii.211

FALSTAFF: We must all to the wars, eh lad? (*Falstaff alone turns at the entrance to the staircase, where he meets the Hostess climbing the stairs.*) Hostess, my breakfast.

68, 75–77

HOSTESS: You owe me money, Sir John. (*Falstaff turns around and, followed by the Hostess and the Prince, walks down the corridor toward the camera as it pans with him.*) And money lent you, four and twenty pounds.

The Prince laughs and points at him admonishingly.

118–141

FALSTAFF: Go, you thing.

HOSTESS: What thing? I am no thing. I am an honest man's wife, and, setting thy knighthood aside, thou art a knave to call me so.

FALSTAFF (*taking a flagon and cup from the ledge of an opening into another room and sitting down in front of the opening. The camera reframes the three in a low angle* MLS.): Setting thy womanhood aside, thou art a beast to say otherwise. (*He takes a drink.*)

HOSTESS: Say, what beast, thou knave, thou?

FALSTAFF: What beast? Why, an otter.

The Prince, laughing, moves into the adjoining room and, at the right, leans on the ledge behind Falstaff.

PRINCE: An otter, Sir John? Why an otter?

FALSTAFF: O, she's neither fish nor flesh; a man knows not where to
have her.

HOSTESS: O, thou art an unjust man for saying so. Thou or any man
knows where to have me, thou knave, thou!

PRINCE: Thou sayest true, Hostess, and he slanders thee most grossly.

HOSTESS (*crossing in front of Falstaff to speak to the Prince*): So he
doth you, my lord, and said you owed him a thousand pounds.

PRINCE (*emerging from the room to stand over Falstaff at the left*):
Jack, do I owe thee a thousand pound?

FALSTAFF (*between the two, rising*): A thousand pound, Hal? A million. (*He shifts the flagon into his right arm to free his other hand.*)
Thy love is worth a million. (*He pats the Prince on the cheek with his
free hand.*) Thou owest me thy love.

PRINCE (*laughing and embracing Falstaff*): Well, my sweet beef, I   183–184
must still be good angel to thee.

HOSTESS (*crossing left to take the Prince by the arm and then stand
behind him*): My lord, he called you a jack and a sneak-cup, and said   142–143
he would cudgel you.

PRINCE: Darest thou be as good as thy word now?   147–154

FALSTAFF (*moving away to the left, and then turning back to face the
Prince. The camera tracks with him.*): Well, Hal, as a man I dare, but
as a prince I fear thee as I fear the roaring of a lion's whelp.

PRINCE: And why not as the lion?

*The camera tracks left again as Falstaff moves through a door into the
adjoining room and reframes him in low angle* MLS *with the Prince and
the Hostess in the foreground on each side of the doorway.*

FALSTAFF: The King himself is to be feared as the lion. Dost thou think
that I'll fear thee as I fear thy father?

PRINCE (*pausing, then turning to face the Hostess*): The money shall be   184–186
paid back again . . . (*He pats her arm and moves out of the shot at
the left.*)

410. MS: *Falstaff stands before a bare wall of the room, flagon in one hand,
cup in the other.*

PRINCE (*off*): . . . with advantage.

FALSTAFF: I like not that paying back. 'Tis a double labor. (*He is about to drink from the cup, when he is distracted by a voice offscreen.*)

H2 II.iv.235–236 DOLL TEARSHEET (*off*): Thou . . .

411. MS: *Doll Tearsheet pulls back the covers and rises from her bed.*

DOLL: . . . whoreson little tidy Bartholomew boar-pig.

W FALSTAFF (*off; overlapping*): How now, Doll.

412. *The camera pans with Doll in* MLS *as she moves toward Falstaff, whose back dominates the left of the frame. She takes the cup from his hand and, putting her other arm around his neck, turns him around with her, as she passes by him. The camera reframes them in* MS *with Doll at the left.*

66–69 DOLL (*close against his chest*): Come, I'll be friends with thee, Jack. Thou art going to the wars, and whether I shall ever see thee again or not, there's nobody cares.

Falstaff bends to kiss her, but she blocks him by drinking from the cup. He pulls away and walks right to a shuttered window. He begins to open one of the shutters. The sound of bells and a horse's hooves are heard on the soundtrack and continue through shot 418.

413. MLS: *Falstaff, seen from outside the window, pulls open the shutters and looks out.*

414. LS: *the Prince on horseback rides toward the camera down the street outside the tavern and out of the shot at the lower left. A morning mist hangs over the street.*

415. *Low angle* LS: *Falstaff leans out of the window.*

FALSTAFF: Hal!

416. LS: *the Prince reins his horse and half-turns in the saddle to face the*

camera. The castle walls are in the background and a tree fills the left of the frame.

PRINCE: Farewell, blown . . .   HI IV.ii.50

417. LS: *Falstaff, as in 415. He waves.*

PRINCE (*off*): . . . Jack!

418. *The Prince, as in 416. He waves and rides away toward the castle.*

PRINCE: Farewell, All-hallown summer!   HI I.ii.162–163

Dissolve.

The Royal Castle

419. *Low angle* MS: *the King in the left foreground, with John of Lancaster partly visible on the right. In the center background, the Prince enters the shot from around a corner. He stops short, seemingly surprised.*

KING (*his first words already audible during the dissolve*): Percy, North-   HI III.ii.118–128
umberland, / The Archbishop's grace of York, Douglas, Mortimer /
. . . (*He pauses when he sees the Prince.*) . . . Capitulate against us
and are up. / But wherefore do I tell this news to thee? // (*Adjusts the
cuffs of his sleeves.*) Thou that art like enough, through vassal fear, /
Base inclination, and the start of spleen / . . . (*The camera tracks left
with the King away from the Prince, past a wall hanging of a medieval king with orb and scepter. He stops, reframed in low angle* MS,
near a low stone archway.) . . . To fight against me under Percy's pay, /
To dog his heels and curtsy at his frowns, / To show how much thou
art degenerate.

420. LS (*from ground level*): *the Prince faces the camera. Soldiers stand at
attention along the arched sides of the long hall. The Prince still stands
where he did when the King began to speak.*

421. *Low angle* MS: *the King, as at the end of 419. He turns away and leaves through the low archway. Martial music begins to sound, and continues into shot 424.*

422. *The Prince, as in 420. He turns and moves purposefully toward an archway at the left.*

423. *The camera tracks with the Prince in* LS *from the side as he strides toward the left down the long assembly hall of the throne room. Soldiers standing at attention against the far wall face the camera. Since the camera is located in a side-aisle, the Prince is for a time obscured by the backs of attendants and by a large stone column.*

424. *Low angle* ELS: *the King seats himself on the throne in the left of the frame. Nobody else is present in the cavernous surroundings.*

1–16

KING: Lords, give us leave. The Prince of Wales and I / Must have some needful conference alone. //

425. ELS: *the Prince is surrounded by courtiers and attendants in the assembly hall beyond the stairs to the throne. All the others bow and begin to back away, taking their leave.*

426. MCU: *the King on his throne.*

427. ELS: *the Prince as at end of 425. He is soon alone and begins to move forward up the stairs. In the silence, only his echoing footsteps are heard.*

428. MCU: *the King's profile.*

KING: I know not whether God will have it so // That, in his secret doom, out of my blood / He'll breed revengement and a scourge for me // To punish my misreadings. Tell me else, / . . .

429. LS: *the King with the Prince standing, back to camera, in front of him. They are framed by pillars in the foreground.*

KING: . . . Could such inordinate and low desires, // Such barren plea-
sures, . . . (*He rises and steps toward the Prince.*) . . . rude society, //
Accompany the greatness of thy blood?
PRINCE (*moving in order to continue facing the King as he begins to
turn away*): So please your Majesty—   18

430. LS: *the King, his back to the camera, with the Prince facing him, both at
right of the frame, with a corner of the throne visible at left.*

KING: Had I so lavish of my presence been, // So stale and cheap to vul- 39–99
gar company, . . . / . . .

431. LS: *the King faces the Prince. Both are at screen left, in reverse of 430.
The high windows above the throne are visible in the background.*

KING: . . . Opinion, that did help me to the crown, // Had left me in reputeless banishment. //

Bells begin to toll, and continue periodically through shot 443.

432. LS: *the King, as at the end of 430. He begins to move down the stairs away from the camera, while the Prince remains stationary.*

KING: The skipping King, he ambled up and down / With shallow jesters and rash bavin wits, // . . .

433. *The camera tracks right, keeping the King in* MCU *as he walks down the stairs, then holding him in* CU *until the end of the shot.*

KING: . . . Mingled his royalty with cap'ring fools, // Grew a companion to the common streets. // So, when he had occasion to be seen, / He was but as the cuckoo is in June, / Heard, not regarded—seen, but with such eyes / As, sick and blunted with community, / Afford no extraordinary gaze, / Such as is bent on sunlike majesty. // (*He turns to look back toward the Prince.*) And in that very line, Harry, stand'st thou; / . . .

434. LS: *the Prince, at the left, still stands at the top of the stairs near the throne.*

KING (*off*): . . . For thou hast lost . . .

435. CU: *the King, as at the end of 433.*

KING: . . . thy princely privilege / With vile participation. Not an eye / But is aweary of thy common sight, / Save mine, that hath desired to see thee more. // (*He turns away.*)

436. *The Prince, as in 434.*

PRINCE: I shall hereafter, my thrice-gracious lord, / Be more myself.
KING (*off*): Harry, for all the world / . . .

437. *Low angle* MLS: *the King approaches the camera in lower left of the frame. The Prince can be seen behind him in the background. As the King stops in low angle* MS, *he blocks out the Prince.*

> KING: . . . As thou art to this hour was Richard then / When I from France set foot at Ravenspurgh; / And even as I was then . . .

438. *Low angle* LS: *the Prince is framed between pillars with light from a high window behind him. He moves forward down the stairs out of the shot at the right.*

> KING (*off*): . . . is Percy now. /

439. *Low angle* MS: *the King, as at the end of 437. The Prince moves into the background at the right.*

> KING: Now, by my scepter, and my soul to boot, / He hath more worthy interest to the state / Than thou.
> PRINCE (*moving further forward on the right*): Do not think so, . . .   129–146
> (*The King turns away from the camera to face the Prince.*) . . . you shall not find it so. // I will redeem all this on Percy's head / And, in the closing of some glorious day, / Be bold to tell you that I am your son. // And that shall be the day, whene'er it lights, / . . .

440. *Low angle* MS: *the King.*

> PRINCE (*off*): . . . That this same child of honor and renown, / . . .

441. CU: *the Prince.*

> PRINCE: . . . This gallant Hotspur, this all-praisèd knight, / And your unthought-of Harry chance to meet. // Then will I make this northern youth exchange / His glorious deeds for my indignities. // This in the name of God . . . (*Momentarily breaks off*)   153

442. *Low angle* MS: *the King, as at the end of 440. The King turns and moves toward the camera out of the shot.*

PRINCE (*off, obscured by the figure of the King*): . . . I promise here.

443. LS: *the King and the Prince in the assembly hall, with the throne in the background. The King moves out of the frame at the right, leaving the Prince alone in the hall.*

170–179   KING: The Earl of Westmoreland sets forth today. // (*Now off.*) On Wednesday next, Harry, you shall set forth. // Our hands are full of business. Let's away.

As the Prince follows the King, the tolling of the bells is clearly heard.

Dissolve.

A Street Near the Tavern

444. *Low angle* LS: *a church tower, with its tolling bells visible. The camera moves down and right to the base of the church wall where soldiers on horseback ride near the wall and through the streets in the foreground. Both streams of the riders move out of the shot on the left. Martial music as in the credit sequence continues on the soundtrack through shot 455.*

445. *High angle* LS: *a narrow street of the town. Soldiers on horseback ride toward the camera, disappearing below it. On the left, townspeople line the side of the street and three women watch from a balcony overhead.*

446. MLS: *Pistol is part of the procession in the street. He walks toward the camera, waving at the crowd.*

447. *High angle* LS: *Pistol seen from behind. He turns to wave to those in the balconies behind him. Soldiers are in the street ahead of him and women line the far side of the street in the background.*

448. *Low angle* LS: *a balcony with three women waving down at the soldiers. In the low foreground, the soldiers' spears and the tops of their heads are visible as they pass to the left.*

449. MS: *Pistol, with his nose high in the air, is obviously full of his own importance. Bardolph, in the helmet and uniform of a foot soldier, moves into the shot from the right and puts his face close to Pistol's.*

BARDOLPH: Pish!   H5 II.i.43–45

PISTOL (*haughtily*): Pish to thee, thy prick-ear'd cur of Iceland. (*He abruptly turns his back on Bardolph.*)

450. MS: *Corporal Nym, with Bardolph behind him, moves to the left through the street with horsemen riding in the background.*

* NYM (*over his shoulder*): We must to the wars together; why the devil   93–95
should we keep knives to cut one another's throats? (*Nym and Bardolph move out of the shot at the left, as Pistol appears at the right in* MS.)

PISTOL: O viper vile! // Know Pistol's cock is up, / . . . (*Holding his*   49, 55–56
dagger in front of him to mimic an erection.) . . . And flashing fire
will follow.

† BARDOLPH (*reappearing from left to stand next to Pistol, shaking his*   97–99
fist): Pistol, pay me the eight shillings I won of you at betting.

PISTOL: Base is the slave that pays. (*He swaggers out of the shot at
the left.*)

† BARDOLPH (*shouting after Pistol*): Shog off!   48

451. *Low angle* LS (*the camera tilted slightly to the left*): *the church, with horsemen partially visible in the lower foreground riding past toward the left.*

452. LS: *horsemen ride past the camera and down the street toward the church tower in the background. Townspeople watch at the left.*

453. *The camera holds on children climbing a staircase until they reach the top in* MCU.

* Bardolph
† Nym

454. *The camera tracks left with soldiers on horseback in* LS, *carrying spears and shields. They are visible over the white-capped heads of women who sit on a low stone wall closer to the camera.*

455. *Low angle* LS: *a balcony at the tavern, crowded with young women. They cheer the riders who pass, partially visible in the lower foreground.*

456. *Low angle* MS (*the camera tilted to the left*): *three young women on the balcony.*

457. LS: *Falstaff walks by himself down the middle of the street, waving to the girls on the balcony. He carries a walking stick.*

458. LS (*from ground level*): *the Chief Justice, with a young attendant behind him. They stand in the middle of the street, with the imposing entrance to a church in the background to their right.*

H2 I.ii.60–63   CHIEF JUSTICE: What's he that goes there?
ATTENDANT: Falstaff, an't please your Lordship.
CHIEF JUSTICE: He that is in question for the robbery?

459. *The camera tracks left with Falstaff in* MS *as he walks backward, looking up.*

DOLL (*off*): Jack!

460. *Low angle* LS: *Doll at a small upper window of the tavern. She blows him a kiss.*

461. *High angle* LS: *Falstaff in the street looking up toward Doll and the camera. He blows her a kiss in return.*

462. MCU: *the Chief Justice at the left of the frame. A mitred bishop is partially visible next to him at the far left. The church entrance is prominent in the right background. The Chief Justice advances out of the shot at the left.*

FALSTAFF (*off*): My Lord Chief Justice . . .   98–104

463. LS: *Falstaff advances down the center of the street. He moves toward the Chief Justice, who stands, his back to the camera, at the lower right. A column of foot soldiers, at the left, passes Falstaff, heading in the direction he has come from.*

> FALSTAFF (*with a salute as a greeting*): . . . I heard say your lordship was sick. I hope your lordship goes abroad by advice. (*Now in* MS *with the Chief Justice.*) Your lordship, while not clean past his youth, has yet some smack of age in him, some relish . . .

464. *Low angle* LS: *Doll leaning out the window in the upper left of the frame.*

> FALSTAFF (*off*): . . . of the saltness of time.

465. MS: *Falstaff and the Chief Justice, the castle walls in the background. Falstaff has passed by the Chief Justice, and now turns back at the right of the frame to face him.*

> FALSTAFF: But I most humbly beseech your lordship to have a reverent care of your health. (*He turns away.*)

466. *Doll, as in 464. A man's arms appear from behind her and pull her away from the window.*

> FALSTAFF (*off*): Ah, my Lord Westmoreland . . .   H1 IV.ii.52–56

467. LS: *Falstaff is seen from a slightly high angle across the heads of the horses of Lord Westmoreland and another nobleman, the horses and riders partially visible in the foreground. An open yard with a bare tree in the center and house with a stone façade are in the background. Bells begin to toll intermittently through shot 478.*

> FALSTAFF: . . . I heard say your lordship had already been at Shrewsbury.

WESTMORELAND: 'Tis more than time I were there, and you too.
77–79   FALSTAFF: What, the King encamped?

468. *Low angle* MS: *Westmoreland and the other nobleman at the right look down in the direction of Falstaff. Houses along the street with people at the windows are visible in the background.*

WESTMORELAND: He is, Sir John. I fear we shall all stay too long.

469. LS: *a group of men move into the shot from the left and then draw up in a line facing the camera in front of the house with the stone façade and its bare tree.*

*NOBLEMAN (*off*): Sir John, methinks your soldiers are exceeding
69–70   poor . . .

470. *Westmoreland and the other nobleman, as in 468.*

*NOBLEMAN: . . . and bare.

38–39   †WESTMORELAND: Never have I seen such . . .

471. *Low angle* MLS: *Falstaff in the foreground, his back to the camera, with the line of men facing him.*

†WESTMORELAND (*off*): . . . scarecrows.
11–31   FALSTAFF: If I'm not ashamed of me soldiers, I'm a sous'd gurnet. (*He begins to turn toward Westmoreland.*)

472. *Westmoreland and the other nobleman, as in 468.*

FALSTAFF (*off*): I've misused the King's press damnably. //

473. *Low angle* MS: *Falstaff faces the camera with his body turned sideways, the line of men behind him.*

*Westmoreland
†Falstaff

FALSTAFF: I pressed me none but good householders. // They've bought out their services, and now me whole charge consists of // younger sons to younger brothers, revolted tapsters, and ostlers . . .

474. MS: *some of the men in the line. They all look shabby, gaunt, and old.*

FALSTAFF (*off*): . . . trade-fall'n, . . .

475. MLS: *Falstaff, as at the end of 471.*

FALSTAFF: . . . the cankers of a calm world and a long peace.

476. MS: *Westmoreland and the other nobleman.*

* NOBLEMAN: We must away all night, Falstaff. (*He rides out of the shot to the right.*)   57–58

477. LS: *Falstaff, his men, and the stone house in the background. In the foreground, the nobleman rides out of shot at the left and Westmoreland, after speaking, rides after him.*

WESTMORELAND: The King, I can tell you, looks for us all.
FALSTAFF (*running forward into the foreground and calling after them*): Goes the Prince with you?   W

The Chief Justice enters the shot from the lower right, followed by the Bishop, and advances toward Falstaff.

† BISHOP: The Prince? You follow him up and down like his ill angel.
CHIEF JUSTICE: Falstaff, you have misled . . .   H2 I.ii.169–170
                                                                     149–150

478. MS: *the Chief Justice faces the camera with the Bishop on the left. Falstaff crosses toward the left behind them. The castle walls are in the background. The camera pans with Falstaff as he moves in a semi-circle with the Chief Justice turning and following him. The camera then reframes*

* Westmoreland
† Chief Justice

the three men in a low angle MS, *with Falstaff in the center and the Chief Justice behind him on the left.*

CHIEF JUSTICE: . . . the youthful Prince.

FALSTAFF: The young Prince has misled me.

141–148   CHIEF JUSTICE: The truth is, you live in great infamy. // Your means are very slender and your waste is great.

FALSTAFF: I would it were otherwise. I would my means were greater and my waist slender. (*He moves out of the shot at the left. The camera tracks left with the Chief Justice and the Bishop, seen from the side, as they follow him.*)

166–168   CHIEF JUSTICE: There's not a white hair on your face but should have his effect on gravity. (*The Chief Justice and the Bishop catch up with Falstaff. The tracking shot continues, now with the three men in low angle* MLS, *and Falstaff the most prominent, slightly ahead of the others.*)

FALSTAFF: His effect on gravy, gravy, gravy.

479. *The camera tracks in a low angle* MS, *ahead and slightly to the side of Falstaff. The Chief Justice and the Bishop are intermittently at his sides during the course of the shot.*

180–197   FALSTAFF: My lords, you that are old consider not the capacities of us that are young.

CHIEF JUSTICE: Falstaff!

FALSTAFF: You do measure the heat of our livers with the bitterness of your galls. //

* BISHOP: Do you set down your name in the scroll of youth?

CHIEF JUSTICE: You that are written down old with all the characters of age?

* BISHOP: Have you not a moist eye, a dry hand, a yellow cheek, . . .

CHIEF JUSTICE: . . . a white beard, . . .

* BISHOP: . . . a decreasing leg, . . .

CHIEF JUSTICE: . . . an increasing belly?

Falstaff takes an apple from his pocket and begins to eat it as he walks.

*Chief Justice

* BISHOP: Is not your voice broken, your wind short, . . .

CHIEF JUSTICE: . . . your chin double, . . .

* BISHOP: . . . your wit single, . . .

CHIEF JUSTICE: . . . and every part about you blasted with antiquity,
   . . . (*The Chief Justice continues offscreen as Falstaff moves out of the
   shot to the left, leaving the Bishop in a low angle* MS, *with a castle
   tower behind him.*) . . . and will you yet call yourself young?

480. MCU: *Falstaff, with houses and passing horsemen in the background.*

   FALSTAFF: My lord, I was born about three o'clock in the afternoon,
      with a white head and something a round belly. For my voice, I have
      lost it with hallowing and singing of anthems.

   * NYM (*off*): Sir John!   H2 II.i.192–193

481. MS: *Nym at the left, a large gnarled tree filling the frame at the right.
   Some of Falstaff's conscripts are partially visible behind Nym.*

   * NYM: Sir John!

482. *Falstaff, as in 480. He turns toward the left at the sound of Nym's voice.*

   * NYM (*off*): You loiter here too long . . .

483. *Nym, as in 481.*

   * NYM: . . . being as we're to take more soldiers in counties as we go.

484. *Low angle* LS: *Nym, framed by the backs of two of Falstaff's conscripts.
   Falstaff passes in front of Nym, waving his walking stick, and moves out
   of the shot at the left followed by Nym and the conscripts.*

   FALSTAFF: On, Corporal Nym.   W

   * BISHOP (*as he and the Chief Justice enter the space just vacated by*   H2 I.ii.231–236
      Falstaff and Nym): Well, be honest, be honest, and God bless . . .

*Chief Justice

485. *Low angle* MS: *Falstaff, with a crowd of women on a balcony behind him.*

   * BISHOP (*off*): . . . your expedition!
   FALSTAFF: Could your grace lend me a thousand pound to furnish
      me forth?

486. *Low angle* MLS: *the Bishop, with the Chief Justice behind him, as at the end of 484.*

   * BISHOP: Not a penny, not a penny. // Fare you well. (*He turns away.*)

487. *Falstaff, as in 485.*

   FALSTAFF: My lord?

488. MCU: *the Chief Justice.*

   CHIEF JUSTICE (*grimly*): Not a penny.

489. *Falstaff is in the foreground in* LS, *seen from the side, with the Chief Justice in the right background. The street behind them is crowded with foot soldiers and horsemen moving toward the left.*

H1 IV.ii.1–4   FALSTAFF: Bardolph, . . . (*Bardolph steps up to Falstaff.*) . . . go thee
      before and fetch me a bottle of sack. //
   BARDOLPH (*extending his hand, palm up*): Will you give me money,
      captain?

490. MS: *Falstaff with Bardolph partly visible, hand extended, in front of him at the right of the frame. Falstaff grimaces, turns, and walks away.*

H2 I.ii.207–209   CHIEF JUSTICE (*off*): Well, God send the Prince a better companion.

----

* Chief Justice

A page leads a donkey laden with a suit of armor across the screen in front of Falstaff.

FALSTAFF (*turning back toward the camera with a guffaw*): God send the companion a better prince! (*He whacks the rear of the donkey with his walking stick.*)

The Rebel Camp, Near Shrewsbury

491. ELS: *horsemen ride from left to right down the slope of an open field. Trees are in the background.*

HOTSPUR (*off*): How now? (*He moves into the shot from the lower left and walks, with his back to the camera, toward the horsemen, who wheel their horses and approach him.*)

VERNON (*still at a distance*): The Earl of Westmoreland, seven thousand strong, / Is marching hitherwards; with him Prince John.   HI IV.i.87–97

492. *Low angle* MS: *Hotspur, in a coat of mail.*

HOTSPUR: No harm. What more?

493. *Low angle* MS: *Vernon on his horse. He dismounts and moves forward.*

VERNON: Further we have learned, / The King himself in person is set forth.

494. *The camera tracks in front of Hotspur, keeping him in a low angle* MS *as he strides along against the background of a cloudless sky.*

HOTSPUR (*smiling*): He shall be welcome too. Where is his son, / The nimble-footed madcap Prince of Wales, / And his comrades, that daffed the world aside / And bid it pass? (*He reaches Vernon.*)

495. MCU: *Vernon, seen over Hotspur's shoulder.*

H1 IV.iii.29

VERNON (*seriously*): All furnished, all in arms. // (*Hotspur moves past him.*)* For God's sake, cousin, . . .

496. *Low angle* MLS: *Hotspur moves into the right foreground. Behind him, Vernon turns toward the camera looking after him. Soldiers can be seen lined up at attention in the far background.*

H1 V.ii.81–86

*VERNON: . . . stay till all come in.
HOTSPUR: O gentlemen, the time of life is short! / To spend that shortness basely were too long / If life did . . .

497. MCU: *Vernon against the background of the sky, with four vertical spears in the left background.*

HOTSPUR (*off*): . . . ride upon a dial's point, / . . .

498. MS: *Worcester, dressed in black with a black hat, against the background of the sky.*

HOTSPUR (*off*): . . . Still ending at the arrival of an hour. /

499. MCU: *Hotspur against the sky.*

HOTSPUR: And if we live, we live to tread on kings; / If die, brave death, when princes die with us!

Justice Shallow's House

500. MS: *Bardolph leans through the upper half of a Dutch door. Rain is falling behind him.*

H2 III.ii.59–66

BARDOLPH: Justice Shallow?

501. MLS: *Justice Shallow, in semi-darkness, descends a crude wooden staircase in his barn. He carries a large book.*

* Worcester

SHALLOW: I am Robert Shallow, sir, a poor esquire of this county, and one of the King's justices of the peace. (*As Shallow approaches the camera, it moves slightly back and to the right to reveal Bardolph in profile, both men now in* CU.)

502. *The camera tracks backward as Shallow advances in* MS *toward it down a passageway of the barn. Bardolph enters the door and walks alongside Shallow.*

BARDOLPH: My captain commends him to you, my captain, sir, Sir John Falstaff, a tall gentleman, by heaven, and a most gallant leader. (*The two men stop and face each other in* MS.)
SHALLOW: He greets me well, sir. (*The camera pans with Shallow as he moves to the right. As Shallow moves out of the shot, the camera continues to pan and reframes on Silence in* MLS, *seated with a pig in his lap.*) He greets me well, sir. (*Off.*): Davy?
SILENCE: He's come hither . . . (*Stuttering.*) . . . bu-, bu-, bu-— 　　　　　w
SHALLOW (*off; overlapping*): Let me see, let me see, where's the roll? 　100–101

503. *Low angle* MS: *Shallow turns toward the camera.*

    SHALLOW: The soldiers—

504. MS: *Silence, with the pig partially visible in the lower foreground. He nods and grunts in assent.*

H2 V.i.31–36   SHALLOW (*off*): Use these men well, Davy . . .

505. *Low angle* MS: *Shallow, in profile, speaks into the ear of Davy, who is turned away from the camera.*

    SHALLOW: . . . for they are arrant knaves, and they will backbite.
    DAVY (*moving back to face Shallow; he is a very young man with a soft voice*): No worse than they are backbitten, sir, for they have marvelous foul linen.
H2 III.ii.85–86   SHALLOW: O, well conceited, Davy! // Look, here comes Sir John . . .

506. LS: *Falstaff enters out of the rain into the shed. People stand outside in the background. Falstaff takes his shield, which he has been using to protect his head from the rain, and his sword, and gives them to a boy who attends him.*
H2 V.i.36–37   SHALLOW (*off*): About thy business, Davy. // (*Enters from the right*
H2 III.ii.86–90   *foreground and moves toward Falstaff.*) Give me your good hand, give me your worship's good hand. Welcome, good Sir John.
    FALSTAFF (*shaking Shallow's hand and moving past him toward the*
H2 V.iii.5–7   *camera*): Good Master Robert Shallow. I'm glad to see you well.
    'Fore God, you have here a goodly dwelling and a rich, . . .
    SHALLOW (*following, his voice overlapping*): Barren, barren, barren.

507. *The camera follows Falstaff and Shallow from behind in* MLS *as they move into a room with stone walls, a heavily beamed ceiling, and a number of tables and benches. Silence stands at the left holding his pig. In the background several men, sitting on a bench by the wall, rise as Falstaff and Shallow come toward them.*

    FALSTAFF: . . . rich.

SHALLOW: Nay, you shall see my orchard, where, in an arbor, we will   1–3
eat a last year's pippin of my own grafting, . . . (*The camera holds
them in* LS.) . . . with a dish of caraways.
FALSTAFF: Have you . . .   H2 III.ii.96–101

508. *The camera pans with Falstaff in* MS *as he passes by several dispirited-
looking men. He then moves across the room to the right, in front of a
long desk with an inkstand.*

FALSTAFF: . . . provided me here with a half a dozen sufficient . . .
(*Glances at the conscripts over his shoulder and pauses.*) men?
SHALLOW (*now behind the desk*): We have, we have, sir. Come, sir,
will you sit? // Let me see, let me see. (*He puts his book on the table
and looks around.*) Where's the roll? Davy! (*He hurries out of a door
near the table.*)
FALSTAFF (*sitting down and reframed by the camera in* MS. *Nym sits
down next to him on the right.*): Robert Shallow. I remember him at   317–338
Clement's Inn like a man made after supper of a cheese-paring. When
'a was naked, he was, for all the world, like a forked radish, with a
head fantastically carved upon it with a knife. // 'A was the very genius of famine, yet lecherous as a monkey. // And now is this Vice's
dagger become a squire, // and has lands and beeves. Well, I'll be
acquainted with him.

509. LS: *Shallow, with Davy following him, seen in a room with large storage
casks. They are framed by a doorway in the foreground. Shallow carries
a piece of paper—the roll—in his hand.*
SHALLOW: I will use him well, Davy, for a friend in the court is better   H2 V.i.30–31
than a penny in the purse. (*He and Davy advance through the door,
the camera then panning right to follow Shallow as he moves to stand*   H2 III.ii.101–103
behind his desk in MS.) Let me see, let me see. Let them appear as
you call, cousin.

*In the background, Silence stands facing Shallow, and Falstaff sits with
Nym at the left, as the men by the wall begin to move toward a bench in
front of the desk.*

510. MS: *three of the men, seen from the back, seat themselves on the bench. At the right, Nym is partly visible as he leaves his seat by Falstaff.*

511. LS: *five men, now seated on the bench.*

90–95   FALSTAFF (*off*): Master . . .

512. MLS: *Falstaff seated at right. Shallow behind him at his desk in the center, and Silence below to the left, lowering a writing board in front of him. Silence now holds the roll.*

W

FALSTAFF: . . . Surecard, as I think?
SHALLOW: Silence! (*Then, as he sees that Falstaff misunderstands.*) Sir John, it is my cousin Silence, in commission with me.
FALSTAFF: Master Silence, it well befits you should be of the peace.
SHALLOW: The same, Sir John . . .

513. CU: *Silence, in left foreground, with Shallow above and behind him.*

SHALLOW: . . . the very same. (*He chuckles.*)

514. MCU: *Falstaff, looking resigned.*

SILENCE (*off*): Your . . .

515. *Silence with Shallow, as in 513.*

SILENCE (*struggling with his stammer*): . . . g-g-good worship is w-w-w . . .
SHALLOW (*reaching over to prod Silence on the shoulder and interrupting him*): Aaah . . .

516. *Falstaff, as in 514. He turns his eyes up toward Shallow.*

30–35   SHALLOW (*off*): . . . I see him break . . .

517. *Silence with Shallow, as in 513.*

SHALLOW: . . . Scoggin's head at the court-gate, when 'a was a crack not thus high. And the very same day did I fight with one Sampson . . .

518. *High angle* MCU: *Falstaff looking up toward Shallow.*

SHALLOW (*off*): . . . Stockfish, a fruiterer, behind Gray's Inn.

519. *Low angle* CU: *Shallow.*

SHALLOW: O Jesu, Jesu, the mad days that I have seen.

520. *Falstaff, as in 514.*

FALSTAFF: Master Silence . . .   **99**

521. *The three men, as in 512.*

FALSTAFF (*tapping the roll with his cane*): . . . let me see your men, Master Silence.
SHALLOW: Let them appear as you call, cousin, let them do so, let   **103–104**
them do so.

522. *Silence with Shallow, as in 513.*

SILENCE: M-mm-mm-—

523. *Falstaff, as in 514.*

SILENCE (*off*): . . . Mmm-mm-—

524. *Silence and Shallow, as in 513.*

SILENCE: Mm-mm-—
SHALLOW (*interrupting*): Moldy!

104–161

525. *The five men, as in 511. One stands up.*

FALSTAFF (*off*): Moldy?

526. *Falstaff, as in 514. He now has a tankard in his hand.*

MOLDY (*off*): Aye, sir.
FALSTAFF: 'Tis the more time thou wert used.

527. *Silence with Shallow, as in 513. Shallow drinks from a cup he now holds.*

SHALLOW (*after considerable chuckling, he taps Silence, who sits impassively, on the shoulder*): Things that are moldy lack use, eh, Sir John?

Silence remains impassive.

528. *Falstaff, as in 514.*

FALSTAFF: Prick him.

529. LS: *Moldy, only partially visible over Shallow's shoulder, advances toward him.*

MOLDY: You could have let me alone.
SHALLOW: O, prick him.

530. *Low angle* MLS: *Moldy.*

MOLDY: My old dame will be undone now for one to do her husbandry and her drudgery.
SHALLOW (*off*): Prick him.

531. *Falstaff, as in 514.*

FALSTAFF: Prick him.

532. *Moldy, as in 529. Looking resentful, he tugs at the earflaps of his cap and turns to leave.*

SHALLOW (*off*): O, prick him.
SILENCE (*off*): P-p-prick him.

533. *Falstaff, Shallow, and Silence, as in 512.*

SHALLOW: Thomas Wart!

534. *Low angle* MLS: *the four men on the bench. Wart rises.*

WART: Yes, sir.

535. *Falstaff, as in 518. He gives Wart a look.*

536. *Wart and the men on the bench, as in 534.*

537. MLS (*camera tilted slightly to the left*): *Nym and Moldy in a doorway at the left.*

MOLDY: There are other men fitter to go than I.

538. *Silence with Shallow, as in 513.*

SHALLOW: Stand aside, Moldy.

539. *Nym and Moldy, as in 537. Nym casually reaches behind him and gives Moldy a push out of the door. On the soundtrack sounds of objects breaking follow.*

540. *Silence with Shallow, as in 513.*

SHALLOW: Shall I prick Wart, sir?

541. *Falstaff, as in 514.*

FALSTAFF: It were superfluous; the whole frame stands upon . . .

542. *Wart, as in 534. Nym appears from the left, takes Wart by the shoulders, and turns him away from the camera.*

FALSTAFF: . . . frames. Prick him no more.

543. *Silence with Shallow, as in 513.*

FALSTAFF (*off*): Who's next?

SHALLOW (*as Silence attempts to speak the name*): Simon Shadow.

544. *Low angle* LS: *Three men on the bench. Shadow rises.*

FALSTAFF (*off*): Let me have him to sit under.

545. *Silence with Shallow, as in 513.*

SHALLOW (*looking toward Falstaff with enthusiastic appreciation*): You can do it, sir, you can . . .

546. *Falstaff, as in 514.*

   SHALLOW (*off*): . . . do it.

   Falstaff looks pleased.

   FALSTAFF: Prick him.

547. *The three men, as in 544. Shadow turns and walks to the left.*

   FALSTAFF (*off*): Who's next?

548. CU: *Silence, seen from the side, trying to force out a syllable.*

549. *Falstaff, as in 514. He presses his lips together, as if to help Silence.*

550. *Silence, as in 548, still trying unsuccessfully to speak.*

551. CU: *Shallow, at the left.*

   SHALLOW: Francis Feeble.

552. *Silence, as in 548. He expels air from his mouth as if giving up his efforts.*

553. *Low angle* MLS: *Feeble, a sturdily built young man, moving forward to stand at attention in front of the bench.*

   FALSTAFF (*off*): What trade art thou, Feeble?

   FEEBLE (*in a high-pitched voice*): A woman's tailor, sir. //

   FALSTAFF (*off*): Wilt thou make as many . . .

554. *Falstaff, as in 514.*

   FALSTAFF: . . . holes in an enemy's battle as thou hast done in a woman's petticoat?

555. *Feeble, as in 553.*

    FEEBLE: I will do my good will, sir. You can have no more.

556. *Falstaff, as in 514.*

    FALSTAFF: Well said, . . .

557. *Silence with Shallow, as in 513.*

    FALSTAFF (*off*): . . . good woman's tailor! Well . . .

558. *Falstaff, as in 514.*

    FALSTAFF: . . . said, courageous Feeble! Thou wilt be as valiant as the wrathful dove or most . . .

559. LS: *Feeble, seen over Shallow's shoulder.*

    FALSTAFF (*off*): . . . magnanimous mouse. Prick me the woman's tailor well, Master Silence, . . .

    Feeble bows to Shallow and turns to go.

560. *Falstaff, Shallow, and Silence, as in 512.*

    FALSTAFF (*tapping the roll on Silence's desk with his walking stick*): . . . deep, Master Silence. //

561. MLS: *Nym in the doorway with Feeble, as he was with Moldy in 539. Once again, Nym gives the conscript a casual push through the door with his arm. Feeble, still rigidly at attention, falls backward with a crash.*

562. *Silence with Shallow, as in 513.*

    FALSTAFF (*off*): Who's next?

SHALLOW: Peter Bullcalf of the green! //

563. *Falstaff, Shallow, and Silence, as in 512.*

BULLCALF (*off, piteously*): O Lord, good me lord—

SHALLOW: What, dost thou roar before thou art pricked?

564. *Low angle* LS: *Bullcalf, the last of the men on the bench, stands before it. He is a burly hulk of a man who speaks in a husky voice.*

BULLCALF: O Lord, sir, I am a diseased man.

565. *Falstaff, as in 514.*

FALSTAFF (*with a hint of mock concern*): What disease hast thou?

566. *Bullcalf, as in 564.*

BULLCALF: A cold, sir, a cough, sir, which I caught with ringing in the King's affairs . . .

567. *Falstaff, as in 514.*

BULLCALF (*off*): . . . upon his coronation day. //

FALSTAFF: We will have away thy cold, and I will give such order as thy friends shall ring for thee. Prick him. (*He begins to rise.*) Is . . .

568. *Falstaff, Shallow, and Silence, as in 512. Falstaff has risen from his bench, Shallow from his desk; Silence makes notations on the roll.*

FALSTAFF: . . . here all?

SHALLOW: Here is more called than your number, sir.

569. *The camera tracks left with Nym from the side in* MLS *as he pushes the new conscripts along a passageway in the barn.*

227–247   BULLCALF (*walking backwards so that he faces Nym*): Good Master
Corporate Captain, sir—

* NYM (*pushing him along*): Go to.

BULLCALF: I had as lief be hanged, sir, as go to the wars.

*The crowd of men has nearly reached the door leading out of doors,
where Falstaff's earlier conscripts stand in the rain.*

MOLDY (*over Nym's shoulder from behind*): Good Master Captain . . .

BULLCALF (*whispering to Nym; the camera holds them in* MLS *at the
right, with men crowding through the door on the left*): Four Harry
ten shillings in French crowns for you. (*He hands the money to Nym
surreptitiously.*)

* NYM (*taking the money; he motions Bullcalf away from the group of
conscripts and pushes him out of the frame at the right.*): Outside!

MOLDY (*coming around to face Nym*): You shall have forty, sir, for my
old dame's sake. She has nobody to do anything about her when I am
gone, and she is old and cannot help herself.

* NYM (*taking the money and pushing Moldy in the same direction as he
sent Bullcalf; the camera pans right with Nym*): Stand aside!

FEEBLE (*encountering Nym while moving toward the door*): Let it go
which way it will . . . (*He begins to move past Nym.*)

570. LS: *Feeble is half-turned in the doorway, his hands on his hips. Behind
him, the conscripts stand in the rain.*

FEEBLE: . . . he that dies this year is quit of the next. (*He turns and
moves out into the yard.*)

* Bardolph

571. MS: *Nym in the passageway. Falstaff enters, crossing from the left to stand next to Nym at the right of the frame.*

> *NYM: Sir, a word with you. I have three pound to free Moldy and   252
> Bullcalf.

> FALSTAFF: Moldy, stay at home till you are past service. (*Claps Moldy   259–279
> on the back as he crosses the frame.*) Bullcalf, grow till you come into
> it. I will none of you. (*Repeats the gesture.*)

> SHALLOW (*off; overlapping*): Sir John, . . .

572. *Low angle of Shallow advancing into* MS *in left foreground, with Silence on the right.*

> SHALLOW: . . . they are your likeliest men.

573. *Falstaff and Nym, as in 571, but now in* MCU.

> FALSTAFF: Will you tell me, Master Shallow, how to choose a man? //
> Now here's Wart. (*Wart enters from the left; since Wart is so short,
> Falstaff, while speaking, puts his hand on the back of Wart's head,
> then pushes him out of the shot at the right.*) 'A shall charge you and
> discharge you with the motion of a pewterer's hammer. // And this
> same half-faced fellow, Shadow. (*As Shadow crosses, Falstaff claps
> him on the back.*) Give me this fellow. He presents no mark to the
> enemy. // (*Repeats the gesture with Feeble.*) And for a retreat, how
> swiftly will this Feeble, this woman's tailor, run off. (*Turns to leave
> frame right.*) Ha, ha, ha. Give me . . .

574. *The camera pans right with Falstaff in* MLS *as he walks by the wall of the shed until he reaches the end of its roof, where Wart, Shadow, and Feeble are lined up.*

> FALSTAFF: . . . the spare men, and spare me the great ones. (*Turns
> back toward the rooms he has just left; the camera holds in* MLS.)

*Bardolph

308   Fare you well, gentle gentlemen. I thank you. (*He passes behind the three new conscripts out into the rain. Nym appears from the left to motion the new men toward the right.*)

575. LS: *Falstaff walks toward an open gate in a high vine-covered wall. Under a tree next to the gate, Bardolph keeps out of the rain.*

306   SHALLOW: (*off*): Sir John, God keep you.

298-300   FALSTAFF (*turning and waving with his walking stick*): Farewell! (*Then walking away, with Bardolph following him.*) Bardolph, give the soldiers coats.

The conscripts begin to follow, entering the shot from the lower left.

576. LS: *Falstaff in open land, as his men move past the camera into the background from the lower left foreground, so that Falstaff is often obscured. Falstaff turns to face his men and wave them on.*

BARDOLPH (*off; incredulous*): Coats!

H1 IV.ii.   FALSTAFF: 'Tis no matter, they'll find linen enough on every hedge.

48-49

H2 III.ii.   SHALLOW (*off*): Sir John!

301-302 W   FALSTAFF: Keep well, Master Shallow!

SHALLOW (*off*): The Lord bless you.

577. *Low angle* LS: *Shallow and Silence stand on a balcony, with a low roof extending before it. They are framed by the branches of trees in the foreground.*

SHALLOW (*as Silence waves*): God prosper your affairs. God send us peace.

The King's Camp Near Shrewsbury

578. ELS: *a military encampment on a plain under a bright sky. Horsemen gallop along the edges of the encampment.*

579. *High angle* LS: *two catapults, partially visible. Horsemen ride by at the top of the frame. A strong wind blows the dust stirred up by the horses.*

580. MLS: *Falstaff stands with a soup ladle in his hand, almost obscured by the dust. Two large kettles over a fire occupy the foreground. Horsemen, shadowy in the dust, ride by in the background. The wind howls.*

581. MS: *King Henry, in a coat of mail, stands in sunlight. His armor is on a frame to the right; soldiers cluster in the far background at the left.*

KING: How now, my Lord of Worcester . . .

HI V.i.
9-29

582. MS: *Worcester advances a few steps. Soldiers, with spears held upright, stand at attention in a line behind him.*

KING (*off*): . . . 'tis not well / That you and I should meet upon such terms. //

583. *The King, as in 581. The camera pans with him as he walks forward a few steps, so that Worcester becomes visible from the rear at the left.*

KING: You have deceived our trust / And made us doff our easy robes of peace / To crush our old limbs in ungentle steel. / This is not well, my lord.

584. MCU: *Worcester, with soldiers behind him.*

WORCESTER: My liege, I do protest. / I have not sought the day of this dislike.

585. MS: *the King with Worcester, as at end of 583.*

KING: You have not sought it, sir? How comes it then?

586. MS: *Falstaff, with a solid line of soldiers on a diagonal from frame left to right behind him.*

FALSTAFF: Rebellion lay in his way, and he found it.

PRINCE (*crossing rapidly behind Falstaff*): Peace, chewet, peace!

587. *The camera pans with the Prince in* MLS *as he passes by the side of the royal tent and joins his father and Worcester. The camera reframes the Prince in* MS, *close to his father but between the two men.*

85–108   PRINCE: Go tell your nephew / The Prince of Wales doth join with all the world / In praise of Henry Percy.

588. *Worcester, as in 584.*

PRINCE (*off*): I do not think a braver gentleman, // . . .

589. MS: *the Prince with his father, as at the end of 587.*

PRINCE: . . . More daring or more bold, is now alive. // For my part, I may speak it to my shame, // I have a truant been to chivalry. // But yet, before my father's majesty, // I will, to save the blood on either side, / Try fortune with him in a . . .

590. *Worcester, as in 584.*

PRINCE (*off*): . . . single fight.

KING (*off*): No, we love our people well; . . .

591. MCU: *King Henry and the Prince.*

KING: . . . even those we love / Who are misled upon your cousin's part; / And, will they take the offer of our grace, / Both he, and they, and you, yea, every man / Shall be my friend again, and I'll be his.

592. *High angle* MCU: *the back of the King's head and shoulders, with the Prince's profile filling the right of the frame behind the King. Worcester, partially visible at the left, faces the King.*

114–115   KING: We offer fair. (*Worcester bows.*) Take it advisedly.

593. LS: *the King and the Prince, with troops and tents in the background. In the foreground, Worcester bows and retires.*

594. *The King and the Prince, as in 591.*

    PRINCE: It will not be accepted, on my life.

    KING: Then God befriend us as our cause is just!   120

595. LS: *the camera pans with Worcester and other horsemen as they cross the screen from left to right, riding out of King Henry's encampment. Camp equipment in the foreground frequently obscures the riders.*

596. LS: *the camera pans with the riders, a tent and animal pens in the background. At the end of the pan, the riders move into the middle distance, while spears, protruding from the back of a cart, dominate the right of the frame.*

The Rebel Camp

597. ELS: (*a crane shot*): *two horsemen approach the camera as they ride over an immense and empty plain. The camera moves lower to show the riders through a dense screen of spears, held vertically. Still in the distance, the riders halt and dismount.*

598. *Hotspur moves forward through a group of soldiers carrying spears into a low angle* MS *as the camera pans with him.*

599. *Extreme low angle* MS (*camera tilted to the right*): *Worcester and Vernon at left of frame; only the sky is in the background.*

    WORCESTER: Good cousin, let not Harry know, / In any case, the offer   HI V.ii.1–2
    of the King. (*The camera pans to follow Worcester as he walks up a slope with Vernon behind him.*)

    HOTSPUR (*off*): Uncle, what news? *The pans shifts to the right to include two knights on the slope and then Hotspur alone in* ELS *at the top of the slope.*

    WORCESTER (*reaching Hotspur*): There is no seeming mercy in   34–40
    the King.

600. *Low angle* MS: *Worcester and Hotspur, with Hotspur turned away from the camera to face Worcester.*

   WORCESTER: He calls us rebels, traitors, and will scourge / With haughty arms this hateful name in us.

₇₅

   HOTSPUR (*wheeling toward the camera to address his men*): Arm, arm with speed!

601. *High angle* LS: *mounted soldiers advance toward the camera up the side of a hill. Farm country is in the background.*

602. *Low angle* MS: *Hotspur with Worcester behind him, as at the end of 600.*

_{75, 92–94}

   HOTSPUR: And fellows, soldiers, friends, // . . . (*Moves left in front of Worcester.*) . . . Let each man do his best; . . .

603. *High angle* MS: *Vernon, with many soldiers standing behind him.*

   HOTSPUR (*off*): . . . and here draw . . .

604. *Extreme low angle* MLS: *Hotspur against the sky, drawing his sword from its scabbard. An empty suit of armor is partially visible in the left foreground. The sky is now overcast and a fine mist is blown across the screen as the wind howls.*

   HOTSPUR: . . . I / A sword whose temper I intend to stain / With the best blood that I can meet withal.

605. *The camera pans with Worcester in low angle* LS *against the sky as he moves toward the left, with soldiers visible against the horizon. The blowing mist is even more pronounced.*

_{45–49}

   WORCESTER: The Prince of Wales stepped forth before the King / And, nephew, . . . (*The pan now includes Hotspur at frame left as Worcester nears him.*) . . . challenged you to single fight.

606. *Low angle* MS: *Hotspur against the sky, with Worcester in profile at the right, only his black hat and cloak visible.*

HOTSPUR: Now by my soul, . . . (*The camera pans left leaving Worcester out of the shot, as Hotspur turns away. He is reframed on the right of the screen, with soldiers at attention carrying spears in the left background.*) . . . I would that the quarrel lay upon our heads, / And that no man might draw short breath today / But I and Harry Monmouth.

The King's Camp, Near Shrewsbury; the Battlefield

607. MS: *the Prince, at the right, is armed; his tunic shows the royal emblems of fleur-de-lys and a heraldic lion. He carries his helmet under his arm. The background is obscured by clouds of dust blown by the wind. Falstaff emerges from the dust, wearing armor to his waist, and stands behind the Prince.*

FALSTAFF: I would 'twere bedtime, Hal, and all well. H1 V.i.125–141

PRINCE (*not turning to look at Falstaff*): Why, thou owest God a death. (*He exits right.*)

FALSTAFF (*now in* MS): 'Tis not due yet: I would be loath to pay him before his day. What need I be so forward with him that calls not on me? Well, 'tis no matter; honor pricks me on.

608. *Low angle* MS: *a group of soldiers in armor. One in the center steps forward with a swagger.*

609. *Low angle* MCU: *Falstaff at left faces the Prince, who stands in profile at the right. The wind howls and the dust blows past them.*

FALSTAFF: Yea, but how if honor prick me off when I come on? How then? (*The Prince looks away from him toward the camera.*) Can honor set to a leg? No. Or an arm? No. Or take away the grief of a wound? No. Honor hath no skill in surgery then? No. What is honor? // Air— . . . (*The Prince looks back at him.*) . . . a trim reckoning! Who hath it? He that died a Wednesday. Doth he feel it? No. // (*The Prince looks away again.*) 'Tis insensible then? Yea, to the dead. But will it not live with the living? No. Why? (*The Prince looks back.*) Detraction will not suffer it. Therefore I'll none of it. Honor is a mere scutcheon—and so ends my catechism.

610. *Extreme low angle* LS: *in the branches of a large tree, four knights in full armor are being lowered in slings toward the camera. Throughout the ensuing battle sequence, the music consists of unaccompanied drums, brass ensembles, and a chorus of women's voices chanting word-lessly. Generally the musical accompaniment remains subordinate to the physical sounds of battle: the neighing of horses, the grunts and cries of the soldiers, the clanging of weapons, and so on.*

611. MS: *soldiers on the ground slowly let out the rope that controls the slings and lowers the men in armor.*

612. *Low angle* LS: *the four knights in 610; the camera pans down as they continue their descent toward their horses. When they are immediately above their horses, attendants help them out of the slings and into their saddles.*

H1 IV.i.118–122   HOTSPUR (*off*): Come, let me taste my horse, / That is to bear me like a thunderbolt / Against the bosom of the Prince of Wales.

613. *Low angle* MCU: *Hotspur in full armor, seen against branches above him.*

HOTSPUR: Harry to Harry shall, hot horse to horse, / Meet, and ne'er part til one drop down a corse. (*He turns away from the camera.*)

614. *Low angle* LS: *a knight in a sling being lowered into the saddle of his*

*horse from ropes running through a pulley at the top of a wooden
scaffold. One attendant holds his horse; another assists him into the
saddle. A similar scaffold is seen in the right background.*

615. *Low angle* LS: *soldiers seen against the sky. They are controlling the
ropes that lower the knights.*

616. *Low angle* LS: *several knights on slings under scaffolds. One scaffold,
on which a knight is being hoisted, dominates the foreground. The other
scaffolds are visible in the background through the haze.*

617. LS: *Nym, Bardolph, and a third soldier pull with great effort at a rope;
in the background, soldiers are dimly seen in the haze.*

618. *Low angle* LS: *Falstaff from behind, in full armor, being hoisted in a sling. He is framed by sections of the scaffold.*

619. *The three soldiers as in 617. They continue to struggle with the rope.*

620. *Low angle* LS: *Falstaff seen against the sky. He is now close to the top cross bar of the scaffold.*

621. *The three soldiers as in 617.*

622. *Extreme low angle* LS: *Falstaff dangles in the sling immediately below the crossbar.*

623. *The three soldiers, as in 617. They lose their hold on the rope and collapse on the ground.*

624. *Falstaff, as in 618, except that now he is plunging toward the ground. After Falstaff disappears at the bottom of the frame a loud crash can be heard.*

625. MS *(ground level)*: *Nym lies on his back, feet toward the camera, the slack rope in his hand. Sounds of a loud crash continue.*

626. LS: *Falstaff sits on the ground at the foot of the scaffold. Behind him, knights with their horses caparisoned ride slowly across the screen to the left.*

627. LS: *a line of rebel knights recedes diagonally toward the upper right on caparisoned horses. They ride slowly forward to the right through the mist. They carry their lances couched.*

628. *Low angle* MLS: *a line of knights on horseback, silhouetted against the sky. The line extends diagonally down the screen toward the left, and the nearest knight, dominating the screen at the right, displays the couchant lion on his shield. The knights hold their horses in place as they couch their lances; then they begin to advance to the left.*

629. *Low angle* MLS: *a group of foot soldiers moving left through the mist. After they pass, Falstaff can be seen behind them, also on foot. He stands sideways to the advancing troops, waving them on with his sword. As his own soldiers begin to trot by him, dressed in a motley array of costumes and moving in no particular order, he turns and lumbers along with them.*

630. LS: *the rebel knights on horseback, silhouetted against the mists. Their line moves forward as in 627, but now at a more rapid canter.*

631. *Low angle* MLS: *Falstaff's men seen from the side against the sky. They carry crude clubs and are advancing to the left. Falstaff is barely visible in their midst.*

632. *The camera pans with the rebel knights in* LS *as they advance through a heavy mist. Their line undulates toward the horizon in the background.*

633. *The camera pans slowly left as the King's knights ride across the frame in low angle* MLS. *They are silhouetted against the mist, with trees seen dimly in the background.*

634. LS: *Falstaff, seen from the back, walks slowly by himself after the advancing troops.*

635. *The camera pans right with the line of rebel horsemen in* LS. *The line, now at full gallop, moves directly past, seen from the side. The horse and rider nearest the camera fill the frame. The rebels give a shout:* "Percy!"

636. LS: *the King's knights advance toward the camera through a wooded landscape, also at a gallop. They give a cry:* "St. George and England!"

637. LS (*ground level*): *the rebel horsemen, seen from the side as they rush by. The shouting continues.*

638. ELS: *the King's knights advance across an open field toward the cam-*

*era. The camera pans to the left with them as they gallop by. The
cheering continues, now accompanied by the martial theme from the
credit sequence on the soundtrack.*

639. *Low angle* LS: *horsemen gallop up a sparsely wooded slope. Several
horses pass immediately in front of the camera. Afterwards, Falstaff can
be seen in the middle distance trudging up the slope.*

640. LS: *the camera pans with the King's knights as at the end of 638.*

641. *The camera pans through shrubbery to hold on Falstaff in* MCU, *his
visor down, partially concealed behind a bush.*

642. LS: *the King's knights rush by the camera in a blur.*

643. LS: *the camera pans right with the first line of rebel horsemen, silhouetted against the clouds of dust raised by their horses. The foremost
riders hold their swords raised in front of them.*

644. LS: *the camera pans left with the King's knights, silhouetted against
dust and sky. They advance toward the camera and wheel past it to the
left, swords and lances at the ready.*

645. *Low angle* LS: *the rebel knights, lances extended, are seen in a blur
from the side riding past the camera. The backs of their helmets gleam
in the sunlight. The side of a horse moving to the right passes by the
camera at pointblank range, obliterating the scene.*

646. *The side of a horse moving to the left passes by the camera at pointblank
range. Afterwards, the heads and lances of the King's knights are visible
silhouetted in* MLS.

647. LS: *the King's knights gallop up a slope, lances extended. Several
waves of horses pass immediately by the camera.*

648. ELS: *the King's knights ride along the ridge of a hill. The rebel horse-*

men ride into the shot from the left, and the shot ends just at the point
when the two armies meet.

649. LS: *the King's knights are seen from the side just as they begin to
engage the rebels.*

650. *The camera tracks left against direct sunlight to show horsemen in low
angle* MS *curbing their horses and raising their swords to strike. From
this point in the battle scene it is virtually impossible to distinguish
between the two armies.*

651. *Another track to the left in low angle* MS *of horsemen in battle. A rider
in the foreground raises his sword to strike as his horse rears.*

652. *The camera tracks right in a blurred* MLS *of horsemen in combat. One
knight drops his sword, and two others slash at each other. The camera
then tracks left, where the knight who has lost his sword swings a mace
at his adversary.*

653. MS: *several horsemen flail at one another with clubs and maces.*

654. *High angle* MS: *the battlefield enveloped in haze.*

655. LS: *three horsemen riding to the right with swords raised become an*
ECU *in silhouette: first, of a horse's head moving left, then of the arm
and part of the head of its rider. The arm, wielding a mace, comes down
twice.*

656. ECU: *the armored back of a rider, then of his extended arm with a
shield warding off a blow from the arm of another soldier. The arm is
then followed by portions of the soldier's tunic and cloak, also in* ECU,
as it moves and turns in the struggle.

657. ECU: *silhouette of the two men in close combat, their heads, shoulders,
backs, and horses' heads visible at different moments. They appear to
circle one another, until one becomes fully visible silhouetted in* MCU
swinging a mace.

658. MS: *a foot soldier brings his mace down on the shield of an opponent.*

659. *The camera tracks right showing the torsos of soldiers in* ECU *as they move toward the left. When they do not fill the shot, the camera shows horsemen riding in both directions in the background. The track concludes by focusing on two men on foot fighting each other with swords.*

660. MCU: *a visored head and an arm strike forward, before they are obscured by riders' and horses' heads in* ECU.

661. MCU: *a horseman in profile faces right and raises his sword. A horse and rider move left in* ECU, *filling the screen. This rider reaches the extreme left of the frame before pitching back into the frame as he is unhorsed.*

662. MS: *Falstaff leans out from behind a tree at screen left. In the background soldiers are fighting. He quickly withdraws behind the tree.*

663. *The camera pans left across a group of archers in* MS *as they draw their bows and release their arrows.*

664. MLS: *a soldier on foot at left wields a mace. Two horsemen gallop across the middle background; the second, apparently struck by an arrow, crashes to the ground with his white horse. The camera tracks left to follow the fallen horse and includes two men in the right background fighting on foot with swords.*

665. *The archers pass by the camera in* ECU *as they rush to the right, the torsos of those closest to the camera filling the screen. Intermittently, between them the heads and weapons of other archers can be seen.*

666. *The camera pans right to show horsemen in* MLS *clustered together, striking at one another with swords and maces.*

667. LS: *the white horse and the men fighting with swords, as at the end of 664. The horse, now riderless, struggles to its feet in the left foreground.*

668. LS: *the white horse stands motionless as a soldier crosses in the fore-ground, very close to the camera. The horse is momentarily alone in the shot.*

669. *The camera pans left away from two foot soldiers fighting to follow in low angle* LS *a series of horsemen riding to the left, outlined against a bright sky. The camera pans back to the right to include the backs of two foot soldiers in the foreground. The shield of one soldier, brought very close to the camera, blacks out the image.*

670. MS: *a foot soldier at right brings down both sword and shield with a clublike overhand motion. Horsemen struggle in the background.*

671. MS: *a soldier at right swings his mace downward in a scything motion. The force of the swing carries his head down and out of the shot, revealing other soldiers fighting behind him.*

672. LS: *the white horse and the two soldiers, as at the end of 667.*

673. *The camera pans away from two soldiers fighting next to the body of a third to include a soldier in* MS *in the left foreground who swings downward with an ax. As the pan continues it includes the soldier who has just been struck from behind by the ax. He flings up his hands and falls forward out of the frame. The first soldier, looking down at his victim, swings his ax again. Behind him, many men struggle.*

674. CU: *the back of a soldier's head as he falls backward toward the lower right. As he continues to fall and strikes the ground, his face becomes visible, still held in* CU.

675. *The white horse and the two soldiers, as in 672. Horsemen gallop by in the background.*

676. MS: *two foot soldiers, only the one at right fully visible, stand still and look ahead. Behind them, half-hidden in mist, another soldier turns backward, whistles, and waves some barely visible comrades forward.*

677. LS: *horsemen in battle, with a small semi-circle of empty field between them and the camera. In the lower left foreground, a foot soldier flails with an ax at someone lying on the ground out of the frame.*

678. *The three soldiers, as in 676, but now the two in the foreground are in* MCU. *As the third soldier waves men forward, the camera pans left to show from the side the men running forward to the right, variously dressed and carrying a variety of weapons. A horseman, riding in the opposite direction, passes very close to the camera and blocks the men from view.*

679. LS: *the men running, now seen from the rear as they move through a low-lying mist.*

680. *Low angle* MS: *the back of a man on foot, wearing a broad-brimmed hat and raising a mace. A rider in full armor gallops by him on the right. The man in the hat begins to fall backwards.*

681. LS: *two men on foot with swords raised, seen within a thick mist. Two horsemen in armor with lances leveled enter from the left and bear down on the foot soldiers. All are seen as dark shapes against the mist.*

682. *High angle* LS: *the two foot soldiers, turning and falling, their swords sailing through the air, as the horsemen ride out of frame at the left.*

683. *The camera pans left, following foot soldiers in* LS *as they run through the mist toward the battle.*

684. *High angle* LS: *several knights on horseback as foot soldiers approach and swarm around them.*

685. *The camera pans left to show two knights on horseback in* MS *grappling with one another. They fall to the ground between the two horses.*

686. *Low angle* MS: *archers silhouetted against the sky, seen from behind as they release their arrows. Two soldiers, entering from opposite sides of the frame, exchange blows in the foreground.*

687. *Low angle* MCU: *the upper body of a soldier wearing a white tunic, as he moves forward to the left delivering a blow. A soldier in chain mail moves across the foreground from the left, partially visible as he stoops to avoid the blow.*

688. MLS: *a group of foot soldiers struggle in combat, seen against a white sky. One soldier falls to the ground in the center of the frame. The body of a soldier passing very close to the camera blacks out the image.*

689. *The camera pans left to follow a soldier in* MS *as he raises his shield and begins to deliver a blow with his mace.*

690. CU: *the back of a soldier as his body turns and he falls down to the left. The soundtrack suggests that he has taken the blow delivered in 689.*

691. MCU: *two men in close combat. One pushes the other out of the shot at the left, then ducks to avoid a two-handed roundhouse swing from a soldier in a black-hooded cloak wielding an ax.*

692. *Low angle* MLS: *the same scene as in 691, now shot from behind the ducking soldier. The man in the cloak moves forward aiming another blow at the soldier, who crouches to avoid it.*

693. CU: *the man in the cloak is carried by his momentum over the back of his crouching adversary. The crouching soldier raises himself and moves offscreen at the left. Other soldiers fighting can now be seen in* MLS *until they are obscured by the back of a soldier passing immediately in front of the camera.*

694. MCU (*ground level*): *the legs of two soldiers who are fighting in the immediate foreground. When their legs are not filling the screen, other soldiers can be glimpsed fighting in the background.*

695. *Low angle* MLS (*ground level*): *soldiers fighting, momentarily obscured by the legs of other soldiers running in the foreground past the camera.*

696. MLS: *two men fight, surrounded by others in hand-to-hand combat. One*

*of the men kicks the other in the chest, knocking him off his feet and out
of the frame in the foreground. The man still standing half turns and
braces himself for another attack. He raises his sword to block a blow
from a soldier with a club, who rushes into the shot from the right.*

697. MS: *the two men fight as at the end of 696. The momentum of the soldier with the club carries him beyond his opponent. The other soldier
thrusts his sword into the back of the man with the club, who falls to the
ground. A soldier, probably the one kicked out of the frame in 696,
enters the shot from the lower foreground and swings a club. The soldier
with the sword crouches and avoids the blow. The other soldier makes a
full turn in front of the camera and begins to strike again.*

698. *Low angle* MLS: *a man swings a spiked club as he moves toward
the right.*

699. *The head of a soldier who has just been struck by a sword pitches past
the camera, which then moves down to show his stunned face in a
momentary* CU.

700. *Extreme high angle* LS: *several men wrestle with each other on the
ground. Another soldier stands above them and strikes at them with a
club.*

701. CU: *the bleeding face of a soldier in a mailed helmet, as he grimaces
in pain.*

702. *The camera pans left in low angle* LS *across several pairs of men in
combat. In the left foreground a man swings a mace downward, missing
an opponent who has a sword.*

703. *Low angle* MLS: *the same two combatants as in 702, against the background of the sky. The momentum of the man with the mace has turned
him away from his opponent, who then strikes him across the back with
his sword.*

704. MCU: *in dense mist, the head and upraised arm of a soldier pitch
backward toward the camera.*

705. *Low angle* LS: *scattered soldiers are silhouetted against the sky. A hooded soldier silhouetted in the foreground stumbles, regains his balance, and turns back toward the opponent behind him.*

706. MS: *a soldier seen from behind against the mist is struck across the face with an ax. He throws his hands up to his face and falls backward toward the camera.*

707. MCU: *the soldier falls to the ground directly in front of the camera, his bloodied face momentarily visible at the end of the shot.*

708. MLS: *horsemen seen through the mist.*

709. MCU: *a hooded soldier moves into a full* CU.

710. *Low angle* LS: *several men on foot surround a horse and armored rider, whom they are trying to unseat.*

711. MCU: *Falstaff, visor down, peeks from behind the trunk of a tree at the right, as a file of horsemen rides forward at the left.*

712. LS: *the men of 710 have unseated the rider and are now dragging him away from his horse.*

713. CU: *a man in a wide-brimmed hat peers toward screen left, with bushes in the background.*

714. *Low angle* MLS: *the unseated rider is pushed backward onto the ground by the men who have been holding him.*

715. CU: *the man in the wide-brimmed hat, as in 713, now peers to the right.*

716. LS: *a horse and armored rider, both being pulled to the ground by several men on foot.*

717. MCU: *the face of a dead soldier in the left foreground. Two figures in cloaks stagger past.*

718. MCU: *Falstaff, visor down, seen partially concealed in bushes, his sword slanted upward.*

719. MLS: *a soldier raises his arm and strikes toward the ground. The hands and chest of a dead soldier occupy the lower right, obscuring whomever the first soldier is striking. An arrow lodged in the chest of the dead soldier intersects the screen diagonally. Horsemen in combat can be seen through the haze in the background.*

720. MS: *the soldier in 719 strikes another soldier who lies beneath him on the ground.*

721. LS: *a horse that has been pulled down on its side. Foot soldiers pin it to the ground, while other soldiers cross to the right immediately in front of the camera.*

722. LS: *the horse seen from somewhat closer. One foot soldier hacks at it with an ax: another, moving away from the camera, leaps over the body of the horse, apparently to attack its fallen rider.*

723. LS: *three men surround a fallen horse and rider. One drives his sword into the fallen rider.*

724. Low angle MLS: *a soldier, seen from the back, removing his sword from the body of a man concealed beneath him.*

725. MS: *a soldier at the right holds his sword down in front of him, thrusting it toward the ground at an unseen opponent, and then raises it as he looks ahead to the left. Horsemen gallop across the screen in the background. The back of a soldier in the extreme foreground blocks the image.*

726. *Parts of horses and riders are visible in MS through a heavy mist as they pass to the right.*

727. MCU: *a dead soldier partially visible in the lower left foreground,*

*his bloodied hand extended. Horsemen move through the mist in the
background.*

728. MLS: *a horseman in the mist rides away from the camera to the right,
as several hooded men, one carrying an ax, run to the left in the
foreground.*

729. MCU: *an archer in the mist draws his bow.*

730. MS: *a soldier, seen from the back and silhouetted in the mist, is struck
by an arrow which enters his back and sticks out of his chest while a
soldier at the right watches. The stricken soldier topples backward out
of the shot at the left. A horse crosses to the right dragging its rider.*

731. MLS: *a soldier, back to the camera, wields a spiked club; near him
another foot soldier holds a mace. They both strike at a horseman with
a lance who rides past.*

732. MCU: *two horsemen in haze ride past the camera, with other horses
visible in the background.*

733. LS: *two men on the ground in lower right of the frame, one rolling in
agony with a lance embedded in his chest.*

734. MS: *Falstaff looks out, framed by the branches of a small tree.*

735. LS: *a large number of horsemen ride down a slope toward the camera.*

736. LS: *Falstaff, sword held in front of him, runs toward the right from one
tree to the next.*

737. LS: *horsemen, seen from the side, gallop to the left across a field with
their lances couched.*

738. LS: *archers, in a line extending from left foreground to right background, with their bows drawn.*

739. MCU: *Falstaff, behind some branches, ducks down.*

740. MCU: *three archers release their arrows toward the right. They then move out of the shot at the right, so that the camera now shows a row of horsemen in LS advancing to the right in line.*

741. *The camera pans right with a single horseman in LS galloping to the right waving his mace above his head. A horseman approaches him from the other direction and, as they pass, they strike at one another.*

742. MCU: *a man in armor falls off his horse directly toward the camera. The camera then follows him in CU as he strikes the ground.*

743. MS: *a blurred image of two riders and horses passes directly in front of the camera.*

744. LS: *a soldier turns, hands in the air, and falls to the ground after being struck by a blow. He is silhouetted against a white sky. He is then obscured by the bodies of soldiers moving immediately in front of the camera.*

745. *The camera tracks with several horsemen in LS as they ride toward the right with their lances level before them. In the foreground men on foot, running or fighting, frequently interpose themselves between the camera and the horsemen. At the conclusion of the shot, other horsemen with lances move across the frame in the opposite direction.*

746. MLS: *a soldier carries a long spear horizontally above his head as he runs toward the left. Behind him a large number of horsemen ride in the same direction. The soldier begins to thrust the spear forward and down, putting his weight behind the thrust.*

747. MLS: *a soldier is impaled by a spear that enters the shot from the left, presumably the spear shown in 746. The soldier turns toward the camera, clutching the shaft of the spear, and begins to sink toward the ground.*

748. MS: *the arms and shoulders of a row of archers as they ready themselves to shoot their arrows.*

749. *The camera moves left with a rider and horse in* LS *silhouetted against a bright background and seen from the side as they topple over into the foreground.*

750. MS: *archers release their arrows. They face right and appear tilted to the left on the screen, but then, as they arise and move out of the shot to the right, it is clear they have been down on one knee, leaning back to gain a greater arc to their shots.*

751. MLS: *a rider in armor at the left of the frame topples from his horse. The camera follows him as he lands on his hands and knees with other horsemen wheeling and passing in the background. A figure passes immediately in front of the camera and blacks out the image.*

752. *Low angle* MS: *a group of archers, each only partially visible, release their arrows and begin to move forward.*

753. LS: *a rider in armor falls from his horse and lies motionless on the ground.*

754. *High angle* MS: *archers releasing their arrows.*

755. *Low angle* MS: *a soldier, silhouetted against a bright sky, pierced in the chest by an arrow. He sinks backward to the lower left and the camera moves with him to show him in profile on the ground as other soldiers continue fighting behind him.*

756. MLS: *one soldier strikes another over the head with a club, sending him crashing to the ground.*

757. MS: *a horse loses its footing as it approaches the camera and falls over on its side, its rider still holding fast in the saddle.*

758. *Low angle* MLS *(camera tilted to the left): two men in combat. One,*

*back to camera, is already falling backward as the other moves to strike
again. A figure passing immediately in front of the camera blacks out the
image so that the actual blow is not seen. When the figure has passed,
one soldier lies on the ground and the other, his club at the ready, turns
and moves out of the shot to the left. The camera stays momentarily with
the man on the ground, then pans quickly up and to the right to include
some horsemen, one of whom impales a soldier with his lance.*

759. MS: *a rider in armor moves to the right. He suddenly throws up his
arms and plunges off his horse toward the camera, which follows the
beginning of his fall.*

760. LS: *footsoldiers, silhouetted in combat. The foreground is dominated
by a horse, lying on its side, twisting and writhing with an arrow in
its side.*

761. *A series of horses, moving very close to the camera, initially black out
any image. After they pass, two men in* LS *are seen struggling, with a
body lying on the ground next to them.*

762. MLS: *a horseman with lance moves to the right and away from the
camera. He unseats another horseman riding toward him, striking him
with the lance. As he then moves further into the background at the
right, a foot soldier crosses the foreground to the left, only his head
visible.*

763. *High angle* MS: *the head and shoulders of a man in armor, apparently
on horseback, with his back to the camera in the lower foreground of the
frame. Beyond him can be seen a rider with couched lance, approaching
him. Other horsemen ride forward in the further background.*

764. CU: *the head and shoulders of the man in armor, still back to camera,
with his sword raised. He suddenly throws his arms in the air and spins
toward the camera, as if struck.*

765. MS: *a helmeted rider with a club raised in his hand. He turns in the
saddle toward the camera, swinging the club as he does.*

766. CU: *the side of the horse in 765; a white horse crosses in the opposite direction even closer to the camera. Portions of the two horses are momentarily visible.*

767. CU: *the studded rear of a rider's saddle. As the rider wheels his horse, the camera moves away to show him in* MS *wearing dark armor, carrying a lance and astride a white horse.*

768. LS: *two horsemen ride toward the camera, with a man on foot partially visible in the left foreground. As the riders pass out of the shot at the lower left, one thrusts his lance into the man on foot.*

769. CU: *a soldier's head falls back onto muddy ground. His face is bloodied and his eyes are closed.*

770. *Low angle* MS: *the rider in 767. He wheels his horse so that his back is to the camera and, with his lance at the ready, charges into a misty background, unseating a horseman coming toward him.*

771. *High angle* LS: *horsemen ride toward the camera, wielding various weapons. A rider in the lead topples from his horse as if struck, falling directly in front of other oncoming horses.*

772. MLS: *several horsemen move to the right against a bright sky.*

773. LS: *Falstaff walks clumsily forward toward the right through a wooded area. Behind him, outside the woods, the battle continues.*

774. *The camera pans right to follow a large number of horsemen seen in* LS *from the side, their swords raised, riding closely bunched together to the right as if making an organized charge.*

775. *The image is first obscured by several horsemen passing immediately in front of the camera. After they move out of the shot Falstaff is seen in* LS *running across a large open area toward woods on the right.*

776. *The camera pans left as a large number of horsemen ride in* MLS *to the*

left and toward the camera before moving out of the shot at lower left. Their armor is different from that of the men in 775, but they too have their swords raised and seem to be in the midst of a charge. As the shot concludes, a horse passes immediately in front of the camera and blacks out the image.

777. *The image is initially blacked out by a horse passing immediately in front of the camera. Afterwards, Falstaff is seen in* LS *running to the left across an open area with trees and bushes in the background. Other horses, also moving left, then black out the screen.*

778. *The camera pans with Falstaff in* LS *running to the left, from a somewhat closer vantage point than in 777. Bright sunlight streams from the right, illuminating the armor on his back.*

779. LS: *Falstaff runs as in 777. Horses passing in front of the camera, moving left, black out the screen.*

780. *The camera pans right across a group of horsemen in* LS, *contending against one another on a rise with a valley in the far background. Then a horse passing in front of the camera obscures most of the action.*

781. *The camera pans left across a battle scene in* LS *crowded with foot soldiers. In the foreground one soldier, half-turned toward the camera, raises his arms to ward off a blow from a soldier who moves into the shot from the right, then reaches up to grab the shaft of the other soldier's weapon.*

782. *Low angle* MLS: *two soldiers struggle with one another, while in the background two others brandish spears.*

783. LS: *many soldiers fight at close quarters. In the foreground one soldier thrusts down with his dagger. Another then crosses close to the camera and obscures the scene.*

784. MLS: *one soldier strikes another with a sword. The second soldier*

jackknifes forward, striking the ground first with his head, while his legs splay into the air. In the background other soldiers stand over several bodies.

785. *Low angle* MS *(camera slightly tilted to the left): archers release their arrows and then move forward to the left, some passing very close to the camera.*

786. *The camera pans left to follow from behind in* LS *a large number of horsemen galloping over an open plain.*

787. MLS: *a horseman in armor tries to control his horse as it slides over on its side heading to the right. Behind him, other horsemen ride to the left.*

788. MCU: *the upper body of a soldier at the left of the shot, as he swings an ax past the camera. The camera pans left to show a cluster of soldiers in* LS, *most carrying spears held at a variety of angles and pointed in different directions.*

789. *High angle* CU: *a soldier on the ground, screaming and writhing.*

790. MS: *a soldier in the foreground turns and bends his head toward the camera; another soldier moves into the shot from the left to his side. Both are in silhouette against a bright sky, as are the men who fight in the background.*

791. MS: *the back of a soldier bends over toward the right in the foreground. The camera moves slightly to follow him as he pulls himself back and then drives his spear downwards with his weight behind it.*

792. *High angle* CU: *a soldier, as in 789, his mouth even more contorted as he screams.*

793. MLS: *silhouetted horsemen ride in both directions.*

794. *Low angle* MLS: *two silhouetted riders and horses as they cross the screen to the left, the riders carrying lances.*

795. *Low angle* MS: *two horsemen in combat. The rider with his back to the camera wards off with his sword a blow from his opponent. He then grabs the reins of the other horse.*

796. MLS: *two horsemen confront one another; one has raised his shield as the other brings his sword forward. Another horse passing immediately in front of the camera blacks out the image.*

797. *The image initially is blacked out by a horse passing close to the camera. Afterwards, a group of horsemen can be seen in* LS *riding to the left, those closest to the camera in silhouette, those further away in sunlight.*

798. MS: *two horsemen in combat face each other from the right and left. The horseman on the left strikes downward with his sword, and the other man begins to topple off his horse toward the camera, so that, as he falls head forward, his legs are silhouetted against the sky above the saddle.*

799. MLS: *a soldier throws up his arms, staggering backward to the right and collapsing on the ground. His body is still visible in the lower foreground as other soldiers run past him to the right.*

800. MLS: *a soldier with a spiked club. The camera pans right to include another soldier, his back to the camera at the right. The soldier facing the camera gives a side-arm swing of the club and the other man doubles over. The first soldier then raises his club high in the air and is about to bring it down on his opponent.*

801. MLS: *a soldier at the left brings his sword down in a high arching movement over the back and shoulder of a man at the right.*

802. MLS: *a soldier at the right brings his mace over his head and down on the back of a soldier who is trying to get up from the ground.*

803. *The camera pans over the heads of horsemen in* LS *at the bottom of the frame silhouetted against the sky.*

804. MS: *a single horseman, silhouetted against the sky, falls backwards toward the camera. As he passes below the frame, the camera holds on the empty saddle.*

805. LS: *two soldiers on foot struggle hand to hand, with horsemen in battle behind them. One soldier knocks the other down and leans over him to strike him again.*

806. MS: *a soldier turns with his back to the camera and slashes downward with his sword across the chest of a soldier facing him at the left. The wounded soldier spins completely around and falls on his back.*

807. MS: *a soldier is held from behind by one man at the right, while another at the left prepares to strike him. The soldier being held kicks the man at the left, knocking him backwards.*

808. *Low angle* LS: *milling horsemen in combat, silhouetted against very bright light. At moments passing horses black out the image.*

809. MLS: *two foot soldiers run to the left in the foreground, as horsemen ride to the right in the background.*

810. MS: *a horseman falls out of his saddle directly in front of the camera as his horse continues out of the shot at lower right.*

811. *The camera pans right across bodies lying in an open field to include two soldiers in* LS *struggling at close quarters. One runs the other through with his sword. As he falls, a group of horsemen rides across the background toward the right.*

812. *Low angle* MLS: *horsemen in combat, silhouetted against the sky. One rider in the right foreground raises his sword. The camera pans right, leaving the rider out of the frame and including a second rider entering from the right. The camera then pans left with the second rider as he thrusts his sword forward into the first rider, now once again in the frame at the left.*

813. MCU: *two soldiers grapple, head to head. They fall out of the frame at
the lower right, followed by a third soldier who enters from the left and
appears to be jumping on top of them. As he disappears, the camera
shows three horsemen beyond in low angle* MLS *as they fight.*

814. LS (*ground level*): *a soldier advances toward the camera, seen through
horses' legs.*

815. *Ground-level shot with camera tilted to the right, first of horses' legs as
they gallop immediately past the camera, then of other riders in* LS *in
the background.*

816. *The soldier, as in 814. The camera pans slightly left to show, through
horses' legs, a soldier kneeling on the ground, his head forward.
The camera tilts upward to show the advancing soldier, now in low
angle* MS, *bring his mace down on the other soldier, who turns and falls
backwards, rolling toward the camera in the lower foreground.*

817. MCU: *the midsection of a rider is seen from the side. The camera holds
this partial view as the rider rears back on his horse, apparently to
avoid the charge of another horseman, seen momentarily in the center of
the frame beyond the rider in the foreground.*

818. *The side of a horse immediately in front of the camera initially blacks
out the image. The horse and its rider, presumably the same figure as in
817, then plunge forward, out of the frame on the right. The camera
moves slightly up and to the left to show other horseman, seen in silhouette, fighting in a confused melee.*

819. *Against an immediate background of fierce fighting, the camera pans
from a soldier in* MCU *striking a blow, to follow the soldier who is
struck. That soldier is first shown with his back to the camera, receiving
a blow to the side of his head. He staggers to the left, turning around
toward the camera and starting to regain his balance. Then he is struck
again from behind and plunges face forward toward the ground.*

820. *High angle* CU: *a soldier, presumably the one in 819, now on the
ground, his face bloody.*

821. *Low angle* MS: *a soldier is ready to strike as the camera pans right to include his opponent, back to camera, his hands raised to ward off a blow.*

822. *Low angle* MS: *a soldier with a club at the left. He raises the club and begins to lower it on an opponent who appears at the right as the camera pans right. The opponent ducks below the frame as the club descends.*

823. MS: *a soldier faces the camera and swings his club from the side against a soldier in full armor who falls backward out of the shot.*

824. *High angle* MCU: *a soldier falls backward onto muddy ground.*

825. *Several soldiers advance to the right very close to the camera. The camera pans with them as they pass and then jump forward onto a pile of struggling soldiers on the ground. In this and in subsequent shots until the end of the battle sequence, the ground is extremely muddy and the soldiers are always spattered or covered with mud.*

826. LS: *horsemen in the muddy field; two foot soldiers struggle in the fore-ground. As they fall out of the frame in opposite directions, a soldier falls and slides through the mud in an open space between the horsemen and the foreground.*

827. MS: *several helmeted foot soldiers are clustered together, their swords locked above them, as they struggle for space to strike a blow.*

828. *High angle* MLS: *two soldiers roll in the mud, fighting hand to hand.*

829. *High angle* LS: *two pairs of soldiers on the ground. One soldier straddles another and beats him with a club, while the other two fight hand to hand.*

830. *High angle* LS: *a soldier in armor is tossed head over heels as he wrestles with another soldier in the mud.*

831. *High angle* LS: *a soldier in armor on his back in the mud as several other soldiers begin to pile themselves on top of him.*

832. *High angle* MS: *several clusters of soldiers still on their feet grapple in the mud.*

833. *High angle* MS: *a soldier close to the camera spins and falls to the ground, where he joins other soldiers struggling with one another in the mud.*

834. MS: *two soldiers on the ground, as two others fling themselves on top of them.*

835. *High angle* MS: *a pileup of several soldiers, their heads visible one below the other.*

836. *High angle* MS: *two pairs of soldiers' legs, as one straddles the other in the mud, their legs moving as they struggle.*

837. *High angle* MS: *horses' legs, as they move through the mud toward the right.*

838. MS *(ground level)*: *horses are seen from the side as they cross to the right in silhouette. After they pass, the camera moves upward to show a portion of the battlefield in* LS, *empty except for the many bodies lying on the field.*

839. MCU: *soldiers entwined together in the mud struggle to get up.*

840. LS: *horsemen, seen from the side, moves diagonally forward toward the right, their swords held vertically in front of them. The camera pans right with them, showing wagons and piles of army supplies in the background.*

841. LS *(camera tilted to the right)*: *a line of horsemen moves diagonally toward the lower right with trees in the background. One horseman*

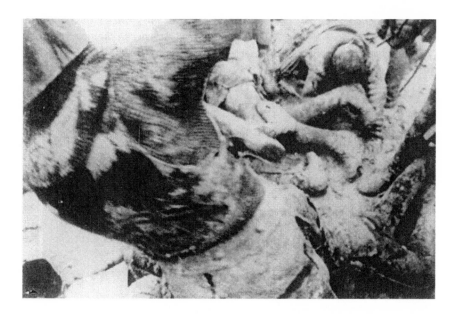

enters at the left and, swinging his horse toward the camera, pulls off his helmet, showing himself to be the Prince.

PRINCE: What, stand'st thou idle here? //   H1 V.iii.39–48

842. LS: *Falstaff, still with visor down, stands alone, with horsemen passing in the background.*

FALSTAFF: Give me leave to breathe awhile. Turk Gregory never did such deeds as I have done this day. (*Waves his sword.*) I have . . .

843. *Low angle* MS: *the Prince on his horse, holding his shield in front of him against his saddle. He looks first at Falstaff, then beyond him.*

FALSTAFF (*off*): . . . paid Percy, I have made him sure.

PRINCE: He is indeed, . . .

844. *High angle* LS: *Hotspur, mounted, seen over the Prince's shoulder at the right, faces him at the left. Falstaff stands between the two, with his back to the Prince. Hotspur's face is visored, so he is as yet unidentifiable.*

PRINCE: . . . and living to kill thee.

H1 V.iv.58–68   HOTSPUR: If I mistake not, thou art Harry Monmouth.

845. MS: *Falstaff, as he turns in the Prince's direction, swings his sword around as if it were a pointer.*

846. *Low angle* MCU: *the Prince.*

PRINCE: Thou speak'st as if I would deny my name.

847. *Low angle* CU: *Hotspur, raising his visor.*

HOTSPUR: My name is Harry Percy.

848. *The Prince, as in 846.*

PRINCE: Two stars keep not their motion in one sphere, / Nor can one England brook a double reign / Of Harry Percy and the Prince of Wales.

849. *Hotspur, as in 847.*

HOTSPUR: Nor shall it, Harry, for the hour is come / To end the one of us. (*He pulls down his visor.*)

850. *The Prince, as in 846. He puts on his helmet.*

851. *Low angle* MS: *Hotspur's horse rears up, the branches of a tree above him. As the horse descends, two men run across in the foreground of the frame.*

852. *The camera pans to the left to show Falstaff peering out in* MS *from behind a screen of bushes.*

853. MS: *the combatants move toward one another, their horses now virtually nose to nose.*

854. MS: *Falstaff moves left across an open space from one clump of bushes to another. He again conceals himself behind the second clump.*

855. MS: *the two men are locked together, their saddles abreast of one another. They sway back and forth, then topple off between their horses.*

856. MS: *Falstaff ducks down behind the bushes.*

857. LS: *the two combatants strike the ground, rolling over and starting to pick themselves up. Hotspur has his back to the camera in the foreground, while the Prince faces the camera in the background. They are in a small clearing in a wooded area.*

858. MS: *Falstaff raises his head again behind the bushes.*

859. MS: *the two men facing each other, seen from behind the Prince. Hotspur strikes at the Prince twice with his sword, and the Prince deflects the strokes with his shield.*

860. CU: *Hotspur, his armored head seen in profile.*

861. MS: *the two men, now with Hotspur in the foreground with his back to the camera. Hotspur strikes at the Prince twice, forehand and backhand, but both strokes are deflected. He then lunges with his sword at the Prince's midsection.*

862. MS: *the two men, seen from the side, as Hotspur, at the left, lunges.*

863. MCU: *Falstaff peers out from behind the bushes.*

864. MCU: *Hotspur, his shield raised as the Prince's sword descends at the right. Hotspur then responds.*

865. MS: *the Prince and Hotspur exchange blows, with the Prince facing the camera.*

866. *Low angle* MS: *Hotspur at the left delivering blows, with only the Prince's shield and sword visible.*

867. *Low angle* MS: *the Prince at the left delivering blows, with only Hotspur's shield visible.*

868. MS: *Falstaff has moved a step or two away from the bushes and is imitating the motions of the fight, as he urges the Prince on.*

869. MCU: *the two men, with the Prince in the background facing the camera.*

870. CU: *Hotspur turns his head and swings his sword upward; the camera moves upward to follow the sword as it crosses with the Prince's sword.*

871. MCU: *Falstaff moves to the left back behind the bushes and continues to shout encouragement.*

872. *Low angle* MCU: *swords crossing under a canopy of trees, with Hotspur's arm moving forward from the left.*

873. MS: *the two men, with Hotspur's back to the camera, as their swords cross close to the ground. They bring the crossed swords upward in a half circle over their heads.*

874. MCU: *the Prince seen over Hotspur's shoulder, as the crossed swords now move in a downward arc.*

875. *The camera pans to follow Falstaff in* MCU, *facing the camera and moving sideways to the right, half-hidden by a screen of bushes.*

876. MS: *Hotspur, facing the camera, brings his sword down and then launches another blow. He is partially obscured at times by the movements of the Prince, immediately in front of the camera.*

877. *The camera pans with Falstaff in* MCU, *as in 875, but now he moves out of the shot to the left.*

878. MS: *the Prince strikes a blow at Hotspur, whose back becomes partially visible at the right. Both are in shadow under a tree.*

879. *Low angle* MCU: *the two men's helmets, Hotspur in the lower foreground facing away, as he crouches to avoid a blow.*

880. CU: *Hotspur at right, with the Prince partially visible to the left.*

881. LS: *Falstaff loses his footing and falls on his back next to a tree.*

882. LS: *Hotspur, at the right, brings his arm forward in an overhand blow, with the Prince partially visible at the left readying himself to receive it.*

883. MS: *the Prince, sword raised, faces the left as he moves backward to the right. He stumbles momentarily, then regains his balance in time to ward off Hotspur's overhand blow. Hotspur enters the shot, partially visible, only as the blow descends.*

884. MCU: *Hotspur faces right, his arm moving forward to deliver a blow. As his sword hand reaches the right edge of the frame, it is blocked and pushed back by the Prince's sword hand.*

885. MS: *the Prince, seen from over Hotspur's shoulder. The Prince delivers a blow and in the foreground Hotspur raises his arm to block it. The two men grapple, now in* MCU, *with the Prince's hand holding Hotspur by the wrist.*

886. MS: *the two men seen from the side as Hotspur pushes the Prince away. The camera follows as the Prince moves backward and reframes both men in* LS *as they begin to circle one another. A blow from Hotspur drives the Prince, now facing the camera, to his knees. He raises his sword defensively; Hotspur swings downward, gripping his sword with both hands.*

887. MS: *the Prince, almost prone on the ground, with Hotspur standing over him to the right and raising his sword to strike again.*

888. MS: *Hotspur at the right, in profile but with his body turned toward the camera as he prepares to swing his sword. The Prince is barely visible at the lower left.*

889. MS: *the Prince, seen from behind Hotspur, as Hotspur's sword descends. The Prince wards off the blow with his sword, but its force knocks him full length on the ground face down. He begins to roll over as Hotspur advances.*

890. *High angle* MLS: *the Prince on the ground at left, with Hotspur at the right, only his arm visible as he raises it above his head to deliver a final blow.*

891. *High angle* MCU: *the Prince, seated on the ground, lunges forward with his sword.*

892. *Low angle* MCU: *Hotspur in profile, his head and two hands with the sword thrown back as the Prince's sword pierces his chest.*

893. MCU: *the Prince pivots while rising and pulling his sword back.*

894. *Low angle* MS: *Hotspur, seen from beside the Prince, slowly lowering his two arms, held close together, over his chest. As the camera moves into* MCU *of Hotspur alone, he drops to his knees and his sword falls out of his hands.*

895. MCU: *the Prince pulls off his helmet and looks down toward Hotspur.*

896. *Extreme high angle* MLS: *the Prince stands over the kneeling Hotspur and removes Hotspur's helmet.*

897. *Low angle* MCU: *Hotspur grimaces in pain, as the Prince's arms reach in from the right and remove the helmet.*

898. *Low angle* MCU: *the Prince brings the helmet toward him.*

899. *Low angle* MCU: *Hotspur, as at the end of 897.*

> HOTSPUR (*looking up to the right toward the Prince*): O Harry, thou   H1 V.iv.76–92
> hast robbed me of my youth! / (*He falls sideways out of the frame at
> the left. For a moment, the camera shows only the boughs of the trees
> in the background; then the Prince, partially visible, leans into the
> shot at the right.*) I better . . .

900. MCU: *Hotspur lies on the ground horizontal to the camera, his head
slightly raised at the left as he props himself on one arm.*

> HOTSPUR (*looking up toward the Prince*): . . . brook the loss of brittle
> life / Than these proud titles thou hast won of me. /

901. MCU: *the Prince, at the right of the frame. A haze obscures much of the
background at the left.*

> HOTSPUR (*off*): They wound my thoughts worse than thy sword
> my flesh. /

902. *Hotspur, as in 900.*

> HOTSPUR: But thoughts, the slave of life, and life, time's fool, / . . .

903. *The Prince, as in 901.*

> HOTSPUR (*off*): . . . And time, that makes survey of all the world, /
> Must have a stop.

904. CU: *Hotspur, face slightly tilted to the left of the frame.*

> HOTSPUR: O, I could prophesy, / But that the earthy and cold hand of
> death / Lies on my tongue. No, Percy, thou art dust, / And food for—
> (*His face glazes over in death.*)

905. LS: *Hotspur lies on his side, propped up on one elbow; the Prince kneels next to him on the right. Hotspur falls over on his back.*

PRINCE: For worms, brave Percy.

906. *The Prince, as in 901.*

PRINCE: Fare thee well, great heart. / Ill-weaved ambition, how much art thou shrunk! / When that this body did contain a spirit, / A kingdom for it was too small a bound; / But now two paces of the vilest earth / Is room enough. This earth that bears thee dead / Bears not alive so stout a gentleman.

907. LS: *Hotspur and the Prince, as at the end of 905. The Prince takes his sword and helmet and begins to rise.*

908. MS: *the Prince, rising.*

98

PRINCE (*after a pause*): Adieu.

909. LS: *a soldier peers out and then retreats behind a tree.*

910. MLS: *the Prince, in an open space with bushes and trees in the background, stops and looks ahead.*

911. *Low angle* LS (*ground level*): *Falstaff, spread out on his back on the ground horizontal to the camera in the lower foreground. A large tree with spreading boughs occupies the background.*

912. LS: *the Prince stands at the top of a gentle slope. The sun behind him makes him cast a long shadow across the slope. He runs down the slope toward the camera.*

101–120

PRINCE: What, . . .

913. *Falstaff, as in 911, with the Prince now entering the shot, partially visible at the right.*

PRINCE: . . . old acquaintance?

914. MS: *the Prince, with the slope in the background.*

PRINCE: Could not all this flesh / Keep in a little life? Poor Jack, farewell! / I could have better spared a better man. //

915. MCU (*ground level*): *Falstaff, his armored helmet in profile. In the cold air, Falstaff's breath is visible through the vents in his visor.*

916. MCU: *the Prince shows by his expression that he realizes Falstaff is alive.*

PRINCE (*emphatically*): Emboweled will I see thee by-and-by. //

917. *Low angle* LS: *Falstaff, with the Prince on the right, as at the end of 913. The Prince crosses the frame to the left immediately in front of the camera and goes out of the shot at left.*

918. *High angle* CU: *Falstaff's head from directly above as he opens his visor so that his eyes, nose, and mouth are visible.*

FALSTAFF: Emboweled? If you embowel me today, I'll give you leave to powder me and eat me tomorrow.

919. LS: *Falstaff lies on the ground with feet toward the camera as two horsemen ride past in the foreground. Two men enter the shot from opposite sides and, reaching Falstaff, begin to help him to his feet.*

FALSTAFF: It was time to counterfeit. //

920. MCU: *Falstaff, seen from the side, as his upper body begins to be pulled up from the ground. The two men assisting him are partially visible.*

FALSTAFF: The better part of . . .

921. *Falstaff, as in 919. He begins to walk forward, with the two men supporting his arms.*

     FALSTAFF: . . . valor is discretion, in the which part . . .

922. LS: *the Page stands in some bushes. He looks with amusement at Falstaff and his two helpers, seen from the back, as they pass from left to right very close to the camera. While they are passing, they block the Page from sight.*

     FALSTAFF: . . . I have saved me life. //

923. *Falstaff, his back to the camera, sees the body of Hotspur on the ground beyond him. He pushes his helpers aside, and moves away from the camera to stand over Hotspur in* LS.

W   FALSTAFF: Zounds, this confounded Percy!

924. MS: *the Page in the bushes.*

124–125   FALSTAFF (*off*): I'll swear I killed him.

925. ELS: *Falstaff, alone in the landscape, leans over Hotspur and picks up his legs by the ankles.*

926. LS: *a single soldier, Prince John, runs forward into a low angle* MS.

157   *PRINCE JOHN: The trumpet sounds retreat.

927. LS: *several soldiers with clubs in a field littered with bodies. A soldier in the foreground turns, as if responding to the voice in 926.*

928. *Low angle* MS: *Prince John, as at the end of 926.*

     *PRINCE JOHN: The day is ours!

*Prince Hal

929. *Several soldiers, as in 927. The soldier in the foreground runs out of the shot to the right. Others lower their clubs.*

930. *The camera tracks left and downward over a section of the battlefield in a high angle* LS. *The shot includes several dead bodies, soldiers holding pairs of riderless horses by the reins, and other soldiers guarding enemy captives.*

931. *The camera pans to the left to show in* MLS *several captives in armor, with the King's horsemen riding up to form a line behind them.*

932. MCU: *King Henry, from the waist up and possibly mounted, takes off his helmet. In the background, knights on horseback are in a line behind him, many holding pennons on poles.*

KING: Thus ever did rebellion find rebuke. / Ill-spirited Worcester . . .   HI V.v.1–15

933. *High angle* LS: *Worcester, seen from over the King's shoulder, with guards behind him.*

KING: . . . did we not send grace, / Pardon, and terms of love to all of you? //

Prodded by a guard, Worcester moves a few steps to the right, now to be seen over the King's other shoulder.

WORCESTER: What I have done my safety urged me to. //

KING: Bear Worcester to the death. //

Worcester moves out of shot at the right.

934. *The King, as in 932.*

KING: Other offenders we will pause upon.

935. MS: *prisoners, seen from the side, are led away across the frame to-*

ward the right. After the prisoners come many soldiers carrying spears and, after them, a line of horsemen.

936. LS: *horsemen in the background pass behind a crudely built open structure and some equipment. Foot soldiers cross the screen in the immediate foreground.*

937. *High angle* LS: *the Prince walks toward the camera through the battlefield. To the left a troop of horsemen ride toward the camera. To the right the ground is covered with dead and wounded soldiers.*

938. MLS: *several horsemen ride across the screen to the left. Behind them other horses are tethered.*

939. LS: *the Prince walks toward the camera, with dead and wounded soldiers on the ground around him. His brother, Prince John, enters from the left and, moving away from the camera, approaches the Prince.*

H1 V.iv.158–159   * PRINCE JOHN (*his first words heard before he enters*): Come, brother, let us to the highest of the field, / To see what friends are living, who are dead. (*A figure carrying a knight in armor over his back by the heels crosses the screen from right to left. The Prince and Prince John stare after him.*)

940. LS: *Falstaff, seen from behind, moves away from the camera with Hotspur, held by the heels, on his back.*

941. MCU: *the Prince, with Prince John at his shoulder. The Prince suppresses a smile.*

942. *Falstaff, as in 940. He comes to a stop, lets the body drop, and begins to turn toward the camera.*

138–146   FALSTAFF: There's your . . .

*Prince Hal

943. *Low angle* MCU: *Falstaff completes his turn.*

   FALSTAFF: . . . Percy. (*He exhales loudly.*)

944. LS: *the Prince and Prince John as at the end of 939. The Prince begins to move toward the camera.*

   FALSTAFF (*off*): If your father will do me any . . .

945. *Low angle* MCU: *Falstaff, as at end of 943.*

   FALSTAFF: . . . honor, so; if not, let him kill the next Percy himself. //

   PRINCE (*off*): Why, Percy I killed.

946. LS: *the Prince moves from the right to kneel beside the body of Hotspur.*

   FALSTAFF (*off*): Didst thou?

   PRINCE: And saw thee dead. (*He turns the body over on its back.*)

947. MS: *Falstaff, turned partly to the side, emphasizing his portliness.*

   FALSTAFF: Lord, Lord, how this world is given to lying.

948. *Low angle* MS: *the Prince, seen from across Hotspur's body.*

949. *Falstaff, as in 947.*

   FALSTAFF: I grant you I was down, and out of breath, and so was he; but we rose both at an instant and fought a long hour by Shrewsbury clock.

950. MLS: *the Prince, seen across Hotspur's body. A figure enters the frame at the left, standing on the other side of Hotspur with only the bottom of his robe visible. The camera moves with the Prince as he rises and*

it also moves left to include King Henry, facing his son with his back to the camera.

951. *Low angle* CU: *the King.*

140–141   FALSTAFF (*off*): I look to be either . . .

952. *Falstaff, as in 947.*

FALSTAFF: . . . earl or duke, I assure you.

953. CU: *the Prince.*

954. *The King, as in 951.*

955. *The Prince, as in 953.*

956. MCU: *Falstaff.*

957. *The King, as in 951. He looks down.*

958. *High angle* LS: *the body of Hotspur, face up and arms extended. His head is at the bottom of the frame.*

959. *The King, as in 957.*

960. *The Prince, as in 953.*

961. *The King, as in 957. He looks up again.*

962. LS: *the King and the Prince face each other over the body of Hotspur. The King walks past the Prince and toward the background where part of the army can be seen moving slowly toward the right of the frame.*

963. MCU: *Falstaff looks to the right toward the Prince.*

964. *Low angle* MS: *the Prince, stands at the left, an empty horizon to the right.*

965. *Low angle* LS: *a single horseman holds his horse in place in front of a line of the King's horsemen.*

966. *Low angle* MS: *the King, his head suddenly plunging forward as he sits in his saddle. Offscreen cries are heard and arms reach up to support him. The King pulls himself upright with an effort and grasps the reins of his horse firmly.*

967. *Low angle* MS: *Falstaff stands in the foreground with soldiers in the background.*

968. *Low angle* MS: *the King, as at the end of 966. He extends his arm in a salute.*

> KING: Rebellion in this land shall lose its sway, / Meeting the check of   H1 V.v.41–42
> such another day. (*He begins to ride off to the right.*)

969. *The camera pans right to follow rows of horsemen in low angle* LS *as they pass from left to right.*

970. *The Prince, as in 964. Horsemen ride by behind him, headed toward the right.*

971. *A horseman rides toward the camera into a low angle* MLS *in the foreground.*

> *HORSEMAN (*reining in his horse*): Falstaff, you are going with Prince   H2 I.ii.212–214
> John of Lancaster against Northumberland.

972. MS: *Falstaff, with soldiers and horses moving in the background. He has now taken off his armor and is dressed in a coat of mail. In one hand he holds a small cask of wine.*

> FALSTAFF: There's not a dangerous action could peep out his head but   221–225
> I'm thrust upon it.

*Chief Justice

973. *The horseman, as in 971. He smiles and rides off to the right.*

FALSTAFF (*off*): Well . . .

974. *Falstaff, as in 972, but the Prince has now moved into the shot at the left and stands facing Falstaff, turned away from the camera and only partially visible.*

FALSTAFF: . . . I cannot last ever, but it was always the trick of our English nation if they have a good thing to make it too common.

211–212   * PRINCE JOHN (*coming from behind Falstaff to stand at the right*): Well, Falstaff, the King hath severed you and Prince Harry.

215   FALSTAFF: Yes, I thank your pretty wit for it. (*Prince John leaves at*
H2 IV.iii.89–129   *the right; Falstaff turns again to the Prince.*) Prince John of Lancaster. Good faith, this same sober-blooded boy doth not love me, nor a man cannot make him laugh. But that's no marvel, he drinks no wine. (*He begins to move left, behind the Prince.*)

975. *Low angle* MS: *the Prince, seen from the back, as Falstaff, behind him, crosses out of the shot at left. The Prince turns to the left to look after Falstaff.*

FALSTAFF (*his last words off*): There's never any of these demure boys . . .

976. MS: *Falstaff approaches a group of soldiers who stand next to a cask of wine so large the Page sits on top of it. Falstaff accepts a tankard from a man in front of the cask, then turns back and tosses the small cask he has been holding toward the camera and out of the shot.*

FALSTAFF: . . . come to any proof, for thin drink doth so over . . .

977. LS: *one of the onlookers catches the cask.*

*Chief Justice

FALSTAFF (*off*): . . . cool their blood, . . . //

978. *Falstaff, as in 976. The Prince enters at right and crosses to stand at left in profile near Falstaff.*

> FALSTAFF (*handing the Prince his tankard, and taking another from the man by the large cask*): . . . that they are generally fools and cowards, which some of us should be too, but for inflammation. (*He drinks.*)

979. MS: *a group of foot soldiers, some raising tankards and all laughing in response to Falstaff's words.*

980. MS: *the Prince faces Falstaff, whose back is partially visible at the right. Soldiers with tankards are laughing in the background. The Prince drinks.*

> FALSTAFF (*off*): A good sherris-sack . . .

981. MCU: *Falstaff holds his tankard in front of him, as if to examine it.*

> FALSTAFF: . . . hath a twofold operation in it.

982. MCU: *the Prince, with a slight smile. Behind him, soldiers are laughing. The smile fades, and the Prince's expression becomes serious.*

> FALSTAFF (*off*): It ascends me into the brain, and dries me there all the foolish . . .

983. *Falstaff, as in 981. He looks upward toward the sky, as if experiencing some grander vision.*

> FALSTAFF: . . . dull, and cruddy vapors which environ it, makes it apprehensive, quick, forgetive, full of nimble, fiery, and delectable shapes, . . .

984. *Low angle* MCU: *the Prince, looking serious.*

FALSTAFF (*off*): . . . which, delivered o'er to the voice, the tongue, which is the birth . . .

985. *Falstaff, as in 981.*

FALSTAFF: . . . becomes excellent wit.

986. MS: *a group of onlookers laughs with delight.*

FALSTAFF (*off*): The second property of your excellent sherris . . .

987. MCU: *Falstaff and the Prince, as at the end of 978. The Prince still stands at the left of the frame, but he now has turned further toward the camera, so that he no longer looks at Falstaff. As Falstaff speaks, the Prince stares past him, not sharing in the general laughter and apparently occupied with his own thoughts.*

FALSTAFF: . . . is the warming of the blood. // The sherris warms it and makes it course from the inwards to the parts extremes. // And hereof comes it that Prince Harry is valiant, . . .

988. *Low angle* MCU: *a virtually toothless man wearing a hood, laughs and cheers. Behind him a row of other men join in.*

989. MCU: *the Prince, as at the end of 982.*

FALSTAFF (*off*): . . . for the cold blood . . .

990. CU: *Falstaff.*

FALSTAFF: . . . he did naturally inherit of his father, . . .

991. *The Prince, as in 984.*

FALSTAFF (*off*): . . . he hath, like lean, sterile, and bare land, manured, husbanded, and tilled with excellent endeavor of drinking good . . . (*The Prince moves out of the frame at the left.*)

992. *Falstaff, as in 990.*

> FALSTAFF: . . . and good store of fertile sherris, that he is become very
> hot and valiant. If I . . . (*Falstaff moves out of the frame to the left.*)

993. LS: *the Prince stands with his back to the camera against a virtually
empty landscape. Falstaff enters at the right, his head and back occupying that side of the frame.*

> FALSTAFF: . . . had a thousand sons, the first . . .

994. MS: *Falstaff, tankard in his hand, is surrounded by smiling soldiers who
raise their tankards.*

> FALSTAFF: . . . humane principle I would teach them would be this: to
> forswear . . . (*He moves out of the frame to the left.*)

995. LS: *the Prince, in the landscape of 993. He turns back to face the
camera. Behind him on the left, a line of horsemen rides slowly away
from the camera toward the horizon.*

> FALSTAFF (*off*): . . . thin potations . . .

996. MS: *Falstaff raises his tankard in the foreground as if making a toast,
with soldiers below him in the background.*

> FALSTAFF: . . . and to addict themselves to sack.

997. LS: *the Prince half turns toward the camera with a tankard raised in his
hand. He turns away to look toward the line of horsemen moving into the
background at his left and then takes a step in their direction. The
laughter of the soldiers with Falstaff can be heard on the soundtrack.*

998. MS: *Falstaff, as at the end of 996. He still raises his tankard in front of
him, but his broad smile begins to disappear.*

999. ELS: *the Prince walks down a slope toward the horsemen in the distance*

at the upper left. As he walks, he lets the tankard in his hand drop to the ground.

Fade out.

1000. *Fade in to* LS *of horsemen crossing the screen from left to right and out of the shot in the foreground while soldiers on foot cross the screen right to left at a higher level in the background. When the soldiers reach the edge of the frame at left they descend to the lower level and follow in the direction the horsemen have taken. The landscape is chalky white and the soldiers are partially obscured by a haze blowing across the screen.*

NARRATOR: From the first, King Henry's reign was troubled with rebellion.

Dissolve.

1001. *Low angle* LS: *gallows with hanged men dangling from them. Soldiers on horseback are partially visible crossing to the right in the lower foreground. All the figures are in silhouette.*

NARRATOR: But in the year of our Lord 1408, the last of his enemies had been vanquished.

Dissolve.

The Royal Castle

1002. ELS: *King Henry sits in a chair at the far side of a room, with a robe covering his legs. The vantage point of the camera is an adjoining room.*

NARRATOR: The King held his Christmas this year at London, being sore vexed with sickness.

H2 III.i.
32-35
*WESTMORELAND (*entering the shot from the right and passing from the room in the foreground into the King's chamber; two other men follow Westmoreland, but stand much further back*): Many good morrows to your Majesty!
KING: Is it good morrow, lords?

*WESTMORELAND: 'Tis one o'clock, and past.

1003. MS: *King Henry closes the book he has been reading and looks up at Westmoreland, partially visible at the right.*

KING: Why, then, good morrow to you all, my lords.

1004. *High angle* MLS: *King Henry turns to look over the back of his chair.*

W   KING: The Prince of Wales.

W   ATTENDANT (*crossing in foreground to stand behind the King at the right of the frame*): My lord?

H2 IV.iv.16–17
KING: Where is he? (*Stands and faces the attendant.*) Is he not with his brother, John of Lancaster?

†ATTENDANT: No, my good lord, he is in presence here.

H2 III.i.104–106
*WESTMORELAND (*off*): Please it your Grace . . .

1005. MCU: *Westmoreland, soldiers standing behind him.*

*WESTMORELAND: . . . to go to bed. // Your Majesty hath been this fortnight ill, / . . .

1006. MLS: *the King stands by his chair as at the end of 1004.*

*WESTMORELAND (*off*): . . . And these unseasoned hours perforce must add / Unto your sickness.

*Warwick
†Gloucester

*King Henry drops the book he carries into the chair as Prince John
enters through a door at right behind the King.*

* PRINCE JOHN (*stopping inside the door*): What would my lord and   H2 IV.iv.18, 50–80
father?

KING (*turning to face him*): Why art thou not at Windsor with the
Prince?

* PRINCE JOHN: He is not there today. (*Crosses to the left foreground
and turns back to face the King.*) He dines in London.

KING: And how accompanied? Canst thou tell me that?

* PRINCE JOHN: With Poins and other his continual followers.

The King walks to the doorway where Prince John had entered.

1007. CU: *the King against part of the doorframe.*

KING: Most subject is the fattest soil to weeds, / And he, the noble
image of my youth, / Is overspread with them. Therefore my grief /
Stretches itself beyond the hour of death. / The blood weeps from my
heart when I do shape / In forms imaginary the unguided days / And
rotten times that you shall look upon / When I am sleeping with my
ancestors. //

1008. *The camera tracks backward to keep the King in* MS *as he moves
forward toward the adjoining room, keeping close to the wall and placing his hand on it as if to steady himself. Westmoreland accompanies
him at the right; Prince John walks behind him.*

WESTMORELAND: My gracious lord, you look beyond him quite. //
The Prince of Wales will in the perfectness of time / Cast off his
followers. //

KING: 'Tis seldom when the bee doth leave her comb / In the dead
carrion. (*As he leans for support on a large chest, the King collapses.*

* Clarence

*When he falls, his hand knocks over the royal crown, sitting on a
cushion on the chest.)*

1009. LS: *King Henry collapses on the floor next to the chest. The clatter of
his crown striking the stone floor is heard. Nobles and attendants immediately surround him, their murmurs of concern audible on the
soundtrack. The camera tracks right with a number of white-robed friars
as they carry the King a short distance to his bed.*

1010. *The camera pans with Westmoreland, as, his back to the camera, he
moves away into* MLS *before a door which is opening; several nobles
crowd into the doorway.*

114–120   * WESTMORELAND: Be patient, lords. You do know these fits / Are
with his Highness very ordinary. //

† PRINCE JOHN (*at first, off, then entering the shot in the foreground
from the right*): No, no, he cannot long hold out these pangs. /
(*Stands at the left as Westmoreland joins him and both look at the
camera toward the King.*) The incessant care and labor of his mind /
Hath wrought the mure that should confine it in / So thin that life
looks through and will break out.

1011. MS: *the King on his bed.*

W   KING (*raising himself up and pointing forward*): The crown!

1012. *High angle* MCU: *the crown on the floor, as a robed arm reaches down
and picks it up.*

H2 IV.v.5   KING (*off*): Set me the crown . . .

1013. MS: *the King turns to the left and stretches out his arm across his pillow
to receive the crown as a partially visible figure enters the shot from the
left and places the crown gently on the pillow.*

* Warwick
† Clarence

KING: . . . upon my pillow here.

1014. MCU: *three attendants look toward the King.*

1015. MCU: *King Henry looks at the crown, which fills the left foreground. He then moves away and toward the right until he moves out of the shot, leaving the crown as the single focus of attention.*

1016. LS: *the King, seen from behind the backs of his attendants, walks in stately fashion to the right in a room crowded with members of the court. Courtiers are visible in the background.*

1017. *Low angle* MS: *several members of the court look toward the King.*

KING (*off*): Let there be no noise, . . .   1-3

1018. ELS: *the King, framed by two columns in the foreground, looks out of a long barred window.*

KING: . . . my gentle friends, / Unless some dull and favorable hand / Will whisper music to my weary state. (*He covers his eyes with his hand.*)

1019. MLS: *an attendant turns away from the camera toward another room. Two other attendants, one in the left foreground, the other in the background, stand looking to the right, apparently toward the King.*

* ATTENDANT: Call for the music in the other room.

1020. *Low angle* MCU: *several members of the court, with solemn faces. A lyrical theme for strings begins on the soundtrack and continues to the end of the scene.*

1021. ELS: *King Henry, as at the end of 1018.*

* Warwick

1022. CU: *Westmoreland and Prince John in profile, with Westmoreland closer to the camera.*

H2 IV.iv.121–128   * WESTMORELAND: The people fear me, for they do observe / Unfathered heirs and loathly births of nature. / The seasons change their manners, as the year / Had found some months asleep and leaped them over.

† PRINCE JOHN: The river hath thrice flowed, no ebb between, / And the old folk, time's doting chronicles, / Say it did so a little time before / That our great-grandsire, Edward, sicked and died.

1023. *King Henry, as in 1021, but with his hands at his sides. He again raises his hand to his face.*

1024. MCU: *King Henry, as he completes the gesture of 1023, brings his hand momentarily across his lower face. He is in profile, lit by the light from the window and shadowed by its bars.*

H2 III.i.4–31   KING: How many thousands of my poorest subjects / Are at this hour asleep! O sleep, O gentle sleep, / Nature's soft nurse, how have I frighted thee, / That thou no more wilt weigh mine eyelids down / And steep my senses in forgetfulness? / Why rather, sleep, liest thou in smoky cribs, / Upon uneasy pallets stretching thee / And hushed with buzzing night-flies to thy slumber, / Than in the perfumed chambers of the great, / Under the canopies of costly state, / And lulled with sounds of sweetest melody? / O thou dull god, why li'st thou with the vile / In loathsome beds, and leavest the kingly couch / A watchcase or a common 'larumbell? / Wilt thou upon the high and giddy mast / Seal up the ship-boy's eyes, and rock his brain / In cradle of the rude imperious surge / And in the visitation of the winds, / Which take the ruffian billows by the top, / Curling their monstrous heads and hanging them / With deaf'ning clamor in the slippery shrouds, / That, with the hurly, death itself awakes? / Wilt thou, O partial sleep, give thy repose / To the wet sea-boy in an hour so rude, / And in the calmest and most

*Gloucester
†Clarence

stillest night, / With all appliances and means to boot, / Deny it to a king? Then happy low, lie down! /

1025. ELS: *the King, as at the beginning of 1023.*

    KING: Uneasy lies the head that wears a crown.

Dissolve.

A Country Landscape

1026. CU: *the Prince, the branches of a tree behind him at the right.*

    PRINCE: Before God, I am exceeding weary.   H2 II.ii.1–5

1027. CU: *Poins, with water and trees in the background.*

    POINS: Is't come to that? I had thought weariness durst not have attached itself . . .

1028. MCU: *the Prince and Poins, with the Prince in profile on the right, Poins facing him and the camera on the left.*

    POINS: . . . to one of so high blood.

    PRINCE: Faith, it does me, though it discolors the complexion of my greatness to acknowledge it.

1029. MS: *the Page, seen over the Prince's shoulder, offers a letter. Bardolph is partially visible behind the Page at the left.*

    BARDOLPH: God save . . .

1030. LS: *the Prince faces the Page, both in profile, with Poins between them, facing the camera and perusing the letter. A pond is immediately behind them, with trees forming a border on the far side. A small tree next to the Prince fills the right of the frame.*

BARDOLPH (*barely visible at the left*): . . . your grace.

PRINCE: Yours, most noble Bardolph. How doth thy master?

BARDOLPH: In bodily health, sir.

118–120   *POINS (*reading*): "John Falstaff, knight, to the son of the King nearest his father, Harry Prince of Wales, greeting." (*Poins and the Prince*
126   *both chuckle.*) "Be not too familiar with—" . . . (*Angrily*) . . . You
106–107   allow this wen to be as familiar . . .

1031. MS: *the Prince and Poins.*

*POINS: . . . with me as your dog!

126–135   PRINCE (*taking the letter from Poins and reading on*): "Be not too
familiar with Poins, for he misuses thy favors so much that he swears
thou art to marry his sister Nell."

POINS (*reaching for the letter and overlapping with the Prince's last few
words*): My lord, I'll steep this letter in sack and make him . . .

1032. *The Prince and Poins, as in 1028.*

POINS: . . . eat it.

PRINCE (*amused*): "Repent at idle times as thou mayst, and so farewell. Thine, by yea and no, which is as much as to say, as thou usest
him, JACK FALSTAFF with my familiars, JOHN with my brothers
and sisters, and SIR JOHN with all Europe." (*To the Page.*) Is he in
London?

1033. *The Page, as in 1029, but with Bardolph more visible at the left.*

144, 152   PAGE: Yes, sir, with Mistress Doll Tearsheet.

*Prince

1034. *The Prince and Poins, as in 1028.*

> PRINCE (*turning to Poins*): Shall we steal upon them, Ned, at supper?   157–158
>
> (*To Page.*) You, boy . . .   160–164

1035. MS: *the Prince stands before Bardolph and the Page, his back to the camera.*

> PRINCE: . . . and Bardolph, no word to your master that I am yet come to town. There's for your silence. (*Hands the Page a bag of coins.*)
>
> BARDOLPH: I have no tongue, sir.
>
> PAGE: And for mine, sir, I will govern it. (*Hal puts his hand on the Page's shoulder approvingly as the Page turns away.*)

1036. ELS: *the Page and Bardolph walk toward the left at the bottom of the screen under a line of trees. A melancholy theme played by the cello is heard on the soundtrack and continues into the next scene to shot 1045.*

1037. *The Prince, with Poins at his shoulder, walks toward the camera into* MS.

> PRINCE: Doth it now show very vilely in me to desire small beer?   5–6
>
> POINS: Tell me, how many good young princes would do so, their fathers being so sick as yours at this time is?   29–31
>
> PRINCE (*turning to look directly at Poins*): A disgrace is it for me to remember thy name or to know thy face tomorrow! (*Turns back toward the camera.*) Do you use me thus, Ned? Must I marry your sister?   13–14   137–140
>
> POINS: God send the wench no worse fortune! But I never said so.
>
> PRINCE (*moving out of the frame at left*): Come, Ned.

1038. MS: *the Prince, his back to the camera, turns as Poins speaks.*

POINS (*off*): I am your shadow, my lord.

1039. MS: *Poins.*

POINS: I follow you. (*He begins to move to the left.*)

1040. MS: *the Prince, as Poins enters the shot from the right. They stand and look in one another's faces. Then the Prince smiles and puts his arm around Poins's shoulder, leading him off to the left.*

Dissolve.

The Tavern in Eastcheap

1041. CU: *Falstaff, his face brightly lit from below against a dark background.*

H1 I.ii.76–77   FALSTAFF: 'Sblood, I'm as melancholy as a gib-cat or a lugged bear. (*The camera pans right with him; then, as he moves out of the shot, it holds in* CU *on Peto and Bardolph, both partially visible.*)

H1 III.iii.12–14   * PETO: Sir John, you're so fretful you cannot live long.

1042. CU: *Falstaff.*

MWW I.iii.37–42   FALSTAFF (*sighing*): Well, there it is. I'll tell you what I am about.

1043. MCU: *Bardolph, with Peto immediately behind him.*

† BARDOLPH: Two yards—and more. //

1044. LS: *the Prince and Poins move to the edge of an overhang that extends out from low eaves above the room. They lean against support beams to listen.*

* Bardolph
† Pistol

FALSTAFF (*off*): Indeed, I am in the waist two yards about. And I am now about no waste, I am about . . .

1045. MLS: *Falstaff stands behind a table, with Bardolph and Peto on the left and the Hostess on his right. He empties his coin purse on the table and she hastily gathers up the few coins that are there.*

FALSTAFF: . . . thrift. // (*Sits down.*) I must turn away some of me followers. // There's no remedy. 4–5, 32

* HOSTESS (*as Bardolph crosses out of the shot in the right foreground*): I will employ Bardolph. He shall draw here for me. 10

*Host

16

30

W

FALSTAFF: A tapster is a good trade. (*In the background, Doll Tear-sheet approaches, dressed in a black cloak and a hat tilted down over one eye.*) Lads, I am almost out at heels. (*Doll now stands at the table between Falstaff and Mistress Quickly, looking down at Falstaff.*) Hello, Doll.

H2 II.iv.39-40

DOLL (*holding up a single coin Mistress Quickly hands her and then tossing it contemptuously away*): Is that all . . . (*As she speaks, the sound of knocking is heard.*)

1046. *The Prince and Poins, as in 1044, now get on their hands and knees and lean their heads over the edge of the overhang.*

DOLL (*off, as the knocking continues*): . . . the comfort you give me?

1047. MLS: *Falstaff, with Doll and the Hostess, as at the end of 1045.*

HOSTESS (*rising and leaving at the right*): Who knocks so loud at door?

39-59

DOLL: Fat muddy rascal.

FALSTAFF (*pulling open the front of Doll's cloak*): You make fat rascals, . . .

1048. *Low angle* MS: *Doll, seen over Falstaff's shoulder in the lower left of the frame as she stands above him.*

FALSTAFF: . . . Doll.

DOLL (*pushing his hands away*): I make them? (*She takes off her hat and puts it on Falstaff's head.*) Gluttony and diseases make them.

FALSTAFF: If the cook helped . . .

1049. *Low angle* MS: *the Prince and Poins, their heads peering over the edge of the overhang.*

FALSTAFF (*off*): . . . to make the gluttony, . . .

1050. *High angle* MCU: *Falstaff, seen over Doll's shoulder. The camera follows him as he rises and then tracks with him as he walks to the right across the room and into a privy.*

> FALSTAFF: . . . you help to make the diseases. We catch of you, O, we catch of you. // For to serve bravely is to come halting off, you know, to come off the breach with his pike bent bravely, . . . (*Opens the gate to the privy and steps behind it.*) . . . and to surgery bravely, to venture . . .

1051. LS: *the Prince and Poins on the floor of the eaves in the upper foreground and Falstaff with his head visible over the privy gate in the lower background, all seen across the width of the room.*

> FALSTAFF: . . . upon the charged chambers . . .

> DOLL (*entering the shot at the extreme lower left and moving toward the privy; overlapping with Falstaff*): Hang yourself!

1052. *Doll, moving into* CU, *with the Hostess behind her.*

> FALSTAFF (*off*): . . . bravely.

> DOLL: You muddy conger!

1053. MCU: *Falstaff, his head above the privy gate. Lowering himself, he disappears behind the gate.*

> DOLL (*off*): Hang yourself!

1054. MCU: *Doll, as at the end of 1052.*

> HOSTESS (*putting her arm around Doll*): You two never meet but you fall to some discord. (*Doll moans softly and, turning away, moves into the background, with the Hostess following her.*) You are both, i' good truth . . .

1055. MLS: *Doll moves toward the camera, covering her mouth with her cloak, followed by the Hostess. Wooden beams occupy the upper foreground and frame the Prince and Poins crouched in the upper left corner.*

HOSTESS: . . . as rheumatic as two dry . . .

1056. *High angle* MLS: *Peto sits on a bench by the wall with his arms folded. He looks upward.*

HOSTESS (*off*): . . . toasts.

1057. *Low angle* LS: *the Prince and Poins peer over the edge of the overhang. The Prince puts his finger to his lips.*

1958. *Peto, as in 1056. He winks.*

1059. *The Prince and Poins, as in 1057.*

26–32   HOSTESS (*off*): I' faith, sweetheart, . . .

1060. *The camera pans left to follow Doll and the Hostess in* MLS *crossing the room. Doll moans frequently and holds the edge of her cloak over her mouth as if she were going to be sick. The Hostess takes some leggings hanging on a line in the room, moves in front of Doll, and fans her by waving the cloth in front of her face.*

HOSTESS: . . . you've drunk too much canary. // How do you now?

DOLL (*now in* LS, *sitting on the end of a bed in the corner of the room*): Better than I was.

HOSTESS (*sitting next to Doll and continuing to fan her*): Why, that's well said. A good heart's better than gold.

1061. *Low angle* MCU: *the Hostess and Doll. Doll lays her head on the Hostess's shoulder.*

HOSTESS: What the goodyear! One must bear, and that must be you.   *60–61*

1062. *Low angle* MLS: *Bardolph comes around a corner and stands next to the privy gate, his back to the camera.*

BARDOLPH: Sir, it's Pistol. He'd speak with you.   *70–74*

1063. *Low angle* MCU: *the Hostess and Doll, as at the end of 1061.*

DOLL (*raising her head quickly and shouting angrily*): Pistol! (*The camera follows her as she jumps up and crosses the room to stand in* LS *near the privy. She turns to look toward the Hostess, still visible at the right.*) The foulest mouthed rogue in England. Hang him, . . .

1064. *The Hostess rises from the bed into low angle* MS.

DOLL (*off*): . . . swaggering rascal!

HOSTESS: Swagger?

1065. *Falstaff, over the privy gate, as in 1053.*

FALSTAFF: Empty the jordan.   *34*

1066. *Low angle* MCU: *the Hostess.*

HOSTESS: If he swagger, let him not come here.   *75*

1067. *Low angle* MS: *Bardolph.*

*BARDOLPH: He's no swaggerer.   *99–101*

1068. *The camera pans left with Falstaff in a low angle* MS *as he walks back across the room from the privy and sits down again behind the table.*

*Falstaff

FALSTAFF: A tame cheater, i' faith. You may stroke him as gentle as a puppy greyhound. Pistol!

1069. MLS: *Pistol enters at right with the Hostess standing at the left near the privy.*

112–130

PISTOL: God save you, Sir John! (*He tosses his hat with a flourish to the Hostess.*)

FALSTAFF (*off*): Pistol, I charge you with a cup of sack. You discharge upon mine hostess.

PISTOL: I will discharge upon her, Sir John, with two bullets. (*He uses his scabbard to imitate an erection and moves toward the Hostess, who screams and slaps at the scabbard with Pistol's hat.*)

FALSTAFF (*off*): Ha, ha, she is pistol-proof, sir; . . .

1070. MCU: *Falstaff holds a goblet in front of him.*

FALSTAFF: . . . you shall hardly offend her. //

1071. LS: *Pistol, scabbard still imitating a phallus, with the Hostess at the left.*

PISTOL (*moving away from the Hostess and toward the camera*): Then to you, Mistress Dorothy, I will charge you. (*He opens his arms toward Doll with romantic extravagance.*)

1072. MLS: *Doll rushes toward the camera, with Falstaff in his chair behind her.*

DOLL: Charge me?

1073. MLS: *Pistol, arms extended, is at the right as Doll enters the shot from the left and runs toward him.*

DOLL: You filthy bung!

1074. MCU: *Falstaff sits in the right foreground with Bardolph, Peto, and a third follower in the background.*

FALSTAFF: Give me my rapier, Bardolph.

1075. MLS: *Doll is seen from the back as she advances on Pistol, who falls to the floor as he backs away.*

DOLL: I'll thrust my knife in your moldy chaps, . . .

1076. *Low angle* MLS: *the Prince and Poins look down from the overhang.*

DOLL (*off*): . . . and you play the saucy cuttle . . .

1077. LS: *Doll stands over Pistol. She kicks him, and the camera moves left with him as he crawls under the gate and into the privy.*

DOLL: . . . with me. //

PISTOL: God, let me not live but I will murder your ruff for this.

1078. MCU: *Falstaff.*

FALSTAFF: Pistol, I would not have you go off here.

1079. MS: *Pistol behind the privy gate, his face first appearing through a peephole in the gate, then above the gate.*

HOSTESS (*off*): Not here, sweet captain.

1080. CU: *Doll.*

DOLL (*in a fury*): Captain!

1081. MLS: *the Hostess at the left holds Doll to keep her away from Pistol, while in the right background Bardolph pulls open the privy gate to reveal Pistol cowering behind it.*

155 BARDOLPH: Pray thee, go down, good captain.

Pistol rushes out of the privy and runs along the room to the right. The camera tracks with him in LS *until he runs up an enclosed staircase and pops his head out of a small interior window above. Doll, who has been chasing him, stops at the bottom of the staircase.*

147–149 DOLL (*partially offscreen as she chases Pistol*): You, a captain! For what? For tearing a poor whore's ruff in a bawdy house?

167–171 PISTOL (*from inside the staircase*): Shall hollow pampered jades of . . .

1082. *Low angle* MS: *Pistol's head protrudes from the window as he looks down.*

PISTOL: . . . Asia / . . .

1083. *Low angle* LS: *the Prince and Poins, their heads visible above the overhang.*

PISTOL (*off*): . . . Compare with . . .

1084. *Pistol, as in 1082.*

PISTOL: . . . Caesars, and with Cannibals, / . . .

1085. MS: *Doll picks up a bowl that is lying on top of a cask and prepares to throw it.*

PISTOL (*off*): . . . And with Trojan . . .

1086. *Pistol, as in 1082. He pulls his head back from the window.*

1087. MS: *Doll throws the bowl. The camera pans left to follow the bowl as it smashes to pieces near the window.*

PISTOL (*off*): . . . Greeks? (*As the bowl shatters, he screams.*)

1088. *Low angle* MS: *the Hostess in the lower left foreground shields her head against fragments from the bowl as they fall from above.*

1089. *Low angle* MS: *the Prince and Poins lean further out to see what is going on below.*

1090. *The camera follows Pistol in* MS *as he tiptoes to the right toward the door.*

1091. MCU: *Falstaff in his chair with Bardolph at the left, presenting him with a sword.*

FALSTAFF: Come.   W

1092. *Pistol, with camera following, as in 1090. He turns in great terror as Falstaff enters the shot, only partially visible, at the extreme left.*

PISTOL (*with a cry of fear*): Nay!

1093. *Low angle* MLS: *Falstaff with his sword in his hand, rolling up the sleeve of his sword arm. Bardolph and another follower stand behind him. Falstaff begins to move forward.*

1094. *Low angle* LS: *the Prince, his mouth agape, and Poins, as they watch.*

* FALSTAFF (*off*): Get thee . . .   199–203

1095. MLS: *Falstaff, as at the end of 1093, moves more rapidly toward the camera.*

FALSTAFF: . . . downstairs!

* Bardolph

1096. *Low angle* MS: *Doll, with the Hostess behind her. They both retreat, Doll looking back toward the fracas.*

PISTOL (*off*): What! Shall we have . . .

1097. *The camera tracks right with Falstaff in* MS *as he runs across the room, underneath low overhangs. Falstaff's shouts and the sounds of combat continue on the soundtrack through 1103.*

PISTOL (*off*): . . . incision? Shall we imbrue? // Why, then . . .

1098. MLS: *Pistol, bent low under a low ceiling, runs with his sword raised.*

PISTOL: . . . let grievous, . . .

1099. MCU: *Falstaff's followers stare after him, with Bardolph in the center foreground.*

PISTOL (*off*): . . . ghastly, . . .

1100. *The camera moves right with Falstaff, seen from the side in a low angle* MCU *as he runs forward, shouting.*

PISTOL (*off*): . . . gaping wounds / . . .

1101. *The camera moves left with Pistol in* MS *as he runs beside a wall, passing behind several wooden beams.*

PISTOL: . . . untwined the Sisters . . .

1102. MLS: *Pistol faces the camera next to a wall on the right as Falstaff enters the shot from the left. Pistol tumbles back out of the frame just as Falstaff draws back his sword.*

PISTOL: . . . Three!

1103. *Low angle* LS: *the Prince and Poins with their heads now entirely below the overhang as they try to follow the action below.*

PISTOL (*off*): Come, Atropos, I say!

1104. *Low angle* LS: *Pistol comes tumbling down a steep staircase and rolls out of the frame in the lower foreground. Falstaff is silhouetted at the top of the stairs.*

1105. *Low angle* MS: *Falstaff returns through the doorway to the room where the chase began. He nonchalantly brushes himself off.*

DOLL (*off*): Jack!   w

1106. *The camera pans right with Doll in* MLS *as she runs up to Falstaff.*

   * DOLL: Are you not hurt in the groin? (*She attempts to look under his*   214–215
    belly; Falstaff looks down and tries to bend.) I thought he made a
    shrewd thrust at your belly. (*As Falstaff begins to breathe heavily, she*
    helps him to sit on the side of her bed.)

   FALSTAFF (*now in* MS *with his back to the camera*): A rascal slave!   219–220

   DOLL (*kneeling in front of Falstaff and taking off his hat*): O you sweet
    little rogue.

   FALSTAFF: A rascal bragging slave!   232

   DOLL (*brushing Falstaff and undoing his jacket; overlapping*): You   213, 220
    whoreson little valiant villain, you. // Poor ape, how you are sweating.

   FALSTAFF: The rogue fled from me like quicksilver.   232–233

   DOLL (*taking up the leggings the Hostess had used earlier and wiping*   221–231
    his face with them): Come, let me wipe thy face. Come on, you
    whoreson chops. (*She takes his face in her hands and squeezes his*
    cheeks.) Ah, rogue! I' faith, I love thee. //

   FALSTAFF: I will toss the rogue in a blanket.

*Hostess

DOLL (*still with his face in her hands*): Do, and thou dar'st for thy heart. And thou dost, I'll canvas thee between a pair of sheets.

Falstaff reaches around Doll's waist to pull her to him and falls back on the bed. The camera moves with him and reframes the two profiled in MCU, *with her face above his.*

1107. MS: *the Page, leaning through a doorway.*

PAGE: The music is come, sir.

FALSTAFF (*off*): Let 'em play.

1108. *Low angle* MS: *the Prince and Poins lie on the floor at one corner of the eaves. The Prince bumps his head on the beam just above him.*

1109. MCU: *Falstaff, in profile, lies face up on the bed.*

FALSTAFF: Play, sirs! (*A melancholy song in the manner of a sixteenth-century folk theme is played primarily by wind instruments and continues intermittently until shot 1149.*)

1110. *Low angle* LS: *the Prince and Poins each lift single boards that form part of the floor on which they lie and, presumably, the ceiling above Falstaff. They look down through the openings.*

1111. *Falstaff, as in 1109.*

281–283   FALSTAFF: What stuff wilt have a kirtle of? I shall receive money Thursday. Shalt have a cap tomorrow.

1112. *Low angle* LS: *the Prince and Poins, as at the end of 1110. The Prince replaces his board, while Poins keeps watching.*

H1 III.iii.14–15   FALSTAFF (*off*): Come . . .

1113. *Falstaff, as in 1109.*

FALSTAFF: . . . sing me a bawdy song to make me merry.

1114. MS: *Doll, lying on Falstaff, draws herself up over his belly and moves toward his head.*

1115. MS: *the Prince and Poins replace the other board and again look over the edge of the overhang.*

1116. MCU: *Falstaff and Doll, her head directly above his.*

FALSTAFF: Thou'lt forget me when I'm gone.

DOLL: You'll start me weeping if you say so.   H2 II.iv.284–286

FALSTAFF: Kiss . . .   269

1117. *Low angle* MLS: *the Prince and Poins are seen from underneath the eaves, so that their heads appear upside down in the lower part of the frame.*

FALSTAFF (*off*): . . . me, Doll.

1118. *Falstaff and Doll, as in 1116. She leans down and kisses him.*

1119. *The Prince and Poins, as in 1117. They withdraw their heads.*

1120. *Falstaff and Doll, as in 1116.*

1121. *Low angle* MS: *the Prince and Poins, the Prince with his head propped against a corner of the eave.*

PRINCE: Is it not strange that desire should so many years outlive   267–268
performance?

1122. *Falstaff and Doll, as in 1116. She lays her head on his chest.*

FALSTAFF: Thou dost give me flattering busses.   275–280

DOLL: I kiss thee with a most constant heart.

1123. *The Prince and Poins, as in 1121. They look below again.*

1124. *Falstaff and Doll, as in 1116.*

FALSTAFF: I am old, I am old.

DOLL: I love thee better than I love e'er a scurvy young boy of them all.
w   (*She slides off his chest to lie next to him in the bed.*) Jack?

FALSTAFF: Eh?

1125. MS: *the Prince and Poins under the eaves. The Prince is leaning far out
over the edge of the overhang.*

241–242   DOLL (*off*): What humor is the Prince made of?

1126. *Falstaff and Doll, as in 1116.*

w   FALSTAFF: The Prince of Wales?

DOLL: Mmm.

FALSTAFF: A good shallow young fellow.

1127. *The Prince and Poins, as in 1125. The Prince pulls himself back and
turns to Poins.*

262–263   PRINCE: Would not this knave have his ears cut off?

245–246   DOLL (*off*): They say Poins has a good wit.

FALSTAFF (*off*): Poins?

1128. *Falstaff and Doll, as in 1116.*

FALSTAFF (*laughing*): A good wit?

1129. *The Prince and Poins, as in 1125.*

    POINS: Let's beat him before his whore.   264

    The Prince begins to slide his leg toward the edge of the overhang.

    FALSTAFF (*off*): The Prince himself is such another; the weight of a   259–261
    hair will not turn the . . .

1130. *Falstaff and Doll, as in 1116.*

    FALSTAFF: . . . scale between their avoirdupois. (*He turns his head
    and looks upward as he hears a noise.*)

1131. *Low angle* MS: *the Prince, hanging by his arms from the edge of his
hiding place.*

1132. MS: *Falstaff and Doll, with Falstaff turning onto his stomach in the bed.
They both look with surprise toward the camera.*

    FALSTAFF (*with a laugh*): A bastard son of the King!   290–291

1133. *The camera follows the Prince as he drops down from the eaves into*
MCU.

1134. LS: *Falstaff and Doll in the bed, with the Prince partially visible on the
far right, as Poins drops into the shot on the left.*

1135. *Poins lands and quickly moves forward into* MCU.

    FALSTAFF (*off*): And thou, art thou not Poins . . .

1136. *Falstaff and Doll, as in 1132.*

    FALSTAFF: . . . his brother?

1137. MCU: *Poins, as at the end of 1135. The Prince can be heard laughing
offscreen. The camera follows Poins as he moves left and joins the
Prince in* MS.

305–307   POINS: My lord, he will drive you out of your revenge, if you take not the heat.

MWW
V.v.155   * PRINCE (*rushing forward and diving toward the camera*): What a . . .

1138. *High angle* MS: *Falstaff, as the Prince lands on top of his belly with his legs sprawled between Falstaff and Doll.*

PRINCE (*leaning his face down into Falstaff's*): . . . hog's pudding, a bag of flax! (*Poins falls on the bed in the foreground, his back to the camera and his arm around Doll. The four heads are pressed close together at the right of the frame.*)

H2 II.iv.324   FALSTAFF (*placatingly*): No abuse, Hal.

MWW
V.v.157   † PRINCE: Old, cold, withered, and of intolerable entrails.

H1 I.ii.82–84   FALSTAFF (*overlapping*): Thou art indeed the rascaliest sweet young prince.

H2 II.iv.308–310   PRINCE: How vilely did you speak of me even now before this . . . (*Takes Doll in both his arms across Falstaff's belly and embraces her.*) . . . honest, virtuous, civil gentlewoman!

317–318   FALSTAFF: Why, Hal, I did not think thou wast within hearing.

314–316   PRINCE (*sarcastically*): Yea, and you knew me as you did when you ran away at the robbery. You spoke it on purpose to try my patience.

1139. MLS: *the Page enters the privy and closes the gate behind him. The squeaking of the gate is very audible.*

327–348   FALSTAFF (*off*): I dispraised thee . . .

1140. MS: *Falstaff, the Prince, Doll, and Poins in the bed, as at the end of 1138. The Prince still embraces Doll.*

*Ford
†George Page

FALSTAFF: . . . before the wicked, that the wicked might not fall in love with thee, // for which thy father is to thank me.

* POINS: See now, whether pure and entire cowardice doth not make thee wrong this virtuous gentlewoman. Is she of the wicked?

PRINCE: Is thine hostess of the wicked? Or . . . (*Points to the left.*) . . . honest Bardolph, . . .

1141. MLS: *Bardolph, sitting on a bench. Peto, next to him on the left, laughs and claps Bardolph on the shoulder.*

PRINCE (*off*): . . . whose zeal burns in his nose, of the wicked? //

FALSTAFF (*off*): The fiend hath . . .

1142. *Falstaff, the Prince, Doll, and Poins as in 1140. Falstaff struggles to raise himself from under the Prince and Doll.*

FALSTAFF: pricked down Bardolph irrecoverable. // (*The camera follows Falstaff as he gradually disentangles himself and, getting on his feet, moves to the left in low angle* MLS *in the background, while continuing to speak. In the foreground, Poins's legs can be seen swinging in the air as he rolls over and leaves the bed. The Prince and Doll then take over the foreground, kissing passionately.*) For the women, one of them is in hell already, and burns poor souls. For the other, I owe her money, and whether she be damned for that, I know not. // But Hal, am I not fallen away . . .

1143. *High angle* MCU: *the Prince kisses Doll's hair as her head lies on his chest. He looks up toward Falstaff.*   H1 III.iii.1-4

FALSTAFF (*off*): . . . vilely when me skin . . .

1144. *Low angle* MLS: *Falstaff, with the Prince's head visible in the lower foreground and Poins's profile partially visible at the far right.*

*Prince

FALSTAFF: . . . hangs about me like an old lady's loose gown? (*The Page comes out of the privy, near where Falstaff is standing, and leaves the shot at the left; Falstaff calls after him.*) Sirrah! You! Giant!

H2 I.ii.1–11   1145. LS: *the Page, in the middle of the room, turns back toward Falstaff. He carries a small pot covered with a cloth.*

FALSTAFF (*off*): What says . . .

1146. *Falstaff, as in 1144.*

FALSTAFF: . . . the doctor to my water?

1147. MS: *the Page, now facing the camera.*

PAGE: He said, sir, the water itself was a good water; but, for the party who owned it, he might have more diseases than he knew of.

1148. *Low angle* MS: *Falstaff, with the Prince lying in profile on the bed in the foreground, and Poins's head in profile at the right.*

FALSTAFF: Men of all sorts take a pride to gird at me. (*The camera follows Falstaff to the left as he moves past the bed into a low angle* MCU, *leaving the Prince and Poins out of the shot.*) The brain of this foolish compounded clay, man, is not able to invent anything that tends to laughter more than I invent or is invented on me. I am not only witty in meself, but the cause that wit is . . .

1149. MCU: *the Prince in profile, with Doll asleep on his chest, and Poins, immediately behind Doll, also in* MCU *and facing toward the Prince.*

FALSTAFF (*off*): . . . in other men.

H2 II.iv.370–371   PRINCE: I feel me much to blame, / So idly to profane the precious time. (*As Poins begins to laugh, the Prince turns away from the*
H2 II.ii.46–48   *camera toward him.*) I tell thee, my heart bleeds inwardly my father is so sick. (*When Poins continues to laugh, the Prince turns back into*
32–45   *profile and his tone hardens.*) Shall I tell thee one thing, Poins?

POINS: And let it be an excellent good thing.

PRINCE: It shall serve among wits of no higher breeding than thine.

POINS (*his smile fading, as he notes the Prince's tone*): Go to. I shall stand the push of your one thing that you shall tell. //

PRINCE: I could tell thee, as to one, for fault of a better, it pleases me to call friend, I could be sad, and sad indeed, too.

POINS: Very hardly upon such a subject.

PRINCE (*turning back to Poins*): Thou think'st me as far in the devil's book as thou and Falstaff.

FALSTAFF (*off*): An old lord of the council . . .   H1 I.ii.87–93

The Prince turns toward the camera.

1150. *The camera moves right to follow Falstaff in low angle* MCU *as he moves past a beam, putting on his robe, and looks down toward the Prince.*

FALSTAFF: . . . rated me the other day in the street about you, sir, but I marked him not; and yet he talked very wisely, and in the street too.

1151. MCU: *the Prince, at the right, with Doll still asleep on his chest.*

PRINCE: Thou didst well, for wisdom cries out in the street, and no man regards it.

FALSTAFF (*off*): Be certain that either . . .   H2 V.i.77–80

1152. *Low angle* MCU: *Falstaff.*

FALSTAFF: . . . wise bearing or ignorant carriage is caught, as men take diseases of one another.

1153. *The Prince, as in 1151.*

   PRINCE: Ned?

1154. CU: *Poins, head tilted to the left.*

   POINS: Yes, my lord?

1155. *Falstaff, as in 1152.*

   FALSTAFF: Let men take heed of their company.

1156. *The Prince, as in 1151.*

H2 II.ii.52–54   PRINCE: What wouldst thou think of me if I should weep?

1157. CU: *Poins, head tilted to the right.*

   POINS: I would think thee a most princely hypocrite.

1158. MCU: *the Prince, his face serious, with the top of Doll's head visible just below his chin.*

1159. CU: *Poins.*

1160. *The Prince, as in 1158.*

H1 II.ii.15–17   FALSTAFF (*off*): I have forsworn . . .

1161. *Low angle* MS: *Falstaff, with Poins standing in profile at the left and the Prince, seated and looking up at him, in the lower right.*

   FALSTAFF: . . . his company hourly any time this two and twenty
      years. (*The camera moves with Falstaff as he advances into the fore-*
      ground, while the Prince suddenly moves out of the shot at the right.)

1162. LS: *the Prince, seen over the top of Doll's head in the lower fore-*
      ground, with Poins partially visible looking toward the Prince from the

far right. The Prince turns back toward his companions, then turns away and begins to leave in the background at the right.

1163. MCU: *the Prince, facing forward and to the right.*

> PRINCE (*softly to himself*): Every man would think me a hypocrite indeed.   H2 II.ii.58–59

> FALSTAFF (*off*): And yet I am bewitched by the rogue's company. If the rascal . . . (*Falstaff appears in the background at the left.*) . . . has not given me medicines to make me love him, I'll be hanged.   H1 II.ii.17–19

> PRINCE (*again to himself*): Let the end try the man.   H2 II.ii.46

> FALSTAFF (*still behind the Prince, who seems oblivious to him*): It could not be else: I have drunk medicines.   H1 II.ii.19–20

The Prince moves out of the shot at the right.

1164. LS: *the Prince, seen over Falstaff's shoulder occupying the left of the frame, walks to the right away from the camera and down a corridor, silhouetted in the light from the door at the end. He passes through the door and begins to descend a flight of stairs.*

1165. MCU: *Falstaff looks after the Prince, his face showing concern.*

> POINS (*off*): My lord. (*His face flashes past in the foreground as he follows the Prince.*)   W

1166. MCU: *Doll turns toward the right.*

1167. *Falstaff, as in 1165. He moves toward the right and begins to move out of the shot.*

1168. *The camera tracks down through the ceiling beams of the main hall of the tavern to show dancers in high angle ELS filling the open space in the center of the room. The music of a gigue is heard on the soundtrack. The Prince can be seen walking through the crowd toward the lower right*

*of the frame, then moving left with the dancers still around him. Finally,
the Prince moves again to the right, as the camera drops closer to ground
level.*

1169. *The camera pans right to follow Falstaff in a low angle* LS *as he walks
behind a long table where the drinkers beat time to the music with
their tankards on the table. Behind him, the balconies are filled with
people clapping with the music. Falstaff moves out of the shot on
the right.*

1170. MS: *the Prince comes toward the camera through a doorway as he
leaves the main hall of the tavern.*

1171. MS: *Falstaff looks for the Prince against a background of dancers and
of people watching from the balcony. The general gaiety contrasts with
Falstaff's expression of bewilderment.*

1172. MS: *Poins moves across the frame to the right and away from the
camera.*

1173. *Low angle* MCU: *three dancers in a line; Falstaff walks behind them,
looking past them to the right. He then puts on his hat and pushes past
the dancers toward the camera.*

1174. LS: *the Prince moves in shadows through a crowded section of the
tavern. He swings his cloak over his shoulders.*

1175. *Low angle* MS: *Falstaff, seen from the back, enters from the right foreground into a group of dancers. A woman hooks her arm under
Falstaff's and pivots him in a circle until he faces the camera.*

1176. *The camera pans left across many dancers, passing Bardolph and Peto,
who are themselves dancing.*

1177. *Low angle* MS: *Falstaff, still dancing in a circle, arm in arm with the
woman of shot 1175. His expression has changed and he is now enjoying
himself.*

1178. MS: *Bardolph and Peto frolic among the dancers.*

1179. *The camera pans left along the side of the densely crowded floor to show Falstaff moving through the crowd in the left background. He pushes his way to the foreground where, in* MS, *he moves out of the shot at the right.*

FALSTAFF: Ooh, a pox . . .   H2 I.ii.254–259

1180. *The camera tracks to the right with Falstaff in* MS *as he passes a number of onlookers at the dance and moves out into the tavern yard.*

FALSTAFF: . . . on this gout, or a gout on this pox, for one or the other plays the rogue with me great toe. Well, 'tis no matter, I have the wars for me color, eh, lad? (*As Falstaff stops with his back to the camera, the Prince runs across the yard and mounts his horse, while several other horses are being led past Falstaff and out of the shot at the right. As Falstaff continues to speak, the Prince rides past without acknowledging him.*) Me pension will seem the more reasonable. A good wit will make use of anything. I shall turn diseases to commodity. (*He turns toward the camera to look after the Prince.*)

1181. LS: *the Prince turns his horse momentarily toward Falstaff and waves, with the castle walls barely visible in the darkness beyond.*

PRINCE: Falstaff!   W

1182. *Falstaff advances toward the camera into* MCU.

1183. *The Prince, as in 1181.*

PRINCE: Good night. (*He wheels his horse around and rides out of the*   W
shot to the left.*)

1184. MCU: *Falstaff, as at the end of 1182. He is now smiling again.*

FALSTAFF: Now comes in the sweetest morsel of the night, and we   H2 II.iv.376–377
must hence and leave it unpicked. // Come, boy . . .

1185. LS: *Falstaff stands on one side of the tavern yard. Two horses cross the foreground, followed by the Page, leading a heavily loaded donkey.*

H2 IV.iii.132–136   FALSTAFF: . . . we'll through Gloucestershire to visit Master Robert Shallow, Esquire. I have him already temp'ring between me finger and me thumb, . . . (*The donkey passes out of the shot at the right; Falstaff turns and follows, as the camera pans to the right.*) . . . and shortly will I seal with him.

1186. *Low angle* LS: *a crowded doorway. Doll bursts through and rushes out toward the right.*

W   DOLL: Jack!

1187. *High angle* LS: *Doll in the gateway to the tavern yard.*

1188. MLS: *Falstaff in the left foreground, with the Page and donkey at the right. The castle walls are visible in the background and the sky is now brighter than in 1181.*

H2 II.iv.236–240   DOLL (*off*): When wilt thou leave fighting o' days and foining . . .

1189. *Doll, as in 1187.*

DOLL: . . . o' nights, and begin to patch up thy old body for heaven?

1190. *Falstaff, as in 1188.*

FALSTAFF: Peace, Doll. Do not speak like a death's-head. Do not bid me remember mine end.

1191. *Doll, as in 1187. She hides the lower part of her face with her robe and begins to cry.*

1192. *Falstaff, as in 1188.*

383   FALSTAFF: Farewell, Doll. (*He turns away and begins to walk into the background.*)

389   DOLL (*off*): Well, sweet Jack.

Falstaff turns and waves.

1193. *Doll, as in 1187. She waves.*

FALSTAFF (*off*): Farewell.

DOLL: Have a care of thyself.

1194. LS: *Falstaff moves out of the shot in the left background, with the Page and donkey following.*

1195. *Doll, as in 1187. She stops waving, and her hand drops limply at her side.*

The Royal Castle

1196. *The Prince, seen from the back, walks from immediately in front of the camera into low angle* MLS. *In the background white-robed friars stand in front of a patterned wall hanging.*

PRINCE: Who saw the Duke of Lancaster?   H2 IV.v.8–11

*PRINCE JOHN (*off*): I am here, brother, . . .

The Prince turns toward the camera.

1197. LS: *groups of nobles in the assembly hall turn toward the camera at the sound of the Prince's voice.*

1198. LS: *Prince John is in the foreground as the Prince advances from the background to stand next to him. Friars and nobles stand against the walls and columns in the background.*

PRINCE JOHN: . . . full of heaviness.

PRINCE (*teasing him*): How now! Rain within doors and none abroad!
    (*Westmoreland enters the shot from the left and joins them. The*

*Clarence

Prince becomes aware of Westmoreland's solemn expression and his own manner changes.) How doth the King?

†WESTMORELAND: Exceeding ill.

The Prince leaves the shot at right.

1199. ELS: *the Prince enters from the left and stands at the foot of the King's bed. His back is to the camera and he is framed by columns in the foreground. The crown is visible on a pillow at the left, next to the King's head.*

20–45   PRINCE: Why doth the crown lie there upon his pillow, / Being so troublesome a bedfellow? // (*He moves to the side of the bed, standing over the King on the left.*) O majesty! / When thou dost pinch thy bearer, thou dost sit / Like a rich armor worn in heat of day, that scald'st with safety. // (*He kneels by the side of the bed.*)

1200. MCU: *the Prince, at the left, with the crown prominent in the lower right foreground.*

PRINCE (*leaning over to touch the King, below the frame*): My gracious lord. My father! //

1201. ELS: *nobles and friars standing by columns and upon a wide staircase in the background. A solemn chant is heard on the soundtrack and continues to the end of the scene.*

1202. MCU: *the King lies in profile in the lower foreground, with the Prince at the left beyond him and with the crown between them.*

PRINCE (*crossing himself*): This is a sleep / That from this golden rigol hath divorced / So many English kings. Thy due from me / Is tears and heavy sorrows of the blood, / Which nature, love, and filial tenderness / Shall, O dear father, pay thee plenteously. / My due from thee is this imperial crown // . . . (*He picks up the crown.*)

†Gloucester

1203. MS: *the Prince rises from his knees with the crown in his hands.*

> PRINCE: . . . Which God shall guard. And put the world's whole strength / Into one giant arm, it shall not force / This lineal honor from me. (*He backs away from the bedside and turns to move out of the shot at the left.*)

1204. ELS: *members of the court standing in the far background within the vast setting of the assembly room.*

1205. *Low angle* MLS: *the Prince at the right carrying the crown enters a pillared room. Looking intently upward to the left, he stops and kneels.*

Dissolve.

Justice Shallow's House

1206. LS: *Silence and Shallow, on either side of Falstaff, seen from behind. They sit on a bench staring into the blaze of a large fireplace. The moment is similar to the one that concludes the precredit sequence of the film, except for Silence's presence.*

> SHALLOW: Ha, cousin Silence, that thou hadst seen that that this knight and I have seen! Ha, Sir John, said I well? H2 III.ii.217–222

> FALSTAFF: We have heard the chimes at midnight, Master Robert Shallow.

> SHALLOW: Ha, Ha. That we have, that we have, that we have.

1207. *Low angle* MS: *the three men, the light of the fire reflected on their faces.*

> SHALLOW: I' faith, Sir John, we have. (*Leans his head against Falstaff's shoulder.*) Jesu, Jesu, the mad days that I have seen. And to think how many of my old acquaintances are dead. 34–55

> SILENCE: We shall all s-s-s-

SHALLOW: Certain, 'tis certain. Death, as the Psalmist saith, is certain to all, all shall die. (*After a long pause, shouts to Silence.*) How a good yoke of bullocks at Stamford Fair?

SILENCE: A good yoke of bu-bu-bu-

SHALLOW (*softly, as Silence struggles to speak*): Death is certain. (*Leans across Falstaff toward Silence.*) And is old Double of your town living yet?

SILENCE (*shaking his head*): D-d-d-

SHALLOW: Dead? (*Silence nods.*) Jesu, Jesu, dead! 'A drew a good bow, and dead! 'A shot a fine shoot. John a Gaunt loved him well and betted much money on his head. Dead! (*Silence makes sympathetic noises; Falstaff, who has been trying to drink from the goblet in his hand but was constantly interrupted by Shallow leaning in front of him, now gets the cup to his lips.*) Dead. (*Pauses.*) How a score of ewes now?

SILENCE: A score of good yuh-yuh-yuh-

SHALLOW: And is old Double dead?

FALSTAFF: Dead.

The Royal Palace

1208. *Low angle* MLS: *the Prince kneeling, the crown on his head. The setting is as in 1205, but several brown-robed friars are now visible, in attitudes of prayer.*

H2 IV.v.47–57   KING (*off*): My lords!

1209. ELS: *the King in his bed, as in 1199. He has now raised himself into a sitting position.*

KING: Lancaster! Westmoreland!

* PRINCE JOHN (*as several men rush in from the left*): Doth the King call?

† WESTMORELAND: What would your majesty?

1210. MCU: *the King raises himself in the bed and turns to the right.*

1211. *The Prince, as in 1208. He gets up off of his knees.*

1212. LS: *the King in his bed, framed by the backs of Prince John and West-moreland in the right and left foreground.*

KING: Why did you leave me here alone?

PRINCE JOHN: We left the Prince my brother here, my liege.

1213. *The King, as in 1210.*

KING: The Prince of Wales?

1214. MS: *several courtiers. None respond.*

1215. *The King, as in 1210.*

KING: He is not here.

PRINCE JOHN (*off*): He undertook to sit and watch by you. //

KING (*turning his head to the left and looking at the pillow*): Where is the crown? (*Angrily.*) Who took it from my pillow? (*He pulls aside the bedclothes and moves abruptly out of the shot at the left.*)

1216. *The camera pans left to follow the king in* ELS *as he walks alone through the assembly hall, past several of its enormous columns.*

* Clarence
† Warwick

109–132 KING: What! Couldst thou not forbear me half an hour? / Then get thee gone . . .

1217. *The camera tracks behind the King in* LS, *then holds as he moves through a narrow space between two columns into a lighted area beyond. In the far distance, members of the court can be seen clustered in a doorway.*

KING: . . . and dig my grave thyself, / And let the merry bells ring to thine ear / That thou art crownèd, not that I am dead. // Pluck down . . .

1218. *The camera tracks slightly ahead of the King, keeping him in* MCU *in partial profile, as he walks to the left down a corridor; members of his retinue are often visible as they follow him down a parallel side aisle in the background.*

KING: . . . my officers, break my decrees, / For now a time is come to mock at form. / Harry the Fifth is crowned. Up, vanity! / Down, royal state! All you sage counselors, hence! / And to the English court assemble now, / From every region, apes of idleness! / You neighbor confines, purge you of your scum. / Have you a ruffian that will swear, drink, dance, / Revel the night, rob, murder, and commit / The oldest sins the newest kind of ways? / Be happy, he will trouble you no more. //

1219. LS: *the King moves to the left across an open space between columns.*

KING: England shall give him office, honor, might, / . . .

1220. *A high barred window, with light from the outside sending shadows of the bars against the stone arch of the window. The King, seen in low angle* MS, *passes below the window and crosses the screen from right to left. His first and last words are spoken offscreen.*

KING: . . . For the fifth Harry from curbed license plucks / The muzzle of restraint, . . .

1221. ELS: *the Prince, wearing the crown, is seen in a pool of light from a high window. His father advances toward him from the immediate foreground, with the Prince facing him.*

KING: . . . and the wild dog / Shall flesh his tooth on every innocent. (*He stops, still several steps away from the Prince.*)

PRINCE: I never thought to hear you speak again.   91–93

1222. *Low angle* MS: *the King falls to his knees, supporting himself on the throne. The Prince enters the shot from behind him on the left and moves across to stand on the stairs below the King at the right of the frame.*

KING: Thy wish was father, Harry, to that thought. / I stay too long by thee, I weary thee.

PRINCE (*taking the King's hand and kissing it fervently*): O pardon me, 138 my liege.

88   KING: But wherefore did you take away the crown?

The Prince reaches up to take the crown from his head.

1223. MCU: *the Prince, with the back of the King's head in the left fore-ground, holds the crown before the King.*

149–151   PRINCE: God witness with me, when I // found no course of breath within your Majesty, / How cold . . .

1224. *Low angle* CU: *the King.*

155–168   PRINCE (*off*): . . . it struck my heart. // Thinking you . . .

1225. *The Prince, as in 1223.*

PRINCE: . . . dead, // I spake unto this . . .

1226. *The King and the Prince, as in 1222. They both hold the crown in their hands.*

PRINCE: . . . crown as having sense, / And thus upbraided it: "The care on thee depending / . . . (*The Prince removes his hands from the crown.*) . . . Hath fed upon the body of my father. / Therefore, thou best of gold art worst of gold. / Other, less fine in carat, art more precious, // But thou, most fine, most honored, most renowned, / Hast eat thy bearer up." Thus, my most royal liege, / Accusing it, I put it on my head, / To try with it, as with an enemy / That had before my face murdered my father, / The quarrel of a true inheritor.

177–185   KING (*laying his hand on the Prince's shoulder*): O my son, / God put it in thy mind to take it hence, / That thou mightst win the more thy father's love, / Pleading so wisely in excuse of it! (*They both look to the right in response to noises offscreen.*)

1227. ELS: *several members of the court stand in the distance, framed by columns in the foreground.*

1228. ELS: *the King and the Prince raise themselves from the side of the steps to the throne, with the throne visible above them in the background.*

1229. ELS: *members of the court gradually advance from the far background into the assembly hall.*

1230. *The King and the Prince, as in 1228. The Prince assists his father as he begins to move slowly up the stairs toward the throne.*

1231. LS: *members of the court, in shadow next to columns in the assembly hall.*

1232. *Extreme high angle* ELS: *the Prince assists his father as the King seats himself on the throne. The Prince then kneels by the side of the throne. The chant of the choir can be heard.*

1233. MCU: *the King, with the Prince visible in the foreground at the lower right.*

   KING: Come . . .

1234. MCU: *the Prince, seen over the shoulder of the King, who is visible at the left.*

   KING: . . . hear, I think, the very latest counsel / That ever I shall breathe.

1235. *The King, as in 1233.*

   KING: God knows, my son, / By what bypaths and indirect crooked ways / I met this crown, // . . .

1236. *The Prince, as in 1234.*

   KING: . . . For all my reign hath been but as a scene / Acting that   197–219
   argument.

1237. *The King, as in 1233.*

> KING: But now my death / Changes the mood, for what in me was purchased / Falls upon thee in a more fairer sort. // Yet, . . .

1238. *The Prince, as in 1234.*

> KING: . . . though thou stand'st more firm than I could do, / . . .

1239. *The King, as in 1233.*

> KING: . . . Thou art not firm enough, since griefs are green. / And all my friends, which thou must make thy friends, / Have but their stings and teeth newly ta'en out, / By whose fell working I was first advanced / And by whose power I well might lodge a fear / To be again displaced. // Therefore, my Harry, / Be it thy course to busy giddy minds / With foreign . . .

1240. *The Prince, as in 1234.*

> KING: . . . quarrels, that action, hence borne out, / May waste . . .

1241. *The King, as in 1233.*

> KING: . . . the memory of the former days. / More would I, . . .

1242. *The Prince, as in 1234.*

> KING: . . . but my lungs are wasted so / That strength of speech is utterly denied me.

1243. *The King, as in 1233.*

> KING (*with great emotion*): How I came by the crown, O God forgive, // . . . (*The Prince bows his head.*) . . . And grant it may with thee in true peace live! (*The King falls back in his seat.*)

1244. *The Prince, as in 1234. He looks up at his father as the King's body slumps over.*

1245. *Low angle* LS: *the King, lifeless on the throne, with the Prince kneeling at his side, both seen in profile from the steps leading to the throne.*

1246. ELS: *the throne, flooded in light from a high window in the background, seen from the end of the assembly hall. Members of the court slowly enter the central area of the assembly hall from both sides of the frame.*

   * PRINCE JOHN: How doth . . .   H2 V.ii.2

1247. *The King and the Prince, as in 1245.*

   * PRINCE JOHN (*off*): . . . the King?

   The Prince rises and turns to face the hall.

1248. *The throne, as in 1246. The members of the court stand, all facing the throne, at various points in the hall.*

   † PRINCE: He lives no more.   5

   * A MEMBER OF THE COURT: God save your majesty. (*All kneel be-*   43
   fore the Prince.)

   PRINCE (*taking a few steps forward to stand at the top of the stairs to*   63, 60–62
   the throne): You all look strangely on me. // I shall convert . . .

1249. *Low angle* LS: *the Prince stands at the far right, the dead King seated in shadow in the background at the left.*

   PRINCE: . . . those tears / By number into hours of happiness.

*Chief Justice
† Warwick

43 *A MEMBER OF THE COURT: God save your majesty. (*All kneel before the Prince.*)

129–134 PRINCE: The tide of blood in me / Hath proudly flowed in vanity till now. / Now doth it turn . . .

1250. *The Prince, as in 1246.*

PRINCE: . . . and ebb back to the sea, / Where it shall mingle with the state of floods / And flow henceforth in formal majesty.

1251. *The Prince, as in 1249. He turns and walks back to the throne, takes the crown from the dead King's hands, and raises it above his own head.*

PRINCE (*looking up at the crown*): Now call we our high parliament.

Justice Shallow's House

1252. *Low angle* LS: *Silence and Shallow, their arms locked as they face in opposite directions, dancing in a circle and singing the melody to which they dance. They are in a large barnlike room in Shallow's house. Falstaff watches them from the background.*

H2 III.ii.14–27 SHALLOW (*as the dance concludes with Shallow's feet becoming tangled in his own long scarf*): I was once of Clement's Inn, where I think they will talk of mad Shallow yet.

SILENCE (*disentangling him*): You were called "lusty Shallow" then.

SHALLOW (*as Silence helps him to a chair at the left*): By the mass, I was called anything. And I would have done anything too, and roundly too. (*He and Silence both attempt to sit at once, and Shallow falls off the side of the chair.*) Oh! (*Falstaff laughs and walks to the far background, where he sits on a bench against the wall.*) Then was Jack Falstaff a boy, now Sir John, and a page to Thomas Mowbray,

*The Prince's Brothers: John of Lancaster, Clarence, Gloucester

Duke of Norfolk. (*Slides forward on his rump until he sits in front of Silence and falls back against Silence's legs.*) Eh, Sir John? (*Falstaff waves his cane.*) O, by the mass, I've had too much sack.

SILENCE: We shall be merry now. Now comes in the sweet of the night.

H2 V.iii.13–14
51–52

Bells begin to toll.

SHALLOW: Davy! (*Davy enters from the right and crosses the foreground to bend down and take one of Shallow's arms. Silence takes the other and they carry him, half standing, half sitting, out of the shot at the right. At the same time, the Page enters from the left in the background and crosses to stand next to Falstaff.*) O, O, Jesus, the days that I have seen. (*The camera pans right briefly with Shallow as he is carried out, leaving Falstaff and the Page visible in the far left background.*)

W

H2 III.ii.225

FALSTAFF: Lord, Lord. How subject we old men are to this vice of lying! This same starved justice has done nothing but prate to me of the wildness of his youth, and every third word a lie.

312–316

SHALLOW (*off*): Sir John!

FALSTAFF: I come, Master Shallow, I come. (*To the Page.*) I will devise matter enough out of this Shallow to keep Prince Harry in continual laughter for the wearing out of six fashions. You shall see him laugh. (*Falstaff begins to laugh.*)

H2 V.i.80–82, 87

DAVY (*entering into the right foreground*): Sir, your worship. There's one Pistol come from the court with news.

H2 V.iii.81–83

FALSTAFF (*getting up from his bench and moving toward the camera*): From the court!

PISTOL (*rushing in from the right as the camera pans left with him, leaving Davy out of the shot; he circles around Falstaff as he speaks*

94–97

excitedly): Sir John, I am thy Pistol and thy friend, / And helter-skelter have I rode to thee, / And tidings do I bring and lucky joys / And golden times and happy news of price. (*He rubs his fingers together, as if feeling coins.*)

86–89

FALSTAFF (*sitting on a chair in the left foreground*): Pistol, what wind blew you hither?

PISTOL: Not the ill wind that blows no man to good. (*He kneels and, picking up one of Falstaff's feet, kisses his boot.*) Sweet knight, thou art now one of the greatest men in the realm.

Falstaff slaps Pistol's arm with his cane, so that he lets go of Falstaff's foot. Silence enters at the right, carrying Shallow in his arms.

111–124

SHALLOW (*as Silence stands him up on the floor*): Give me pardon, sir. If, sir, you come with news from the court, // I am, sir, under the King, in some authority.

PISTOL (*getting to his feet and facing Shallow*): Under which king, Besonian? Speak, or die.

SHALLOW (*backing off to stand within Silence's protective arms*): Under King Harry.

PISTOL: Harry the Fourth, or Fifth?

SHALLOW: Harry the Fourth.

PISTOL (*making an insulting gesture to him*): A foutra for thine office! / (*He dashes forward to the extreme right foreground, turns and kneels, facing Falstaff.*) Sir John, thy tender lambkin now is king. / Harry the Fifth's the man.

FALSTAFF (*after rising, pausing, and then advancing to the extreme foreground, as the camera tracks back and holds him in low angle MS*): What, is the old king dead?

PISTOL (*reappearing at the left from behind Falstaff's shoulder*): As
nail in door.

FALSTAFF: Away! Saddle my horse! (*He pushes Pistol backwards and
leaves the shot on the right. The camera then pans right to show first
Pistol, then Shallow and Silence following. Off.*) I know the young   137–138
king is sick for me.

1253. CU: *a staircase wall, as first a Page and then a second figure pass
downwards, both immediately in front of the camera.*

FALSTAFF (*off*): Master . . .   124–141

1254. LS: *Falstaff moves away from the camera through the open shed at-
tached to Shallow's barn. Shallow and the Page follow close behind him.*

FALSTAFF (*stopping and turning*): . . . Shallow, choose what office
thou wilt in the land, 'tis thine. Pistol, . . . (*Pistol enters from the
foreground.*) . . . I will double-charge thee with dignities. // Master
Silence, . . . (*Silence enters at the left.*) . . . my Lord Silence, be
what thou wilt. I am fortune's steward. Come, Pistol, . . . (*He turns
and moves off through Shallow's yard and out of the shot at the left,
his voice trailing away in the distance.*) . . . utter more to me, and
withal devise something to do thyself good.

1255. ELS: *Falstaff, followed by the others, enters from the right and crosses
the top of a rise in a snowy landscape. Bells are tolling on the
soundtrack.*

FALSTAFF: Let us take any man's horses; the laws of England are at my
commandment. Blessed are they that have been my friends, and woe
to my Lord Chief Justice! (*Falstaff moves out of the shot at the left,
with the others strung out behind him.*)

London: A Street and Cathedral

1256. *The camera pans left with the new king in* ELS, *his head intermittently
visible over a mass of helmeted heads and standards with pennons that*

*crowd the foreground. The King rides slowly to the left of the frame.
Processional music is heard on the soundtrack.*

1257. *Low angle* MCU: *cheering commoners, crowded together.*

1258. *Low angle* LS: *the King rides to the left and toward the camera, framed
by a foot soldier standing at the left and a horseman in profile on
the right.*

1259. *Low angle* CU: *a cheering commoner at the right, with others behind
him to the left.*

1260. *Low angle* LS: *the King, seen from the back, rides toward the left past
cheering crowds in the background.*

H2 V.v.40   PISTOL (*off*): There roared . . .

1261. *High angle* LS: *a portion of the crowd, densely packed together. Pistol
and Bardolph are forcing their way through the crowd, moving toward
the camera.*

PISTOL: . . . the sea, and trumpet clangor sounds.

1262. ELS: *the King faces toward the camera as he rides to the left. The
camera looks over the heads of a crowd of foot soldiers and through
many standards and pennons.*

1263. *High angle* LS: *a portion of the crowd. Falstaff and Shallow slowly push
their way toward the right through the crowd.*

1264. *The King, as in 1262, but now moving past the camera and away from it.*

1265. *High angle* LS: *the crowd, seen through a series of upright shafts that
act as bars in the foreground of the shot.*

1266. ELS: *the King, barely visible at all, crosses toward the left through an
extremely dense cluster of standards and pennons in the foreground.*

Dissolve.

1267. LS: *the King rides forward toward the camera and through an entranceway, with cheering crowds in the background.*

1268. LS: *a procession of white-robed friars enters the cathedral, seen through another dense cluster of standards and spears and over the heads of several rows of soldiers. Formal sixteenth- or early seventeenth-century ceremonial music for brass ensemble accompanies the procession within the cathedral.*

1269. LS: *Westmoreland, carrying a sword, its hilt raised as a cross, is seen through standards and over the heads of a single row of soldiers.*

1270. LS: *friars, seen from the side and back, move to the left along the aisle between soldiers. They wave censers and the smoke of the incense rises above them.*

1271. LS: *a mitred bishop advances toward the camera, preceded and followed by friars, and accompanied by soldiers in coats of mail with lances raised in front of them.*

1272. LS: *white-robed friars, seen from the back and over the heads of soldiers, move forward into the assembly hall.*

1273. ELS: *the friars, only partially visible over the heads of many soldiers and through many lances, dispense incense.*

1274. High angle LS: *soldiers, all in coats of mail and all carrying lances, move slowly in procession up the aisle.*

1275. MLS: *Falstaff and Shallow move into the assembly hall, with soldiers at attention, seen from the back, in the foreground.*

> FALSTAFF: Come with me, Master Robert Shallow. I will make the   5–28
> King do you grace. I will leer upon him as 'a comes by, and do but
> mark the countenance he will give me. // (*Falstaff pushes his way
> between two of the soldiers in the foreground.*)

1276. LS: *Falstaff, in an open space near a column and apart from the crowd and the procession, is moving away from the camera.*

FALSTAFF: O, if I had time to . . . (*He stops and turns back to look toward Shallow.*) . . . make new liveries, I'd have . . .

1277. *Shallow moves between the two soldiers and stops in* MCU.

FALSTAFF (*off*): . . . bestowed the thousand pounds I borrowed of you.

1278. LS: *Falstaff, as at the end of 1276. He advances toward the camera into* MCU.

FALSTAFF: 'Tis no matter; this poor show doth better. This doth infer the zeal I had to see him.

1279. MCU: *Shallow, as at the end of 1277.*

*SHALLOW: It doth so.

1280. MCU: *Falstaff, as at the end of 1278.*

FALSTAFF: It shows my earnestness of affection—

1281. *Shallow, as in 1279.*

*SHALLOW: It doth so.

FALSTAFF (*off*): My devotion—

SHALLOW: It doth, it doth, it doth.

1282. *Falstaff, as in 1280.*

FALSTAFF: As it were, to ride day and night, and not to deliberate, not to remember, not to have patience to shift me, but to stand . . .

1283. *Shallow, as in 1279.*

FALSTAFF (*off*): . . . stained with travel, and sweating with . . .

*Pistol

1284. *Falstaff, as in 1280.*

> FALSTAFF: . . . desire to see him, thinking of nothing else, putting all affairs else in oblivion, as if there were nothing else to be done but to see him. (*He turns away toward the procession in the background.*)

1285. *Shallow, as in 1279.*

1286. ELS: *the King walks toward the left in the procession, barely visible through a foreground densely crowded with soldiers' helmeted heads and spears.*

1287. LS: *the camera tracks left with Falstaff as he moves behind rows of soldiers at attention who face the camera. Falstaff peers out over them, looking toward the procession.*

1288. *The camera pans left to follow the King from the side in low angle LS as he slowly proceeds. Soldiers with spears fill the foreground.*

1289. LS: *the camera pans left with Falstaff as he now moves among the soldiers, looking up and to the left after the King.*

1290. *The King, as in 1288. He has now moved farther away to the left.*

1291. *The camera moves to the left with the King in LS, seen in profile over soldiers in the foreground.*

1292. *Low angle LS: white-robed friars, seen from the back, are obscured by the silhouetted figure of a soldier who occupies most of the lower foreground.*

1293. *Low angle LS: massed spears dominate the background above the heads of soldiers who occupy the foreground and look to the left toward the procession.*

1294. LS: *white-robed friars are seen from the rear until they are blocked out by a silhouetted figure in the immediate foreground.*

1295. MLS: *the friars move forward toward the left. The heads of soldiers are in the lower foreground.*

W

    FALSTAFF (*off*): God save thee!

1296. LS: *the Bishop, seen through spears and soldiers who dominate the foreground, moves to the left in advance of a row of friars. Hearing Falstaff's voice, he stops and turns. The ceremonial music stops.*

1297. *Falstaff pushes between two knights in the formal row bordering the processional aisle and moves into* MS, *alone in the aisle.*

44–72

    FALSTAFF: God save thee, my sweet . . .

1298. *Low angle* MLS: *the King, his back to the camera. He stops, but does not turn.*

    FALSTAFF (*off*): . . . boy! //

1299. *The camera tracks back as Westmoreland advances in the aisle into* MCU. *He carries a ceremonial sword in front of him.*

    *WESTMORELAND: Have you your wits? Know you what 'tis . . .

1300. MCU: *Falstaff, with soldiers carrying shields and lances forming a line across the background.*

    *WESTMORELAND (*off*): . . . you say?

    FALSTAFF (*gesturing toward the King*): My King! (*He sinks to his knees.*) My . . .

1301. LS: *the King is seen from the rear at the left as Falstaff kneels in the right foreground.*

    FALSTAFF: . . . Jove!

*Chief Justice

1302. *High angle* MCU: *Falstaff.*

   FALSTAFF: I speak to thee, my heart!

1303. *The King, with Falstaff, as in 1301.*

   KING (*still with his back to Falstaff*): I know thee not, old man. Fall to thy prayers. / (*He begins to turn.*)

1304. *Extreme low angle* MS: *the King.*

   KING: How ill white hairs become a fool and jester! /

1305. *Falstaff, as in 1302.*

   KING (*off*): I have long . . .

1306. *Low angle* MCU: *the King, at the left of the frame.*

> KING: . . . dreamed of such a kind of man, / So surfeit-swelled, . . .

1307. *High angle* MS: *Falstaff, kneeling.*

> KING (*off*): . . . so old, and so profane, / But being awaked . . .

1308. *Low angle* CU: *the King, looking directly ahead.*

> KING: . . . I do despise my dream. /

1309. *Falstaff, as in 1302.*

1310. *The King, as in 1308. He now looks down toward Falstaff.*

> KING: Make less thy body hence, and more thy grace. / Leave gorman-
> dizing. Know the grave doth gape / For thee thrice wider than for
> other men. /

1311. *Falstaff rises from his knees into* MS *and begins to laugh.*

> KING (*off, imperiously*): Reply not to me with a fool-born jest. /

1312. *The King, as in 1304.*

> KING: Presume not that I am the thing I was, / For God doth know, so
> shall the world perceive, / That I have turned away my former self. /
> So will I those that kept me company. /

1313. MLS: *Falstaff stands alone, a large open space in the hall behind him,
> with the lines of soldiers in the far background.*

> KING (*off*): When thou dost hear I am as I have been, / Approach
> me, and thou shalt be as thou wast, / The tutor and the feeder of
> my riots. /

1314. MLS: *the King at the left, with Falstaff standing, back to the camera, in
> the right foreground.*

KING: Till then, I banish thee, on pain of death, / . . .

1315. MS: *Falstaff again kneels, but now as if weary and defeated. The Chief Justice now stands behind him at the left.*

KING (*off*): . . . As I have done the rest of my misleaders, / . . .

1316. *Low angle* MS: *the King.*

KING: . . . Not to come near our person by ten mile. /

1317. MS: *Falstaff kneels at the right. Behind him there is open space with the Chief Justice and the soldiers in the far background.*

1318. *The King, as in 1306.*

KING (*now speaking much more softly, as if to Falstaff rather than the assembled multitude*): For competence of life I will allow you, / That lack of means enforce you not to evil. / And, as we hear you do reform . . .

1319. *Falstaff, as in 1317.*

KING (*off*): . . . yourselves, / We will, according to your strength . . .

1320. *The King, as in 1304.*

KING: . . . and qualities, / Give you advancement. (*He looks up.*)

1321. *The Chief Justice advances several steps.*

KING (*off*): Be it your charge, . . .

1322. *The King, as in 1304.*

KING: . . . my lord, / To see performed the tenor of . . .

1323. MCU: *Falstaff.*

KING (*off*): . . . our word.

1324. *The King, as in 1306.*

1325. *Falstaff, as in 1323.*

1326. *Low angle* MS: *the King turns away from the camera and resumes his processional walk up the aisle.*

1327. *Falstaff, as in 1323.*

1328. LS: *the King, seen from behind, moves further along the aisle, with soldiers at attention lining the way at the right of the frame.*

1329. *Falstaff, as in 1323.*

1330. MLS: *a squadron of soldiers, lances held vertically, passes between columns and move out of the shot at the left. Falstaff appears from the right*

*just as the last of the soldiers are passing. He moves slowly and he turns
in the right foreground to face Shallow, who now can be seen standing
against a wall in the center background.*

FALSTAFF (*quietly*): Master Shallow, . . .   74-91

1331. LS: *Falstaff stands in isolation next to a column.*

FALSTAFF: . . . I owe you a thousand pound.

1332. *Shallow advances toward the camera into* MS.

SHALLOW: Yes, Sir John, which I beseech you to let me have home.

1333. MS: *Falstaff, with columns in the background.*

FALSTAFF: That can hardly be, Master Shallow. Do not you grieve
   at this.

1334. MS: *Shallow, as at the end of 1332.*

FALSTAFF (*off*): Look you, . . .

1335. *Falstaff, as in 1333.*

FALSTAFF: . . . he will seem thus to the world.

1336. *Shallow, as in 1334.*

1337. *Falstaff, as in 1333.*

FALSTAFF: I shall be sent for in private to him.

1338. MS: *Falstaff in the right foreground, as in 1330, but Shallow is now
   facing him from next to a column.*

FALSTAFF: Fear not for your advancement. I shall be the man yet. I
   shall make you great. (*He moves out of the shot to the right.*)

SHALLOW (*calling after him*): I cannot well perceive how, unless you should give me your doublet . . . (*He crosses to the right into* MLS.) . . . and stuff me out . . .

1339. *Low angle* ELS: *Falstaff, his back to the camera, walks toward the castle walls, their turrets obscured in darkness.*

SHALLOW (*off*): . . . with straw.

1340. MLS: *Shallow, as at the end of 1338.*

SHALLOW (*as he moves out of the shot at the right*): I beseech you, . . .

1341. ELS: *Falstaff walks toward the castle walls in the background. Silence, Pistol, and Bardolph stand, backs to the camera, in the foreground. They are joined by Shallow, who enters from the left and stands among them. Falstaff, in the distance, is framed by the four men in the foreground, two at either side.*

SHALLOW: . . . Sir John, let me have five hundred of my thousand.

FALSTAFF (*turning*): Sir, . . .

1342. MCU: *Falstaff turns toward the camera.*

FALSTAFF: . . . I will be as good as my word.

1343. *Falstaff, as in 1341.*

FALSTAFF: This that you have seen was but a color.

SHALLOW: A color that I fear you will die in.

FALSTAFF: Fear no colors. Come.

The four begin to advance.

1344. ELS: *the four men walk alongside a castle wall and leave the shot at the left. Falstaff's Page remains standing against the wall, facing the camera.*

FALSTAFF (*off*): Go with me to dinner.

1345. LS: *Falstaff, half turned toward the camera. He turns away and, leaning on his cane, begins to walk toward a lighted archway at the far left.*

1346. ELS: *Falstaff, as in 1341, but with the foreground now empty. He continues to walk toward the archway.*

1347. ELS: *the Page still stands in front of the wall, dwarfed by its height.*

FALSTAFF (*off, in a whisper*): I shall be . . .

1348. LS: *Falstaff, now in a darkened area with the lighted archway in the background, has stopped and looks back toward the camera.*

FALSTAFF: . . . sent for soon . . . (*Pauses.*) . . . at night. (*He turns back and continues to walk toward the archway.*)

1349. ELS: *the Page, as in 1347, but seen from an even greater distance.*

1350. ELS: *Falstaff moves slowly through the archway.*

The Cathedral, exterior

1351. LS: *Prince John, the Bishop, and the Chief Justice emerge from the cathedral. As they advance toward the camera, it tracks forward to meet them in a low angle* MLS.

98–102   * BISHOP: I like this fair proceeding of the King's. /

* WESTMORELAND: But all are banished . . .

PRINCE JOHN: . . . until their conversations / Appear more wise and modest to the world.

* CHIEF JUSTICE: He hath intent his wonted followers / Shall all be very well provided for.

H2 V.iv.9   DOLL (*off*): Thou damned . . .

1352. *High angle* MS: *Doll, surrounded by soldiers who push her along to the left, as she struggles against them.*

DOLL: . . . tripe-visaged rascal! Jack! Jack Falstaff!

1353. *Low angle* MS: *the Sheriff on horseback.*

H2 V.v.92   † SHERIFF: Go, carry Sir John Falstaff to the Fleet.

1354. MS: *Bardolph, in a crowd with Pistol and Peto. They are seen from the back, but Bardolph turns toward the camera.*

* Prince John
† Chief Justice

BARDOLPH: The Fleet?

1355. *The camera pans left to follow the Page in* MS *as he worms his way through the crowd, all seen at waist height. The camera reframes him in* CU.

    PAGE: Come quickly. You must come to my master. O poor heart,   H5 II.i.84-85
    sweet man. Come to him. He is very sick.

1356. CU: *Pistol has bent down to hear the Page, and now he begins to straighten up.*

1357. *Bardolph, in the crowd, advances into* MCU.

    *BARDOLPH: The King is a good King, but it must be as it may.   128-129

    Dissolve.

A Battlement

1358. *Low angle* MLS: *the King crosses to the right in front of assembled nobles under a bright sky.*

    KING: Now, lords, for France. // We doubt not of a fair and lucky war.   H5 II.ii.182-193
    // (*He turns back and moves out of the shot at the left.*) Then forth,
    dear countrymen.

    † WESTMORELAND (*at the right, flourishing a flag*): The signs of war
    advance: / . . .

1359. *High angle* MS: *the King, seen from behind. Beyond and below him are several lines of soldiers with spears and beyond them a crowd of people who surge up against the soldiers and cheer.*

    † WESTMORELAND (*off*): . . . No King of England if not King of
    France!

*Nym
†King Henry V

1360. MCU: *the King, at the right, with the Chief Justice slightly behind him at the left. In the background, pennons flutter in the wind.*

40   KING (*turning to the Chief Justice*): My lord Chief Justice, / Enlarge the man committed yesterday.

W   CHIEF JUSTICE: Falstaff?

1361. MCU: *the King, seen over the Chief Justice's shoulder.*

45–46   *NOBLEMAN (*off*): Let him be punished, Sovereign, . . . (*Now he appears from the left and goes behind the King.*) . . . lest example / Breed, . . .

1362. MCU: *the nobleman, at the right and looking toward the left. Another nobleman stands at his shoulder, to screen left.*

     *NOBLEMAN: . . . by his sufferance, more of such a kind.

54–57   KING (*off*): If little faults . . .

1363. *Low angle* MCU: *the King looks to the right toward the nobleman.*

     KING: . . . proceeding on distemper / Shall not be wink'd at, how shall we stretch our eye / When capital crimes, . . .

1364. *The nobleman, as in 1362.*

     KING (*off*): . . . chew'd, swallow'd, and digested, / Appear before us?

1365. *The King, as in 1363. He turns to the left, toward the Chief Justice.*

41–42   KING: We consider / It was excess of wine that set him on.

*Scroop

The Tavern Yard

1366. *The camera pans right to follow Poins in* MS *as he walks through the main hall of the tavern.*

1367. LS: *the Hostess and the Page sit outdoors on either side of the door that leads into the tavern yard. Poins walks through the door and into the yard. The camera tracks with him to the right as he crosses the yard, passing Bardolph and Peto sitting on a bench. Poins comes to a stop behind a large coffin, set up on a crude sled in the middle of the yard.*

   POINS: Falstaff?   W

1368. LS: *the Page, sitting on the doorstep.*

   * PAGE: Falstaff is dead.   H5 II.iii.5

1369. LS: *Bardolph and Peto on the bench.*

   † PETO: The King has killed his heart.   H5 II.i.88

   BARDOLPH: Would I were with him, wheresome'er he is, either in   H5 II.iii.7–45
   heaven . . .

1370. *High angle* MS: *the Page.*

   BARDOLPH (*off*): . . . or in hell.

   HOSTESS (*off*): He, sure, is not in hell.

1371. MS: *the Hostess leans against the tavern wall, her head tilted back.*

   HOSTESS: He's in Arthur's bosom, if ever a man went to Arthur's
   bosom. 'A made a finer end, and went away and it had been any

*Pistol
†Hostess

Christian child. 'A parted ev'n just between twelve and one, ev'n at the turning o' the tide; for after I saw him fumble with the sheets, and play with flowers, and smile upon his finger's ends, I knew there was but one way; for his nose was as sharp as a pen, and he babbl'd o' green fields. "How now, Sir John?" quoth I, "what, man? be of good cheer." So 'a cried out, "God, God, God!" three or four times. Now I, to comfort him, bid him he should not think of God; I hop'd there was no need to trouble himself with any such thoughts yet. So 'a bade me lay more clothes on his feet. I put my hand into the bed and felt them, and they were as cold as any stone; then I felt to his knees, and they were cold as any stone; and so upward and upward, and all was cold as any stone.

1372. *The Page, as in 1370.*

1373. *Bardolph and Peto, as in 1369.*

1374. ELS: *the Hostess and the Page sitting by the door, seen over the heads of Bardolph and Peto in the foreground. Bardolph and Peto get up and move toward the left.*

　　* PAGE: He cried out o' sack.

1375. *High angle* LS: *the tavern yard with the coffin partially visible in the lower center. Peto gets behind the coffin and prepares to push. Bardolph moves out of the frame in the foreground as he goes to the front of the coffin. In the background, the Page and the Hostess still sit by the door.*

　　BARDOLPH: And of women.

　　HOSTESS: Nay, that 'a did not. // (*She gets up and walks forward as Peto begins to push the coffin out of the frame in the lower foreground.*)

　　† PETO: He said once, the devil'd have him about women.

*Nym
† Boy

HOSTESS (*as she moves slowly out of frame at the left, following the coffin*): 'A did in some sort, indeed, handle women. //

1376. LS: *Bardolph pulls and Peto pushes the coffin through the wooden gate to the tavern yard.*

PAGE (*off*): Do you not remember, 'a saw a flea once stick upon Bardolph's nose, and 'a said it was a black soul burnin' in hellfire?

The camera tracks upward, so that it looks out over the open fields beyond the tavern fence and emphasizes the great walls of the city in the background.

BARDOLPH: The fuel is . . .

1377. ELS: *outside the tavern fence, the coffin, the (now) three men with it, and the Hostess following it, are all seen from the side.*

BARDOLPH: . . . gone that maintain'd that fire. That's all the riches I got in his service.

1378. *High angle* ELS: *above the tavern yard looking down on the Hostess standing in front of the tavern gate and looking out into the country beyond, where the coffin is slowly being moved toward the right of the frame.*

NARRATOR: The new king, even at first appointing, determined to put on him the shape of a new man. This Henry was a captain of such prudence and such policy that he never enterprised anything before it forecast the main chances that it might happen. So humane withal, he left no offense unpunished nor friendship unrewarded. For conclusion, a majesty was he that both lived and died a pattern in princehood, a lodestar in honor, and famous to the world alway.

Production credits scroll upward against a background film loop of densely packed rows of nobles, clerics, and soldiers. They stand against the side wall of a large church underneath stained glass windows and amid tall pennons. A drum beats a processional rhythm on the soundtrack.

Interviews

Interviews

One of the interviews Welles had with Juan Cobos (an editor of the Spanish magazine *Griffith* and an assistant director of *Chimes*) and with Cobos's colleague Miguel Rubio is an excellent source for discovering Welles's intentions in the film. After the interview was translated into Spanish for *Griffith,* an edited version of the original appeared in *Sight and Sound,* and it is that version, further edited to include only material relevant to *Chimes,* that is reprinted as the first interview here.

The second interview is a recent one with Keith Baxter. Born in Wales and trained as an actor at the Royal Academy of Dramatic Art, London, Keith Baxter has had a distinguished stage and screen career since his debut in both media in 1957. In addition to his successes in modern dramas

(such as his prize-winning performances in *A Man for All Seasons* and *Sleuth*), he has performed in many classical plays by such authors as Sheridan, Congreve, Shaw, Chekhov, and especially Shakespeare. He has been associated with the Chichester Drama Festival in England both as an actor and as a writer; one of his own plays, *Cavell,* was performed there in 1982. Baxter played Prince Hal in the stage version of *Chimes at Midnight* (Belfast and Dublin, 1960) and later in the film. He was with Welles in Spain during the entire period the film was shot (1964–65), and is therefore uniquely qualified to describe its production and to discuss Welles's intentions and practices as a director. The interview with Bridget Gellert Lyons printed here took place in London on February 19, 1988.

Welles and Falstaff

Juan Cobos and Miguel Rubio

Chimes at Midnight is based on the Falstaff scenes from both parts of *Henry IV,* with Welles as Falstaff, John Gielgud as Henry IV, Keith Baxter as Prince Hal, Jeanne Moreau as Doll Tearsheet. This is Welles' third Shakespeare film, and *King Lear* is among his several projects. More than ten years ago, however, as his interviewers reminded him, Welles told an Edinburgh Festival audience that he doubted whether there could be a happy marriage between Shakespeare and the cinema:

Orson Welles: When I made that remark I was trying to please my public. That was purely demagogic. I had to give a two-hour lecture to an audience which didn't like my *Macbeth.* I had to make friends with them, and the first way I could do this was to admit that probably I partly agreed with them about *Macbeth.* To an extent, that was as close as I could go in saying so. . . . But for Shakespeare you mustn't make a museum. You must find a new period, you must invent your own England, your own epoch, on the basis of what you have learned through research. The drama itself dictates the kind of world in which it is going to happen.

In Chimes at Midnight, *as in all your films, you don't give much value to landscape as such. There's a rather stylised and unreal feeling about it, so that a scene like the robbery at Gadshill ends up looking a bit like a set.*

Oh, that's sad to hear. Really? Well, to an extent I wouldn't object to that criticism . . . to an extent. I may have to submit to the criticism, because it may be true, but I regret it if the country doesn't seem real. But it mustn't seem *perfectly* real. In other words, one of the enemies of the film is of course the simple, banal fact, the tree or rock that looks as it looks to anybody who takes a picture of his family through a camera on Sunday. So we have to be able to invest what is real, by reason of the photography, position of the lights, the conception, with a character, sometimes with a glamour, sometimes with an allure or a mystery which it doesn't have. To that extent it must be treated as a décor.

From *Sight and Sound* 35 (Autumn 1966): 158–161.

I feel that there is almost an aesthetic problem here, one which is almost never resolved in costume pictures. I don't know why I say almost: I would say never in the history of films, with the possible exception of some films of Eisenstein. Films which I don't particularly admire in themselves, but which have solved the problem that the real world outside—sky, clouds, trees and so on—doesn't seem to have anything to do with the décor. No matter how convincing the set, whether it's a real place or made out of cardboard, as soon as people in costume ride out on their horses it's suddenly banal, it's modern. You see a perfectly-made costume, actor wearing it correctly, everything is all right: he goes outside, and it's suddenly a location. You feel the trucks behind him and everything. I don't know why. In *Henry V,* for example, you see the people riding out of the castle, and suddenly they are on a golf course somewhere charging each other. You can't escape it, they have entered another world.

The only place where you don't feel this is in Westerns, and Japanese pictures which are like Westerns because they are a tradition. And it's a tradition in which the clothes, and nature and so on, have learned to live together. But I believe the problem can be solved, and I *think* I solved it to some extent in *Othello,* and more here. What I am trying to do is to see the outside, real world through the same eyes as the inside, fabricated one. To create a kind of unity.

The seventy minutes we have seen of your Don Quixote *seems to translate just that ideal world which Cervantes dreamed for his characters.*

That's the problem, isn't it? The people must live in their world. It is a fundamental problem for the film-maker, even when you are making apparently the most ordinary modern story. But particularly when you have a great figure of myth like Quixote, even like Falstaff, a silhouette against the sky of all time. These are people who have more life in them than any human being ever had. But you can't simply dress up and *be* them, you have to make a world for them.

You originally had certain ideas about the photographic look of Chimes at Midnight, *a kind of grading which would give the images almost the quality of an old engraving. In the first print we saw, you used this for the credit titles, which came up over the characters present at the coronation. Why did you change this?*

They weren't able to do it in the lab. It would have produced an extraordinary effect, I think, and it's my great sorrow that it hasn't been done. In fact, the film would have been lit in a completely different way if I had known that this process was likely to fail.

The Greatest Good Man

From reading the plays, one had the feeling that the film might have been gayer than you made it.

It's a very sad story: perhaps it should be happier, and that may be a failure on my part. But I also think that it is funnier in the English version than in Spanish. The Spanish version loses very little in the serious story, even though you can't expect a popular audience to appreciate that speech of the King on sleep unless it is an English audience. There is a density in what Shakespeare wrote that cannot be changed, and you must understand that every time you come to a speech of that kind you must fail except in English. You just have to sit still and say "well, we lost it." Luckily this picture only has one speech like that; but there are technical difficulties of translation for the jokes. All the same, the thing that most concerns me about the film and my own performance is that I am not as funny as I expected to be. That was part of what preoccupied me all through the shooting: the more I studied the part, the less funny he seemed to be.

Falstaff is a man defending a force—the old England—which is going down. What is difficult about Falstaff, I believe, is that he is the greatest conception of a good man, the most completely good man, in all drama. His faults are so small and he makes tremendous jokes out of little faults. But his goodness is like bread, like wine. . . . And that was why I lost the comedy. The more I played it, the more I felt that I was playing Shakespeare's good, pure man.

I have played the part three times in the theatre and now in the film, and I'm not convinced that I have realised it properly yet. It's the most difficult part I ever played in my life, and there are at least three scenes in the film that I would like to do over again from my point of view as an actor. I feel he is a wit rather than a clown, and I don't think much of the few moments in the film when I am simply funny, because I don't think that he is. But I can see that there are scenes which should be much more hilarious, because I directed everything, and played everything, with a view to preparing for the last scene. The relationship between Falstaff and the Prince is not the simple, comic relationship that it is in Shakespeare's *Henry IV, Part One,* but always a preparation for the end. And as you see, the farewell is performed about four times during the movie, foreshadowed four times.

There is a wonderful moment after the play-acting at the tavern, when they are talking about Falstaff's banishment ("banish plump Jack, and banish all the world . . .") and the Prince says "I will. . . ."

That's the clearest of all those farewells. And you discover in making the film that the death of the King, and the death of Hotspur, which is the death of chivalry, and Falstaff's poverty and Falstaff's illness run all through the play. Comedy can't really dominate a film made to tell this story, which is all in dark colours. But the basic thing is the innocence. The interesting thing about this story is that the old King is a murderer, an usurper, and yet he represents the legitimate idea. So Hal is the creation of a legitimate Prince who must betray the good man in order to become a hero, a famous English hero. The terrible price of power which the Prince has to pay. In the first part of the play, the Hotspur subplot keeps the business of the triangle between the King, his son and Falstaff (who is a sort of foster father) from dominating. But in my film, which is made to tell, essentially, the story of that triangle, there are bound to be values which can't exist as it is played in the original. It's really quite a different drama.

The film has become a sort of lament for Falstaff?

Yes, that may be true. I would like to think that. . . . The film was not intended as a lament for Falstaff, but for the death of Merrie England. Merrie England as a conception, a myth, which has been very real to the English-speaking world, and is to some extent expressed in other countries of the Medieval epoch: the age of chivalry, of simplicity, of Maytime and all that. It is more than Falstaff who is dying. It's the old England, dying and betrayed.

The Magnificent Ambersons is also a lament for an epoch which has ended.

Not so much for the epoch as for the sense of moral values which are destroyed. In the case of *Ambersons*, they are destroyed by the automobile, in the case of *Chimes*, by the interests of power, duty, responsibility, national grandeur, all this kind of thing.

All your films are stories of a failure with a death in it . . .

Almost all serious stories in the world are stories of a failure with a death in it. . . . But there is more lost paradise in them than defeat. To me that's the central theme in Western culture: the lost paradise.

The Shape of Poetry

Along with The Magnificent Ambersons, Chimes at Midnight *seems to be one of the most personal of your films, perhaps because these two are the most lyrical.*

Yes, I agree. I don't know whether lyrical is the right word, but there is a more personal feeling in those films, a deeper emotion. Yes, because people think of my films as being violent and sometimes cold, but I think *Ambersons* . . . this picture represents more than anything else what I would like to do in films. This question of 'an Orson Welles style' is all exaggerated anyway. I don't think that my films are dominated by style. I have a strong style, or different ones, I hope, but I'm not a formalist. The great majority of critics, whether they treat me well or badly, always treat me as a formalist. And I'm not a formalist!

How do you conceive scenes? They seem to be conceived rather like poems, with a kind of musical flow.

Music. Music and poetry. It's that rather than simply visual. The visual side comes out of a method of thinking, if thinking is the word. I hate to use pompous words like 'creating,' but I'm afraid you have to. With me, the visual is a solution to what the poetical and musical form dictates. I don't begin with the visual and then try to find a poetry or music and try to stick it in the picture. The picture has to follow it. And again, people tend to think that my first preoccupation is with the simple plastic effects of the cinema. But to me they all come out of an interior rhythm, which is like the shape of music or the shape of poetry. I don't go around like a collector picking up beautiful images and pasting them together.

Is that why editing is so important to you?

It's very central. I believe in the film as a poetic medium. I don't think it competes with painting, or with ballet—the visual side of films is a key to poetry. There is no picture which justifies itself, no matter how beautiful, striking, horrific, tender . . . it doesn't mean anything unless it makes poetry possible. And that suggests something, because poetry should make your hair stand up on your skin, should suggest things, evoke more than you see. The danger in the cinema is that you see everything, because it's a camera. So what you have to do is to manage to evoke, to incant, to raise up things which are not really there.

Do you think Chimes at Midnight *does this?*

That's what I am reaching for, what I hope is true. If it is, then I'm reaching maturity as an artist. If it isn't true, then I'm in decadence, you know? But what I am trying to discover now in films is not technical surprises or shocks, but a more complete unity of forms, of shapes. The true form, the interior, the musical form of a picture. I believe that you should be able to enjoy a picture with your eyes closed, that a blind man should be able to enjoy a movie. We all say "the only movies are silent movies," but they have been talking now for forty years, so we have to say something in them. And when something is said, or a sound is made, or there is music, whatever occurs must have in it—just technically, I'm not thinking of poetry now, only technically—a shape which is immediately recognisable, so that you see that the whole thing has a shape, just as the image does. And the interior conception of the author, above all, must have a single shape.

Blows and Counterblows

Chimes at Midnight *was originally designed to open with the assassination of Richard II and the landing of Bolingbroke in England. Why did you change this? The part of the Bolingbroke scene which was shot was full of extraordinary visual ideas—all the flags, and the future King waiting by the camp-fire, cold and hungry.*

We shot one day on the assassination, and it didn't seem to me that the scene was sufficiently clear: instead of explaining the political background, it would tend to obscure it and confuse the audience. Also, four or five days work were necessary to complete it, and I didn't want to put the producer to that expense.

The Bolingbroke scene looked very interesting . . . but that's what divides the men from the boys, the people who can really do it from the others. What a director must have is a capacity to throw out his most beautiful shots. A film is often ruined, in my opinion, by a director who can't bear to get rid of something just because it's beautiful. Do you remember the shots of the two old men, Falstaff and Shallow, walking in the snow? Fine, marvellous shots, which I took out. Now, I could have indulged myself and had all the cinema clubs in the world say "Look! How beautiful!" But those shots would have hurt the real, internal rhythm of the picture. And when things won't be as useful to the total film as you expected, then you must be willing to abandon them immediately.

When you were filming the battle sequence you shot longish takes, then fragmented them in the cutting-room.

On the first day I tried to do very short pieces, but I found the extras didn't work as well unless they had a longer thing to do. They didn't seem to be really fighting until they had time to warm up. That's why the takes were long, since there was no way of beginning the camera later and cutting. But I knew I was only going to use very short cuts. For example, we shot with a big crane very low to the ground, moving as fast as it could be moved against the action. What I was planning to do—and did—was to intercut the shots in which the action was contrary, so that every cut seemed to be a blow, a counterblow, a blow received, a blow returned. Actually it takes a lot of time for the crane to move over and back, but everything was planned for this effect and I never intended to use more than a small section of the arc in each case.

You edit very dynamically, breaking up your long takes with constant movement. Is that because you are apprehensive about boring the public?

Because I am so easily bored, I think the public probably is. You people who love the cinema are not as easily bored by it as I am. In other words, if I had to make films only for people who *fundamentally* love the movies, then I could be longer. But I would be false in it, because I believe that the point of boredom is very easily reached. If it isn't reached this year, it will be later. It's one of the things that dates films, that makes them seem old-fashioned, when you don't have the courage to keep it moving. . . . I believe that films should be able to tell a story quicker than any other medium. Instead the tendency, in the last ten years particularly, has been to get slower and slower, and for the director to indulge himself in what you call visual ideas. If we don't have speed, I think we are basically betraying the medium. But nowadays serious directors are permitted to ask the public anything they like, at any length.

I do not like verbosity; I don't like wasted time. I like concentration in every art. And although I know that I lose, that the public loses, a great deal because of the concentration, I also hope that somebody will see one thing and someone else will see another. I think you make a very thin movie if everything in it is going to be exactly clear. I don't want to criticise my contemporaries, but there are some directors who are considered very great who make one effect and only that effect. You can go back again ten times, and you will only admire exactly the same thing again. I don't think a film should be entirely evident: there should always be something else to see when you go again. . . .

The last scene at Justice Shallow's house, in which Pistol brings the news of Hal's accession, was originally shot in one five-minute take. Then you intercut it with shots of the King's castle, breaking it up and losing some minutes of this scene of the old men in front of the fire.

I had a reason for that. I believe that as it is cut now, it tells the basic story better. If you are making a film in which you are not completely at the mercy of your narrative, then anything that is interesting can give itself its own length. The scene was in itself a good one, a little like a photographed scene from the theatre, and what remains now is what I thought was good about it. What was there before seemed to me to reduce the interest of the film after the big scene of the King's death. In other words, what you had was something beautiful, well-conceived perhaps by the director, admirable cinematically but not dramatically.

You sometimes do several retakes of the same scene on different days. Do you think the scenes over and decide on a retake without even seeing the rushes?

Yes. The rushes aren't important to me. I don't really shoot a 'retake' in the classic American sense of the word: a shot that has been studied by everybody and has been discovered to be wrong technically. I make a retake because *my* work wasn't good enough.

Sometimes you shoot a scene which seems perfect, and then do it over again. Is that because you think that there was something in it that didn't work after all?

Well, it wasn't perfect. . . . You can only do that, though, where you are working on the same set. I never go back for a retake on a set that's finished with; that's a luxury I can't indulge in. In Cardona we didn't retake anything, because I had to finish John Gielgud's part in two weeks. I knew when he left that I would have all the work we later did with doubles. That wasn't second thoughts: I knew I would have to use doubles because I only had him for two weeks and he plays a part that runs almost as long as mine. . . .

Interview with Keith Baxter

Int.: I'd like to ask you first of all whether you've seen *Chimes at Midnight* recently and how you feel about the film at this point.

KB: Yes, I saw it four years ago after not seeing it for twenty years. I was very moved by it, not because I was absorbed in my own performance—that's clearly a boy who doesn't exist any longer. As I hadn't seen it in so long it was all very fresh, and I was able to watch it with a very detached attitude. The film has a wonderful vitality about it; I do think it's the greatest Shakespeare on film.

Int.: So do I! Can we start even before the beginning? I've heard that Welles was able to begin filming *Chimes* only by pretending that he was going to film *Treasure Island*. Is there any truth to that?

KB: Yes, he got the money for the film by persuading the producer that he was really going to shoot *Treasure Island*. He said, "I will make *Treasure Island* if you allow me, at the same time, to make *Chimes at Midnight.*"

Int.: Why did that make it more palatable to the producer?

KB: Oh, because he didn't want a Shakespeare film. He thought *Treasure Island* could sell with Orson. (And Orson subsequently did play Long John Silver in some terrible movie version of *Treasure Island,* though not for the same producer.) But that's how Orson got the money. And indeed we did shoot in Alicante the departure of the good ship *Hispaniola,* using a British eighteenth-century man-of-war that had been used in the film of *Billy Budd.* The idea was that we would do some location footage, then stop and film *Chimes,* and then go back to *Treasure Island.* Of course we never did. But we were all contracted—I was contracted to play Dr. Livesey, and Tony Beckley to play Israel Hands. I don't think John Gielgud ever knew that he was also contracted to play Squire Trelawney, because of course Orson had no intention of making the film. But Orson did get the money to build Mistress Quickly's tavern by telling the producer that it was also the Admiral Benbow Inn. You must remember that the producer, Emiliano Piedra, was a very young man, mesmerized—as we all were—by Orson, who could charm the birds off the trees. Piedra is now the most important producer in Spain, and Welles gave him the last script he wrote shortly before his death.

Interview with Bridget Gellert Lyons printed with the permission of Keith Baxter.

Int.: You were the only major actor besides Welles himself to be in both the stage and film versions of *Chimes.* Can you talk a little about the relationship between the two versions?

KB: We put the stage version of *Chimes* on in Belfast in 1960; Welles discovered me. After opening in Belfast, we were supposed to play in Dublin, and then Paris, Amsterdam, Brussels, Athens, Cairo, and back to the Royal Court in London. We never got beyond Dublin because Orson got bored and decided he didn't like the company. But on the last night, coming back to England, he said to me on the ship, "This is only a rehearsal for the movie, Keith, and I'll never make it unless you play Hal in that, too." And then we did it almost five years later, by which time, thanks to him, my career had taken off. But from the beginning it was always geared to the cinema. As you know, the subject matter had long fascinated Welles. He had experimented with it in *Five Kings,* and it was a process in which the outlines of the story kept getting clearer. He always saw it as a triangle basically, a love story of a Prince lost between two father figures. Who is the boy going to choose?

When Welles started filming, I was very conscious that his concept was exactly as it had been in Ireland, but now—working in his preferred medium—he was able to refine and concentrate the action and the emotional intensity of the story. I think the play was probably less melancholy: it was less everything! But the story of Hal, Falstaff, and the King was the same. There were practical differences, of course. For example, in the play a narrator (Hilton Edwards) appeared onstage from time to time reading from Holinshed's *Chronicles;* a tiresome device, but necessary when so much of the text had to be truncated to make one play out of two. In the film these same passages are voice-overs by Ralph Richardson and work beautifully. Also Reginald Jarman, who played the King, was not Gielgud, and Gielgud's own intensity added the kind of darkness that suited Welles's scheme very well.

Int.: Was there a set script for the film of *Chimes?*

KB: Absolutely, and we just about never deviated from it. Every line of it was shot and used, including the parts from Holinshed's *Chronicles.* I cannot remember one scene that was not used—oh yes, only one. It was a summer scene where we are riding to the Gadshill robbery. Apart from that scene, and a short bit where Orson kissed Margaret Rutherford for some reason, the script was all used. It was a very meticulous one.

Int.: Did Welles shoot any additional scenes that were not in the script?

KB: Yes, he shot two sequences for the beginning of the film that were never used. One was the murder of Richard II, and the other was a scene where Richard's coffin is presented to Henry. There was a sweet fellow—Oscar Pelissier, I think his name was—and he was Richard II. Poor Oscar had to stay during all the shooting; he didn't speak a word of English. On the very last day of location in Cardona, they filmed the murder of Richard II in the deserted castle—he's pursued by soldiers and then killed, whoomp, and then the film was to start. The other scene, which was shot with Gielgud, was not Gielgud in court, but was in fact Gielgud on a deserted hillside, outside a tent, with a very stormy sky, which we shot at Colmenar outside Madrid; and then over the hillside came this huge procession of bishops led by Northumberland, carrying a coffin. And they dump the coffin at Henry's feet, saying "Lord Henry Bolingbroke, we come to thee with thy buried fear (etc.)." Orson shot both those scenes and didn't use them. He always said to me, "You have to kill your babies, Keith." He said the murder of Richard II looked like the murder of Thomas à Becket; it seemed like a cliché. And indeed the empty horizon and the people walking over also seemed trite. So he got rid of them. Well, that's normal. In a film, one always shoots scenes that never appear.

Int.: When did Welles decide on the precredit sequence of Falstaff and Shallow in the snow?

KB: The film version was always planned to start with the snow sequence. That would have been followed by either the murder of Richard II, or by Northumberland's procession, or indeed by both scenes. But the old men walking through the snow was always planned as the opening of the picture.

Int.: Did working with such a careful and complete script mean that Welles defined everything very fully for his actors? Did you feel you had enough freedom in shaping your role?

KB: Orson always saw things very clearly, very precisely. He had a very definite idea of what he wanted to do with the relationship between Falstaff and Hal and he certainly thought of Falstaff as the great, good man. I'm sure he felt like that partly because he was playing Falstaff. But the scene late in the film between Gielgud and myself, which is very tender, he didn't in any way attempt to negate that or to diminish it. On the contrary, because he was wise enough not to do that, he in fact enhances the sadness.

In terms of shooting, he knew in his head what he wanted to accomplish. He was the most extraordinary director, but if I was asked to give a specific instance of his direction I couldn't. I think he was so secure in his own genius, and one uses that word advisedly, that he was incredibly relaxed about it. So you felt you were very free. His imprint is on every frame of the picture, but one didn't feel in any way intimidated by him. On the contrary, one felt released by him. It was a wonderfully liberating experience for an actor. And anybody could say anything. John is notorious, as he would be the first to say, for making suggestions. Orson would listen to them all, and maybe throw them all out, but he was never too grand to accept one and use it if he thought he could make something wonderful out of it.

Int.: Did Welles rely on the script to rehearse scenes before he shot them?

KB: If it was a very simple scene, as with Gielgud's soliloquies or mine, he often didn't rehearse, because we both knew our lines. Orson would say, "Let's rehearse on camera." In the famous "Uneasy lies the head" scene, there was the window, with the light outside, and Orson said, "John, just walk up to the window, and bring your eye down level with this grille. We've got a light there for your eyes, and we're going to shoot it in a long shot, and a close shot." And then he said, "Let's do it." And John did it. And the Spanish crew applauded—I don't think they'd ever heard one man speak so long without interruption.

So he didn't necessarily rehearse. But he would if it was something complicated, like the first tavern scene. Most directors either move the actors or move the camera. Orson would move both at the same time, and that is tricky. In the tavern, the camera track was laid like an *S,* and the actors as well as the camera were made to move in very intricate ways. So we did rehearse that first scene; it took about three days to shoot it. And he also had lots of extras running around there—the ones playing the tavern girls and so forth—and that he certainly rehearsed.

Another scene that he reheased for about four days was the one late in the film with Alan Webb, Walter Chiari, and the boy, where Pistol comes in and says the king is dead. Orson had a very specific idea about that scene. He wanted the camera to be still, and so he rehearsed it like a stage scene. He never really felt it came off, but I think it comes off marvelously. It's a low shot, and when Welles rushes into the foreground with "What, is the old king dead?" the effect is wonderful.

The only soliloquy of mine that we did rehearse didn't come off well at all. It's my first long speech, "I know you all," with a wink at the end. I cringe every time I see it. We were near Alicante launching the *Hispaniola* for *Treasure Island* and had nothing to do while the second crew was on the boat. So Orson said we'd just talk about *Chimes* and go through some of our soliloquies. It's the thing I think I do least well in the film. I hate it.

Int.: Do you still hate that part?

KB: Hate it, loathe it with a passion. Orson agreed. I said why did you make me wink, and he said we'd never rehearse again.

Int.: Were bits of comic business, such as your bumping your head, impromptu or were they planned?

KB: I bumped my head on the tavern set one day by accident and it seemed a good bit of business to use sometime later. Orson would ask "When are you going to do that bump-your-head business?" and I would say "I'll surprise you." So one day I did it and he said "I didn't think that was much of a surprise." When we saw the rushes, he announced, "Now everyone, watch out for Keith's Big Surprise." Luckily two people kindly laughed and I asked Orson what he thought of it. "*Very* subtle," he said.

Int.: There was always a good deal of improvisation connected with the making of the film, wasn't there?

KB: There certainly was. I can give you a very good example of Welles's improvisation. He had a location in Barcelona—an extraordinary thirteenth-century courtyard with narrow pillars—very elegant, very pretty—that he planned to use for a scene between Poins and myself. It's the scene where I say I'm very sad. When we got there it turned out to be a holiday weekend, and the palace with its courtyard were open to the public by law. So there was no way of stopping people from coming in, and we had to abandon that location. Later I kept asking Orson when we were going to do that scene, because I thought it was an important one, and he would say "I don't know. I see water, I see water."

He had already designed this grey velvet robe with a high collar (which he jokingly called my "frock") for me to wear in that scene—Orson designed all the clothes, you know—but when I'd ask, he'd say, "I see water in it, maybe lying on a boat, with a boy playing a guitar or something." One day we were filming in the Casa de Campo, which is this huge park right in the middle of Madrid where all the battle scenes were shot and where a lot of the film was shot. We were doing the Gadshill robbery. Frequently Orson would go marching off with the viewfinder to find a shot for the next scene, followed only by the lighting man and the camera operator, while we all waited around having a cup of coffee or something, until someone would say "Right," and we'd go to the next setup. This time a man came rushing back to me and said "Mr. Welles says you are to put on your grey frock." The trucks with all the costumes had to follow us everywhere, because you never knew what scene was on. Orson had found a sort of boating pond near where we were. It was about ten o'clock in the morning in

November, and this whole ugly boating pond—really very ugly—was totally covered by a grey mist; you could see no sky and very little background. Orson said "We have five minutes to shoot, the mist is clearing. We have to shoot on Keith, and then we can shoot the reverses later." By the time we shot the reverses the mist had disappeared; there were cars going past on the other side hooting, and this very ugly concrete pond was full of little toy boats. But he saw what he wanted and said "Let's shoot that scene!" So we shot the mastershot within ten minutes. That's improvisation.

Int.: And he was able to work so fast!

KB: Very fast.

Int.: That's a great example. And that scene comes off magnificently.

KB: Yes, but of course it couldn't have been done if he hadn't known that he was working with actors who knew all their lines for the whole film—had them in their heads as he himself did.

Int.: May I ask you a different kind of question? Welles said in an interview after the film was completed that Shakespeare was making an important historical statement in the rejection of Falstaff. Did he talk about that while making the film?

KB: He always saw the film as an elegy for "Merrie England." He felt that Shakespeare was looking back on the world of Richard II, that the age of chivalry died with the murder of Richard. In the play it dies with Hotspur. All of Hotspur's lines are in poetry; a lot of Hal's are in prose. And the great bravura poetry of Hotspur is all very gay, beautiful, heroic, chivalrous. That England died with the beginning of the Lancastrian reign and the introduction of gunpowder; London began to change and Welles felt very much that Shakespeare was looking back and presenting Falstaff as the actual personification of that pastoral earlier England, just as we look back at Georgian England or Colonial America with a kind of romanticism because that was two hundred years ago. People realize that life is very different in 1988 from what it was in 1788, but they don't always realize that Shakespeare writing in 1599 about 1399 was also looking back two hundred years with that remembrance of things past, that kind of sadness. And it was something, of course, that Orson in his own life felt.

Int.: Did the tone of the film change as he was shooting?

KB: Yes, I think it did. Orson realized, halfway through the shooting, that this was a very sad film, much sadder than he had intended it to be. But what he himself was and what the film expressed about him had taken over. Subconsciously, he was always projecting the end of the film onto the beginning. He wanted the moment in the tavern when I say "I do, I will" to be a signal. It was a much more potent signal than he realized, because the film had begun to take on a darker texture.

Orson had to stop shooting the film just before Christmas 1964 because he ran out of money. When he started shooting again at the end of February, the trees were out in the Casa de Campo. There was one specific tree, a great tree in an empty meadow, that was in blossom, and Orson said to me, "You know, we don't have one scene of summer in this film, Keith." And we tried to shoot one, riding to the Gadshill robbery. Orson found a sort of leafy lane, but it didn't work. He never tried to reshoot it and I think by then he had begun to realize that winter, and the movement of the film toward winter and cold and bleakness, was in fact what he wanted. In the end, although all the skylarking about at the beginning of the film isn't really successful, in a way that's right. It shouldn't be successful.

Int.: Then you don't think those scenes in the tavern work very well?

KB: Well, not as comedy. People complain, with justice, that *Chimes* isn't a very funny film, but that's because Orson was never a good clown. He could be a buffoon, but he was not a great clown. The early comedic scenes are rather uneasy, and don't really come off well, but that's because Welles himself never felt that kind of gaiety. He wasn't that sort of person.

You're always faced with that problem doing the two plays in the theater. If they are tremendously comic, the sweep of the story and its tragedy and the coldness of the King in the royal scenes doesn't work, and if that works, very often the comedy doesn't work.

Int.: The "darker texture" you mentioned earlier is certainly conveyed by the black-and-white photography. Did Welles want to shoot in black and white or was that economic necessity?

KB: The producer meant the film to be shot in color, but he really couldn't raise the money, and thought it more important to shoot *Treasure Island* in color. Although it's so much easier to sell a color film, Orson had tremendous resistance to it because he always said that no film yet had found the way to photograph a human face in color without makeup. And nobody in *Chimes at Midnight* wears any makeup, except Orson himself, because he was only fifty, and Alan Webb, who was given a longer nose.

You can see the results of Welles's choices when you compare *Chimes* with Olivier's *Richard III*. There everything is in color, the actors all wear makeup and all wear wigs—and they all look like actors. They're wonderful performances, of course, especially Larry's own performance, but it's very much a piece of stagecraft. *Chimes at Midnight* has this extraordinary naturalism about it and one reason for that is because it is shot in black and white. Orson said once that if he put it into color every actor's performance would be diminished by ten percent. I'm sure he was pleased the film was to be in black and white, and once he began shooting he strove to get this very cold, very bleak effect, with a very grainy texture.

Int.: Welles said he hated the fancy-dress kind of historical film, but *Chimes* creates a strong sense of a distant period, doesn't it?

KB: Although Orson was a modernist director, his taste was very Gothic, and all his films have a tremendously Gothic feel. In most of them, it's because of the sets (that extraordinary house in *Ambersons*, for instance) and because of the lighting. In *Chimes*, he's able to be Gothic because it is an authentically Gothic period, but the historical setting meant he had to find a device when we all got disguised for the Gadshill robbery. Because to the modern eye, the costumes the actors are wearing are already a disguise. So we needed to wear something that the film audience would recognize as a disguise and not just another costume change. Orson suddenly hit on the idea of dressing us all up as friars. Of course, it wasn't an accident that he chose friars, because that also thickened the religious atmosphere. Even the woods helped to create this atmosphere; the light comes through the trees like in a cathedral. I can never smell incense without thinking of the film, because incense was used all the time—in the woods and elsewhere—so that the light would be diffused.

Int.: Did Welles ever talk about the film as a reflection of his personal involvements? In a sense, he had two fathers himself, and I wondered if he ever mentioned that connection to you?

KB: I don't think so. If anything, he identified himself with Falstaff as a father figure. Orson did have a deep attachment for me, as he had earlier for Tony Perkins, whom he directed in *The Trial*. When Orson was setting up *Chimes,* Tony went from California all the way to Madrid to see him. He didn't actually come out and say he wanted to play Prince Hal but that was in his mind. But because I had played the role with Orson on stage, he wanted me to do it. At that time, Orson was very possessive about me—I don't mean in any restrictive way at all, but I was very much pulled into the family.

Of course, Orson had three children, all girls, and I suspect that like lots of men he would have liked to have a son. So in the film Hal is Falstaff's surrogate son. Hal turns to Falstaff for the love he is not getting from his father.

Int.: Is that how Welles defined the relationships among the King, Hal, and Falstaff?

KB: Welles very much wanted to make the King and Hal and Falstaff equal partners—a triangular relationship. In the theater, as you know, when you do both halves of *Henry IV*, the King doesn't come out awfully well, because there are too many other glittering performances. Hotspur comes off wonderfully in the first part, but in this version there wasn't room for Hotspur to steal the picture. It's no accident that when Olivier did the play for the Old Vic he chose to play Hotspur; Hotspur was the hero.

Int.: It's very possible, though, to see the play with Hal as the hero. After all, Hal is the one who becomes the great king. But that is not the way the film comes out.

KB: It isn't, of course, the way Welles felt about it. When we finally finished the coronation speech ("I know thee not, old man"), I said "Well, Orson, I feel very sad, as though the part is over, and I really think I'd like to play Henry V." And he said, "Why would you want to do that? He's a most awful shit." According to Orson, Henry V has nothing to do with Prince Hal. And he hasn't, you know. If you look at Henry V, there's this great wooing scene with Kate, the Princess of France, in which the King acts as if he's never bedded a girl before and has no experience of life at all; he's just a common soldier. "Kate, kiss a soldier," etc. That has nothing to do with Prince Hal.

Orson was so romantic about the Plantagenets, but he thought the Tudors and the Lancastrians were terrible. That's why the King in the film is always surrounded by soldiers—sort of black storm troopers. It's not underlined, but all the King's soldiers are in dark armor; Hotspur's armor is silver. Welles wanted that feeling that Hal was going into the cold.

Int.: Then the coronation scene where you reject Falstaff is supposed to show Hal going into that world of public and joyless responsibility.

KB: Yes, it's a long series of shots, many of them silent, with me dressed in that elaborate robe of state. It says a great deal for Orson that, although he felt so strongly that Hal was a monster, the shot of Falstaff looking at me—proud of me for being so magnificent—is terribly moving.

Int.: That's interesting, because I find a lot of pride in the shot and most critics of the film haven't.

KB: Real pride, saying, "Look, this is my boy."

Int.: Yes, the boy has grown up and he's splendid.

KB: No doubt about that. It was always wonderful playing that scene on the stage with Orson because he never cheated.

In the film, Orson was usually behind the camera when I did my speeches, but not in that scene. He knelt the whole time, and then he said he wanted to shoot the reverses immediately. He didn't move and they shot the reverses right over my shoulder, with that marvelous face looking at me.

Int.: It's interesting that with all of Shakespeare's language to draw on, Welles made some of the film's most stunning moments without any language. The end of the coronation scene that you've just described is one example, but there are also the shots in which you and Gielgud look at each other after the battle, and nothing is said.

KB: Well, that is an example of Welles's originality. In *Henry IV, Part 1*, there's a reconciliation after Shrewsbury between Hal and the King. Welles, of course, couldn't have that because the film was going on through *Part 2*. So he invented that moment when the King walks in, and Falstaff produces Hotspur's body, saying "There's your Percy." It was Welles's idea that the King waits for me to say "I did it."

Int.: But you don't come through.

KB: No, and by the time I do, the King has turned his back on me. But Gielgud's part and mine were shot four months apart. Gielgud did his looks in Cardona at the end of October on his last day of shooting and I did my looks in Madrid in April. But Welles knew exactly what he wanted. He just said "John, look here, look over there," while John was just standing on a tuft of grass. But when I did my looks, John was in New York on stage, so in those shots whenever the King does cross the camera it's John's double. You watch that scene next time, now that I've told you, and you will see that it is John's double. And John sitting dead behind me on the throne is not John, but a double.

Int.: I know that Gielgud was not the only actor who could be with the film for only a limited time. That must have made the filming complicated.

KB: Once somebody came, everybody had to shoot on them all the time. Gielgud would be there for three weeks, so we had to shoot on Gielgud all the time—all the things with Gielgud. And anybody who had a scene not with Gielgud had to wait. When Jeanne Moreau arrived, anything with her had to be done. We had Margaret Rutherford for four weeks; she was going back to London to do a play, so we had to shoot all her stuff.

Int.: Despite all the coming and going, Welles made excellent use of his actors—Gielgud, for instance.

KB: Welles made a brilliant choice there because Gielgud had been a great Richard II, but he wasn't the obvious casting for Henry Bolingbroke. Orson said he wanted to play him as somebody who is ill and dying and it was John's idea to play him as a monk, with a skullcap and a pectoral cross. He felt he couldn't bring the kind of robustness of Henry Bolingbroke, but what he could bring was the haunted quality of a man who is at the end of his life and feels he's committed that terrible sin. So when he says "God knows by what crooked path I won the crown," that guilt which Gielgud conveys was based on John's suggestion that Henry was somebody who had become obsessed with religious scruples at the end of his life.

Int.: Welles made a more controversial choice, didn't he, when he asked Jeanne Moreau to play Doll Tearsheet?

KB: Jeanne got a lot of bad notices unfairly—lots of people said what is a French woman doing playing Doll Tearsheet. But Orson said these were the wars, and Calais and Dunkirk were British ports, and Doll Tearsheet was some hooker that they picked up in Calais. That's absolutely legitimate. One forgets that at the time of Richard II the language of the English court was French. To this day when the Queen signs an act into law the actual words used—"la reyne le veult"—are Norman French. It's totally legitimate that Jeanne should have played Doll and should be French. She came to do the role after her success in *Jules and Jim*, and when journalists wondered why she would come for five days to play Doll, she said without any affectation, "Orson Welles asked me."

Int.: Did Welles have problems casting any of the roles in the film?

KB: There were problems getting somebody to play Justice Silence. Hilton Edwards, who ran the Gate Theatre in Dublin and who gave Welles his first professional acting job in the thirties, was flown out to Spain to play Silence. We were chasing the snow at the time, looking to shoot what became the opening sequence of the film, and we found snow in a place called Lecumberri in the Basque country. But Hilton got ill there and had to go back to Dublin. Welles had the snow though, even if he had no Silence, and it had taken considerable trouble to find snow, so he said "I've got to shoot the scene now." First he wanted me to be Silence; he said "It will be a long shot and we'll keep you in the back, and when we choose the actor, we'll dress him in whatever you've chosen to wear." Finally, we both agreed this was madness, so he had to shoot the scene that day without Silence. That is why there is just Falstaff and Shallow in the opening scene, although in the reprise of the scene later in the film, Silence is sitting with them in front of the fire.

Welles took the loss of Hilton very calmly, even though he needed a replacement desperately. I put Orson in touch with someone in London who found him an actor, but after all the arrangements were made, the actor failed to show up when Orson expected he would. Then Orson's wife, Paola, who was Italian, suggested Walter Chiari. So Orson rang up Walter, who was a big star in Rome then, and he said he'd come right away.

Int.: Was it Chiari's idea to play Silence as a stutterer?

KB: No, that was Orson's idea. Orson felt it would be very funny to have Silence only able to say, f—, f—, f—; it would be sort of low and vulgar. But it was Walter's idea to have a pig on his lap, and it was Walter's idea to pad out his cheeks.

Int.: With actors from many different countries, like Fernando Rey and Walter Chiari, there must have been a good deal of dubbing. Is it true that Welles dubbed several of the other voices himself?

KB: Every word of the picture is post-synched because we shot in real locations, and so the whole soundtrack was done after the shooting. But as I remember, the only major actors who were dubbed were Marina Vlady and Fernando Rey, because they had very strong foreign accents. Most of the very minor roles were dubbed, because Welles cast them with local Spanish people. Michael Aldridge does about three voices in the film. Orson does at least two. One of the recruits Shallow presents for Falstaff is Orson's voice. The sheriff's rather pompous voice when I'm in bed in the tavern—"My lord"—that's Orson. We all did assorted voices in the crowd scenes. I can always hear my own voice shouting "Esperance!" among the battle noises. Some of my post-synching I did in Paris with Jeanne Moreau, because she was shooting a film there. I also post-synched in two different sound studios in Madrid, and in a sound studio in London.

Int.: It's not surprising, then, that sometimes the sound synchronization is less than perfect.

KB: That's true, there isn't a word of the film that was shot in direct sound. There are disadvantages, of course, because it's quite difficult sometimes to get consistent quality. But the huge advantage was the authenticity of the locations. The castle in which we filmed the throne-room scenes was in a place called Cardona, in the mountains near Andorra, and it was a wonderful Spanish Gothic cathedral or monastery that had fallen into disrepair. It's now been restored as a very glamourous Parador Hotel by the Spanish government. I haven't been back there since, but in those days it was extremely cold and primitive. You can see the steam coming out of our mouths as we were shooting there, even though we were inside. The first day of shooting, Orson said "No *wonder* the boy went to the tavern!" All of that coldness and bleakness was gained by shooting there; you couldn't reproduce that scene in a studio.

Int.: Then was the tavern the only location created for the film?

KB: Yes, the tavern was designed and built by Welles. As I said before, he got the money by claiming he would be using the set for *Treasure Island*. It was built in what was a sort of Les Halles area of Madrid—very down-market. It was a warehouse and Orson reconstructed the whole thing. The nooks and crannies and tiny rooms at the Tavern were all planned by Welles in his design. All the other settings, they're all real houses, real places, real streets. The wonderful house where Falstaff hears the King is dead, that's a real house near Lecumberri.

Int.: I was reading in one account that Welles finally didn't like the tavern set and had it all changed.

KB: No, not at all, that's absolutely wrong. The set was finished while we were in Cardona. When we got back to Madrid, we went with Orson to see the set. We all thought it was an incredible set, but Orson felt it needed aging. He said it's got to look as though this is a tavern in 1400 that was built in 1200. So we were all given hammers, blowtorches, or brushes with blacking on them, to age the set, to bring it down.

Int.: Do you remember some of the details of where and how the battle sequence was shot?

KB: Orson shot virtually all of it in the Casa de Campo, the big park in Madrid. At first he had about a hundred and fifty people on horseback for the charge that begins the battle, but I think he had them for only two days, or possibly four days. Of course, he often reversed the negative; he was very good at all those tricks. But he never had those men again. So the rest of the battle was filmed usually with not more than twelve or fourteen people. In the shots of me walking through the deserted battlefield (a sequence shot at Colmenar), those bodies were all dummies and the dead horses were dummies, and not very good dummies because we couldn't afford it. We even had dummy half-horses that they put a bit of baggage on to hide the missing parts.

During the period when the producer had run out of money and we were waiting to raise more money to shoot things like the coronation scene, Orson would go out to the Casa de Campo with about a dozen people—they were just extras, waiters and such who were paid about a hundred pesetas a day. They would do bits of backlighting for the battle scene. Something like the feet pushing in the mud was actually shot indoors. They wet down some earth inside the warehouse where we had the tavern set; the result, of course, is astonishing.

Int.: That is amazing; I had no idea the battle sequence used so many illusionistic tricks.

KB: Well, Orson was a conjurer, you know. He would say "Audiences will look at what you tell them to look at."

Int.: Are there other examples of Welles's conjuring in the film that you can remember?

KB: Welles needed to begin the battle scenes and we had no armor. I had to persuade Gielgud that Orson thought it would be much more interesting to shoot the preparations for battle with John in his under-dress. They found a suit of armor in Madrid which they put outside John's tent, on a sort of clothes-horse. But in fact it's for a man of about five foot seven, practically a dwarf. John is six foot. But Orson said if you put in on a clothes-horse, as long as he never wears it, it'll never matter. As long as he has a helmet which he takes off in a close shot, that's all you need. And that's why you never see John in armor—at that time, there was no armor. When you see me in armor, it's because we shot those scenes much later. For my costume, he found some old chain mail, and I wear a leather tunic that Jayne Mansfield had worn in *The Sheriff of Fractured Jaw,* which had been shot in Spain. Around the bottom I wear a sort of scalloped velvet which came off Stephen Boyd's horse from *The Fall of the Roman Empire.* I said to Orson, "What did people wear under their armor?" He said "I don't know, but nobody else will know either."

Of course, I always saw the bits that don't show up on the screen. For example, John was terrified of horses, and so was Norman Rodway. When Norman takes off his helmet, and says "If I mistake not, thou art Harry Monmouth," he's actually sitting on the shoulders of two men who are bouncing him, because he couldn't bear to sit astride a horse. I do all my own riding in the film, but John loathed riding and Norman couldn't get on a horse. So the long shot of John collapsing on the horse—that's not him at all—and when he's sitting on the horse, that's a terrible old nag that was firmly held and was cropping grass and regurgitating it all the time that John was saying "Bear Worcester to the death."

Remember, Orson often invented these tricks because he had to. Sometimes he had to cover because he was using actors who weren't going to be there very long. For example, Margaret Rutherford, more than anybody else, is shown reacting to the play scene in the tavern between Hal and Falstaff. But she never saw the scene. Orson just said "Come in here and sit down and now laugh, Margaret." So she was doing all this rocking back and forth with laughter and clapping her hands and she had no idea! I mean, yes, she knew what the scene was, but she never saw us do it. Sometimes he had to cover because he couldn't afford to do anything else. For example, when I'm riding to my coronation with the crowds there, many of those figures are cardboard cutouts, with a bit of scarf pinned on them to blow in the wind.

Int.: You were with the film from beginning to end. Did you make any uncredited appearances?

KB: Oh, yes. I can't remember them all specifically now, but I do remember that at the time I counted fourteen appearances in the film where I'm not playing Hal. Often in the battle scenes or with a crowd of extras, because it was too complicated to explain to them what to do or when to stop or when to move, Orson would just say "Follow Señor Baxter." I would be put into whatever the costume was, and they would be told when he stops, stop; when he moves, move. There are scenes in the battle where I'm walking and then scenes when I'm riding—not as Prince Hal. There's a short scene after Falstaff learns of the King's death where Falstaff, Shallow, and Silence are running through the snow, chasing after each other. Walter Chiari had already gone, so that's me, running behind Shallow. We're actually running across sheets, because the snow had gone by then and Orson simply had white sheets laid on the top of the turf. But it was all a kind of conjuring trick, all part of the game of making movies.

I'm not sure, but I think my hand may even have made a special appearance. When Orson was putting the film together, he suddenly discovered that he needed to have a hand to pick up the King's crown after it falls. We just used the kitchen floor of my flat and put a couple of flagstones down with the camera right there.

Int.: You've already mentioned the main locations for the film. Could you give me some idea of the sequence in which the scenes were shot?

KB: We first did a week in Madrid with prebattle scenes: the challenges to the King, etc. All the Gielgud scenes that were not in the castle we did in his first week. The scene that was never used, Northumberland with Richard's coffin, was done in Colmenar just outside Madrid on the first day of shooting. Gielgud had just arrived and this was a scene where he didn't have to say anything—they just shot this thing coming toward him.

Then we went to Cardona to finish all the royal scenes: all the scenes in court, the King's confrontations with me, and his death. When Gielgud left Cardona, the Hotspur scenes with Marina Vlady were also shot in the same castle, around the back of it. My scenes at the end of the film where I say "Enlarge the man committed . . . ," was shot at Cardona, on a deserted battlement. A bit of my coronation was shot there too—some interiors with me walking through. And on our last day in Cardona, Orson shot the (unused) murder of Richard II. Then we returned to Madrid and did the Gadshill robbery in a wood in the Casa de Campo while the leaves were falling, and we filmed the scene by the boating lake between Hal and Poins. After that we started in the tavern and completed everything with Jeanne Moreau and Margaret Rutherford.

Then we went west to shoot against the walls of Avila; to the little medieval town of Pedraza for street scenes; then north to Soria searching for snow; and further north to the Basque area for the Shallow and Silence locations, returning to Madrid in December to start filming the battle sequences in the Casa de Campo. We had to shut down from Christmas 1964 to February 1965, but I stayed around. Orson wouldn't let me return to England (but of course I didn't want to return; I wanted to finish the film), and he continued to shoot small sequences for the battle even while we were shut down. When we really began again in February, we did a number of my long speeches. We shot the rest of the coronation in a church near Madrid. Then, in March, when all the other actors had left, we filled in the holes; we did the closeups for the play scene in the tavern, the rejection speech ("I know thee not, old man"), and most of Falstaff's big speeches.

Int.: It sounds as if some of the meatiest of Welles's own scenes were left for last.

KB: That's true. Partly he couldn't spare the time earlier, but also he was crippled with funk, strangely enough. It was his life's ambition to make this film and also to play Falstaff. He wanted this to be his statement. You felt that there was a great deal of him in Falstaff—this sort of trimming one's sails, always short of money, having to lie, perhaps, and to cheat. He obviously felt there was a lot of himself there in the character. But when you suddenly have the chance of your dream coming true, of doing what you've always wanted, you get a terrible attack of jitters. Also he'd seen Ralph Richardson play Falstaff and I think that frightened him a bit, too.

I can't tell you how he put off getting into makeup. He was forced into makeup when Margaret arrived, because he had a couple of scenes with her, and he was forced again with Jeanne Moreau to do the scenes with Doll. But when Jeanne and Margaret had gone, he wouldn't do the other scenes for months, especially his big speeches. We eventually did those alone, virtually alone. I should think it was April before we actually got around to doing the last closeups.

Int.: So Welles delayed because he had such an emotional investment in the film. Did he have similar problems when he was editing it?

KB: Yes, but that went beyond his feelings about Falstaff. He could never bear to leave a picture alone. He'd cut and cut and cut. Luckily, the man who was then running the Cannes Festival came to Madrid and saw a rough cut. He was so enthusiastic about it that he wanted the film for the festival. The producer needed to sell the film, so Welles was pressured into finishing the editing and then leaving it alone.

Int.: But despite Welles's obsessiveness, especially with regard to this film, it sounds as if he was great fun to work with.

KB: Absolutely. It was very larky making the film. We all had a lot of fun; it was wonderful, hilarious. There's a scene where I lift Gielgud up and help him up the stairs to the throne just before he dies. You can't really see it, but I stumbled a little, and then John stumbled, and Orson, who was up behind the camera, called out, "You're like the Dolly Sisters!" I mean, in the middle of the shooting!

Once a week or so, the rushes would be assembled in some cinema wherever we were filming, and we would all go off late at night to see them and we roared with laughter at all the mistakes. Orson adored that. Nobody laughed louder at any bad choice of acting than he did himself at his own performance. A lot of people who are serious about making films feel that means they have to be terribly solemn, but Orson never behaved that way. There was a tremendous amount of laughter.

Margaret Rutherford used to say that working with Orson was like walking where there was always sunshine. I felt that way too.

Reviews and
Commentaries

Reviews

osley Crowther, the influential film critic for the *New York Times,* was hostile to *Chimes* after seeing its opening at the Cannes Film Festival in 1966. He repeated his negative comments when the film was released in New York in 1967 and undoubtedly contributed to the film's failure to gain a substantial audience. (In addition to the excerpt reproduced here, Crowther offered a summary judgment six days later for the Sunday *Times* which accused Welles of "disgusting indulgence" and called the film a "dreary come-down" from *Citizen Kane.*) Other reviewers were less acerbic, but only Judith Crist among these early American reviewers found the film a major work. A more balanced view, some weeks after the film's first appearance, was that of Pauline Kael, but even she took as her point of departure its probable commercial failure. While early responses in England were mixed also, some English critics, interestingly, were less insistent on the authority of the Shakespearean texts and therefore more understanding of Welles's innovations. The most positive early responses came from France, a country whose film critics and scholars have always been especially admiring of Welles. The two samples included here (translated by the editor of this volume) are characteristic of French film criticism in tending to regard Welles as the creator of a body of work with consistent features, rather than in concentrating exclusively on this film.

New York Times

Bosley Crowther

Nothing has happened to Orson Welles' *Chimes at Midnight* since I saw it last spring at the Cannes Film Festival to cause me to alter my opinion of it. Although they have changed the title to *Falstaff* (which some people called it at Cannes) and are said to have tried to do something to make the dialogue track less fuzzy and incomprehensible than it was, it is still a confusing patchwork of scenes and characters, mainly from Shakespeare's *Henry IV, Parts 1* and *2*, designed to give major exposure to Jack Falstaff, performed by Mr. Welles. And it is still every bit as difficult as I found it then to comprehend what several of the actors are saying, especially Mr. Welles.

This difficulty of understanding Mr. Welles' basso profundo speech, which he seems to direct toward his innards instead of out through his lips, makes it all the more difficult to catch the drift of this great, bearded, untidy man who waddles and cocks his hairy eyebrows and generally bluffs his way through the film.

Is this Falstaff a truly jovial person? Does he have a genuine wit and a tavern-companion's grand affection for the fun-loving scapegrace, Prince Hal? Has he, deep down, a spirit of rebellion against stifling authority? Or is he merely what he looks like—a dissolute, bumbling, street-corner Santa Claus?

Evidently Mr. Welles' reading of Falstaff ranges between a farcical conception of him and a mawkish, sentimental attitude. He makes the old pot-bellied rascal an armor-plated buffoon in the midst of a wild and brutal Battle of Shrewsbury, in which Prince Hal slays the brave Henry (Hotspur) Percy (for which Falstaff claims credit, of course).

He makes him a sort of Jackie Gleason getting off one of his homilies when he gives the great apostrophe to Honor, much of which I simply couldn't understand. And he chokes up like a soap-opera grandmother when he is suddenly banished by the new Henry V, giving out with the cruel "I-know-thee-not-old-man" speech. Mr. Welles runs the gamut, as they say.

But he is still an inarticulate Falstaff. It is a big, tatterdemalion show, and it has no business intruding so brashly in the serious Shakespearean affairs of the

From the *New York Times*, March 20, 1967.

Lancasters, the Percies, and the Mortimers, which Mr. Welles does get to from time to time in this freely selected composite of scenes from Shakespeare, as it were. . . .

The picture, a Spanish-Swiss production, was shot in Spain, so that the scenery, especially that around the walled city of Avila, has a noticeable Spanish tone. Mr. Welles' black-and-white cameras are very busy most of the time, rushing around and sweeping in for mammoth close-ups. This accentuates the patchwork effect.

Mr. Welles has always wanted to play Falstaff. Now he's had his chance. Those who are interested may see him at the Little Carnegie.

New York World Journal Tribune

Judith Crist

O rson Welles's long-awaited *Chimes at Midnight* has arrived under the title of *Falstaff,* a title change that pays fitting tribute to the actor-director's superb portrait of Shakespeare's mountainous rogue.

And yet the original title was more in the mood of the dramatic history Welles has constructed [out of] five plays, a history of merry rompers grown old, their games aglow in their own memory but seen for their own crassness through the cool eyes of youth growing to maturity. It is a doddering Shallow's "Jesu—the days that we have seen!" that evokes an aged Falstaff's "Aye—we have heard the chimes at midnight"—and our awareness that the players are as worthless as the game.

This is the fascination of the Welles characterization of Falstaff. Intentionally or not, he has killed the charge of betrayal and ingratitude on Hal's part in his denial of his erstwhile companion upon his crowning. The heart does not go out to the old and foolish wastrel: Welles' Falstaff is a Rabelaisian behemoth, amusing, outrageous, imaginative, lusty—and quite unlovable. We had as lief believe that he died of the pox or cirrhosis of the liver or just general excess as suspect that his heart was broken by his rejection by the king.

The Welles chronicle—on screen it is Holinshed's, narrated by Sir Ralph Richardson—is culled from Shakespeare's *Richard II, Henry IV Parts I* and *II,* and *Henry V* and *Merry Wives of Windsor.* We see a troubled Henry IV facing rebellion by the Duke of Northumberland and his son, Hotspur, the young Percy who is all that the roistering Prince Hal is not. Through the wars we see Hal as a spoiled carouser, one who, however, despite his personal revolt against his father and jealousy of young Percy is aware of the worthlessness of his crasser companions. And finally we see him as a young man coming of age, aware of the betrayals by friends and foes alike and conscious of where duty lies. . . .

So excellent a cast has Welles rallied for his history that we get a rounded tale, one dominated now by John Gielgud's proud and deeply troubled Henry IV, now

From the *New York World Journal Tribune,* March 21, 1967.

by Keith Baxter's saturnine but vulnerably boyish Prince Hal, now by Norman
Rodway's fiery and youthful Henry Percy and only intermittently by his own
Falstaff.

Above all, there is the Wellesian respect for language, so that always there is
the Shakespearean flow, the poetry that provides the drama. Coming on the heels
of [Franco Zeffirelli's] *The Taming of the Shrew,* this film, stark, simple, concentrating on word and performance, serves as a reminder of where the substance of
the plays lies. . . .

The Times [London]

John Russell Taylor

When Orson Welles' *Falstaff* film was playing in Paris last year *Une Semaine de Paris,* with one of those Freudian slips for which French printers have a peculiar gift, persistently advertised it as *Crimes at Midnight.* Tempting to suggest that the crimes in question are against Shakespeare, but this would not be fair to Welles. His Falstaff, even if not the Falstaff we are familiar with, is a careful creation, intelligently thought out. The interpretation is highly personal, but perfectly fair. Only, it is not really very interesting.

Welles' Falstaff is conceived, as it were, from the end backwards. This is a hollow, rather sad Falstaff, not the big comic character who takes over the Henry IV plays willy-nilly, but a man born to affliction and rejection, living for most of the time in a fool's paradise which we at once recognize as such. The tone of the film which embodies him is dark, almost tragic. The moments of comedy are subdued, the action of the central battle sequence is doom-laden, and the final rejection of Falstaff comes as no surprise to anyone but himself. It is a Falstaff tailored, no doubt, to Welles' own qualities as an actor, which have never been importantly comic. As a director, therefore, he has chosen to put Prince Hal instead of Falstaff at the center of the drama.

This burden Keith Baxter as Prince Hal does his best to bear and his performance is by far the most telling in the film. Few others get much of a chance and some of the casting (Margaret Rutherford as Mistress Quickly, Jeanne Moreau as Doll Tearsheet) is bound to seem unnecessarily perverse unless the players are given room to justify it. The film is often visually splendid, if spectacularly un-English (the film was made in Spain, and looks it). It is certainly far more successful than Welles' last, *The Trial,* and yet there is inescapably something vital missing. Perhaps, after all, it is just Falstaff.

From *The Times* [London], March 23, 1967.

The New Statesman

John Coleman

Harder going to bring this [speaking lines well] off with Shakespeare and harder when the evidences of dubbing are all too often apparent, but Orson Welles's *Chimes at Midnight* has other resounding virtues. This is a movie drawn from the Welles Falstaff-play of several years ago, an arrogant (if you like) vehicle for a large talent. Its material may be found in the two parts of *Henry IV*, together with snippets from *Richard II, Henry V,* and *The Merry Wives of Windsor.* If Shakespeare found Falstaff's popularity so great he felt obliged to resuscitate him in *The Merry Wives,* as they say, then a kind of chop-logic should allow Mr. Welles his own liberties. I must say he takes them to some point. His swaggering knight is physically huge, strawberry-nosed: for a few crazed instants on the battlefield—in dark, swollen armour—the spitting image of Jarry's Ubu. The compilation film turns out to be substantially about spurning, the priggish new King rejecting the old fellow-roisterer. Welles himself has said: "The film was not intended as a lament for Falstaff, but for the death of Merrie England . . . the age of chivalry, of simplicity, of Maytime and all that. . . . It's the old England, dying and betrayed." This makes a sort of sense, and Welles from the beginning stresses the hazards of Falstaff's situation *vis-à-vis* Hal; Keith Baxter's Hal is a nasty piece of work, as is Shakespeare's, and constantly toys with good Sir Jack like some fat puppet. Welles has been reproached for playing down the early fun and revelry in favor of pathos: I can't see why. His interpretation is more reasonable than most.

Nor is his film devoid of humor: anything but. The scenes between Falstaff, Shallow (Alan Webb) and Silence (Walter Chiari) are excruciatingly well-conceived. Chiari's direst of stammers and Welles's eye-rolling impatience with it rate preservation alone. There are oddities of casting: Jeanne Moreau goes for little as Doll and Margaret Rutherford, great actress though she is, looks uneasy as a naughty old inn-keeper and procuress (though one sees why she is there when she comes to deliver the tremendous account of Falstaff's death). The battle

From *The New Stateman*, March 31, 1967.

scenes are very painful to watch, as battle scenes should be, chopped into bruising fragments by the editing as swords chop flesh. The men roll and rattle at last in grey mire, undignified statues of themselves. I suspect this is a film we shall return to with increasing admiration and affection. The Welles *Falstaff* has more subtlety to it than may meet the purist's eye.

The Spectator

Penelope Houston

tonnez-nous, Orson! This has been the demand made regularly to Orson Welles, seldom in vain, seldom left unsatisfied. One still approaches a Welles film in the expectation of a particular quality of excitement and surprise. And perhaps part of the slight sense of letdown one feels on first seeing his *Chimes at Midnight* is that it seems so unastonishing: a film of great sobriety, some bleakness, only intermittent visual flair, a film which seems to turn its back on brilliance.

That, at least, was how I felt about it after last year's Cannes Festival. But festival impressions can be notoriously unreliable, and at a second viewing it's the bone structure of the film, the line Welles has cut through his source material in the two parts of *Henry IV,* that commands attention. The flesh, on occasion, may be weak—uneven performances, some shaky post-synchronization, and an odd sense that John Gielgud's haggardly majestic Henry IV has barely been introduced to anyone else in the cast. But the bones are impressively strong and simple.

A lament for the death of Merrie England . . . ! is how Welles has summed up the film. And in case Merrie England may suggest tourist-board images of maypoles, thatch, and dancing on the green, Welles interprets it as a nobler conception, dying not in mellow autumn but with a wintry nip in the air. Over this version of the Falstaff story hangs the shadow of its ending: the Prince's rejection, Falstaff's death of a broken heart. What destroys Falstaff is cold power; and the film is shaped (as Welles' movies so often have been) into a study of how power overtakes those who want to exercise it.

Inevitably the Shakespearean balance of comedy is upset. Keith Baxter's cool, conniving Prince Hal is nobody's boon companion and this wary Machiavellian seems to be using horseplay as a chance to test out his own authority. So Welles' Falstaff becomes a man play-acting on borrowed time, until the Prince chooses to bring down the curtain. Falstaff stumbling about the battlefield, a mammoth sardine inside his armour, or beaming under a saucepan-lid crown, or enlisting

From *The Spectator,* March 31, 1967.

his amateur retinue, is the happy doom-haunted innocent at large. Playing him in a grizzled and jovial make-up, Welles contrives to look more like some Father Christmas banished from the toy department than a victim of medieval *realpolitik*.

For the shift of emphasis does diminish Falstaff, underlining every intimation of mortality, leaving him vulnerable as a foolish, fond old man. I suspect this wasn't necessarily Welles' intention, but that it was almost bound to follow from working the play, as it were, backwards, concentrating on the cold inevitability of the Prince's inheritance. What remains is less Falstaff as a great comic presence than Falstaff as a concept—"the old England, dying and betrayed." And, in spite of some emphatically Spanish settings, Welles' maytime England comes through as a sad, lost dream, a memory for garrulous old women (Margaret Rutherford's Mistress Quickly) and quavering old men who once heard the chimes at midnight.

The New Republic

Pauline Kael

You may want to walk out during the first twenty minutes of *Falstaff*. Although the words on the soundtrack are intelligible, the sound doesn't match the images. We hear the voices as if the speakers were close, but on the screen the figures may be a half mile away or turned from us at some angle that doesn't jibe with the voice. In the middle of a sentence an actor may walk away from us while the voice goes on. Often, for a second, we can't be sure who is supposed to be talking. And the cutting is maddening, designed as it is for camouflage—to keep us from seeing faces closely or from registering that mouths which should be open and moving are closed. Long shots and Shakespearean dialogue are a crazy mix. It's especially jarring because the casting is superb and the performance beautiful. It's not hard to take Shakespeare adapted and transformed by other cultures—like Kurosawa's *Throne of Blood*, a *Macbeth* almost as much related to Welles's as to Shakespeare's—but the words of Shakespeare slightly out of synch! This is as intolerable as those old prints of *Henry V* that the miserly distributors circulate—chewed up by generations of projection machines, crucial syllables lost in the splices. The editing rhythm of *Falstaff* is at war with the rhythm and comprehension of the language. Welles, avoiding the naturalistic use of the outdoors in which Shakespeare's dialogue sounds more stagey than on stage, has photographically stylized the Spanish locations, creating a theatrically darkened, slightly unrealistic world of angles and low beams and silhouettes. When this photographic style is shattered by the cuts necessary to conceal the dialogue problems, the camera angles seem unnecessarily exaggerated and pretentious. But then despite everything—the angles, the doubles in long shots, the editing that distracts us when we need to concentrate on the dialogue—the movie begins to be great. The readings in *Falstaff* are great even if they don't always go with the images, which are often great, too.

Welles has brought together the pieces of Falstaff that Shakespeare had strewn over the two parts of *Henry IV* and *The Merry Wives of Windsor*, with cuttings

From *The New Republic*, June 24, 1967.

from *Henry V* and *Richard II*, and fastened them into place with narration from Holinshed's Chronicles (read by Ralph Richardson). Those of us who resisted our schoolteachers' best efforts to make us appreciate the comic genius of Shakespeare's fools and buffoons will not be surprised that Welles wasn't able to make Falstaff very funny: he's a great conception of a character, but the charades and practical jokes seem meant to be funnier than they are. This movie does, however, provide the best Shakespearean comic moment I can recall: garrulous Falstaff sitting with Shallow (Alan Webb) and Silence (Walter Chiari), rolling his eyes in irritation and impatience at Silence's stammer. But Welles's Falstaff isn't essentially comic; W. C. Fields's Micawber wasn't either: these actors, so funny when they're playing with their own personae in roles too small for them, are not so funny when they're trying to measure up. The carousing and roistering in the tavern doesn't seem like such great fun either, though Welles and the cast work very hard to convince us it is. Oddly, we never really see the friendship of Prince Hal—played extraordinarily well by Keith Baxter—and Falstaff; the lighter side in *Henry IV, Part I* is lost—probably well lost, though we must take it for granted in the film. What we see are the premonitions of the end: Hal taking part in games that have gone stale for him, preparing himself for his final rejection of his adopted father Falstaff in order to turn into a worthy successor of his father the king. And we see what this does to Falstaff, the braggart with the heart of a child who expects to be forgiven everything, even what he knows to be unforgivable—his taking the credit away from Hal for the combat with Hotspur (Norman Rodway). Falstaff lacks judgment, which kings must have.

John Gielgud's Henry IV is the perfect contrast to Welles; Gielgud has never been so monkishly perfect in a movie. Welles could only get him for two weeks of the shooting and the makeshift of some of his scenes is obvious, but his performance gives the film the austerity it needs for the conflict in Hal to be dramatized. Gielgud's king is so refined—a skeleton too dignified for any flesh to cling to it, inhabited by a voice so modulated it is an exquisite spiritual whine. Merrie England? Falstaff at least provides a carcass to mourn over.

Welles as an actor had always been betrayed by his voice. It was too much and it was inexpressive; there was no warmth in it, no sense of a life lived. It was just an instrument that he played, and it seemed to be the key to something shallow and unfelt even in his best performances, and most fraudulent when he tried to make it tender. I remember that once, in *King Lear* on television, he hit a phrase and I thought his voice was emotionally right; it had beauty—and what a change it made in his acting! In *Falstaff* Welles seems to have grown into his voice; he's not too young for it anymore, and he's certainly big enough. And his emotions don't seem fake anymore; he's grown into them, too. He has the eyes for the role. Though his Falstaff is short on comedy, it's very rich, very full.

He has directed a sequence, the battle of Shrewsbury, which is unlike anything he has ever done, indeed unlike any battle ever done on the screen before. It ranks with the best of Griffith, John Ford, Eisenstein, Kurosawa—that is, with the best ever done. How can one sequence in this movie be so good? It has no dialogue and so he isn't handicapped: for the only time in the movie he can edit, not to cover gaps and defects but as an artist. The compositions suggest Uccello and the chilling ironic music is a death knell for all men in battle. The soldiers, plastered by the mud they fall in, are already monuments. It's the most brutally somber battle ever filmed. It does justice to Hotspur's great "O, Harry, thou hast robbed me of my youth."

Welles has filled the cast with box-office stars. Margaret Rutherford, Jeanne Moreau, Marina Vlady are all in it (though the girl I like best is little Beatrice Welles as the pageboy). And Falstaff is the most popular crowd-pleasing character in the work of the most enduringly popular writer who ever lived. Yet, because of technical defects due to poverty, Welles's finest Shakespearean production to date—another near-masterpiece, and this time so very close— cannot reach a large public. There ain't no way.

Cahiers du Cinéma

Serge Daney

Welles says of Falstaff "that he fights a battle that has already been lost." And further, "I do not believe that he is looking for anything. He represents a value. He is goodness." There is something very astonishing in the fact that power and genius—unanimously acclaimed as such—should celebrate only hopeless causes or grandiose falls, and that a man like Welles, whose influence on his colleagues is so undeniable, embodies in his art only those who have been defeated. Admittedly this is obscured by an impressive technology, but nonetheless his protagonists tend to be worn out by life, betrayed by those close to them. An extraordinary fate decrees that a man who is too strong can only come to a bad end. And yet from Kane to Falstaff, from pomp to nakedness, from a corpse one doesn't see to a coffin that is carried away, it is always the same story: that of a man who misuses his power.

. . . The conquest of power (aspiring to it, living up to it, obtaining it by force) is precisely what Welles deals with the least. For him, this kind of power is represented by the witches who create Macbeth and the intuition which propels Quinlan. Welles's films start where others end; when everything has been won, the only thing left is to be stripped of all knowledge as death approaches: Quinlan yesterday, Falstaff today.

Welles's work, faithful to Shakespeare in this respect, is a reflection on the very idea of Power: that excess of freedom which nobody can pursue without finding degradation and ridicule at the end. Power is an evil that gives life only to those who do not already have it. Heroic undertakings, actions that succeed in changing the course of events, intricately woven plots: these belong to men of the future, who are born to "tread on kings," men to whom it is granted, at least once in their lives, to shake the world. Kings have other cares; their triumph, like repression or the fruitless re-creation of the past, confers no prestige by definition. Defeat is the only adventure left to them.

Absolute power destroys true power, reducing it to futility. "If there is a sense of reality," Musil says, "there must also be a sense of the possible." And a little

From *Cahiers du Cinéma* 181 (August 1966):27–28.

further on he adds, "God himself undoubtedly prefers to talk about his creation as potentiality." When power is too great, the possible consumes reality, dooming it in advance: one action is then no more necessary than another; good and evil are interchangeable and equally meaningless. A man like Citizen Kane, who is master of the possible at the age of twenty, winds up being the slave of his whims, surrendering bit by bit to a power that has neither object nor echo, and to action which is arbitrary and foolish, useless and wasteful, which never involves him fully but which distances him more and more from others (like the career of a singer who has no voice, or the collections heaped up at Xanadu). He who has the power to do the most achieves the least, or uses only a fraction of his power. The laws of humor require that a prodigious expenditure of energy results in a strictly useless life.

In film after film as his work develops and as Welles grows older, the inclination to mockery grows stronger, to the point of becoming the very subject of the film Welles considers his best, *The Trial*. Everywhere and always, power is in bad hands. Those who have it either do not know enough (Othello, who believes Iago; Macbeth, who is the victim of wordplay), or too much (Arkadin, Quinlan, the lawyer Hastler)—all doomed to act for nothing out of excessive naiveté or intelligence.

In terms of money, the life of John Falstaff is a failure. Shortly before dying, he observes that his friend—the doddering but shrewd Robert Shallow—has succeeded better, and he resolves to cultivate his friendship. Only Falstaff's sudden death, of which there has been no warning, spares him what would undoubtedly have been a last disillusionment. Falstaff was not born to receive, but to give—indiscriminately and without hope of return—or, if he has nothing, to give him*self* theatrically. Welles calls this prodigality the goodness of Falstaff (and the character himself remarks: "I am not only witty in myself, but the cause that wit is in others"—a good definition of genius). That Falstaff—whom Shakespeare especially wanted to be ridiculous—should have become a moving character as imagined and then embodied by Welles, is not very surprising. His death is not the mysterious and legendary disappearance of a Kane, but the prosaic and unadorned event into which the end of the world must be read (although nothing is really emphasized). "If all the year were playing holidays," says the young prince, "to sport would be as tedious as to work." Of what is Falstaff guilty? Not so much of having misused his power, since he hardly has any, being a comic character and one without real courage or authority into the bargain. Perhaps of having been intemperate in his use of words, of having turned his power of parody into an interminably hammy act, an unproductive and tiresome one, where talent, if there is any, asserts itself to no purpose. Even more surely, he is guilty of having survived the squandering of his energy for so long (indicated by the wordplay on "waste" and "waist"). And even more seriously, he is the victim, rather than the guilty one, in making a bad use of his feelings, since he chooses as his friend the very person who will betray him.

Welles's work offers especially many examples of breaches of confidence (*The Lady from Shanghai*) or betrayed friendships (*Othello*). The strange and scandalous complicity that links the young prince and Falstaff for so long reveals more and more clearly that which is never spoken: the differences in their natures. But there would be no mutual fascination if each of them did not feel himself as radically Other: they are symbols of two worlds that are inimical but complementary, opposite sides of the same coin. On one side there is Falstaff, who lives off his past, off what he already is, in the gradual entropy of a freedom that has deliberately been abused. On the other, there is the future Henry V, who is nothing yet, who will perhaps be a great king if he discovers the proper relationship between the expenditure of effort and the object to be attained: the austerity and discipline which make the use of power possible.

Cahiers du Cinéma

Pierre Duboeuf

The almost monstrous egocentricity of the characters Welles played in his films in the past was seductive only because it was accompanied by a more or less discernible degree of vulnerability. Beyond self-affirmation, some scattered but explicit signs betrayed anxiety and weakness: a certain irritation in the movement of the eyebrows, the tension of the gaze, which was sometimes extreme, or some hesitation in the character's demeanor gave him a dimension of pathos and gave rise to that sense of fragility which the most instinctive power emits. Once the weakness or the sensitive point has been perceived, the attraction was as irresistible as the initial repulsion had been strong.

Falstaff gives us an inverted reflection of this moral picture, which Welles has devoted himself to refashioning in film after film. It isn't that the film shows a changed posture on Welles's part, or a new orientation for his art, but rather that in the course of the same kind of investigation, he makes a sort of moral discovery. The primitive power that energized him in the past has lost its edge, to the point where the components of his portrait have been modified, not so much in themselves as in the way they are recombined. Formerly, crass power crushed the character's underlying virtues; today, degraded and ridiculed by age, that same power lets one see what was latent and barely perceptible before: vulnerability and a certain goodness, the final form which power or weakness takes and which determines the emotional tone of the film.

. . . For the distance is great from the gloomy shot of *Othello* from which Welles's tense face emerges to the milky, pure whiteness of *Falstaff;* there is a great distance, too, from the willful, dominating countenance of Kane or Arkadin to the wide range of expression and the abandon touched with melancholy of Jack Falstaff. In the process, Welles has lost his visual aggressiveness, and if an extreme low-angle shot reappears from time to time, it is rather like a nostalgic reference to the past. But he bends with Rembrandt-like anxiety over his own face, aware that there are other harmonies—accents less brilliant but more human that he substitutes for the bright flashes of the past, so that the glacial image of old Kane, reflected to infinity in the mirrors of Xanadu, effaces itself before that of a king's jester, which is closer to life.

From *Cahiers du Cinéma* 181 (August 1966), 28–31.

Commentaries

The three essays reprinted in this section have been chosen to give a range of perspectives on *Chimes*, especially themes not developed in my Introduction. C. L. Barber's essay on the function of misrule in Shakespeare's *Henry IV* is notable for its sensitivity and balance on a subject that has long divided conservative from liberal responses to the history plays. Dudley Andrew places Welles's emphasis on time and death in *Chimes* within the context of his filmic language in general. And Michael Anderegg explores a subject that has distressed some viewers of the film: the lack of prominence that it sometimes gives to Shakespeare's language.

Rule and Misrule in
Henry IV

C. L. Barber

> If all the year were playing holidays,
> To sport would be as tedious as to work . . .

The two parts of *Henry IV,* written probably in 1597 and 1598, are an astonishing
development of drama in the direction of inclusiveness, a development possible
because of the range of the traditional culture and the popular theater, but realized only because Shakespeare's genius for construction matched his receptivity.
We have noticed how, early in his career, Shakespeare made brilliant use of the
long standing tradition of comic accompaniment and counterstatement by the
clown. Now suddenly he takes the diverse elements in the potpourri of the popular chronicle play and composes a structure in which they draw each other out.
The Falstaff comedy, far from being forced into an alien environment of historical drama, is begotten by that environment, giving and taking meaning as it
grows. The implications of the saturnalian attitude are more drastically and in-
clusively expressed here than anywhere else, because here misrule is presented
along with rule and along with the tensions that challenge rule. Shakespeare
dramatizes not only holiday but also the need for holiday and the need to limit
holiday. . . .

Mingling Kings and Clowns

The fascination of Falstaff as a dramatic figure has led criticism . . . to center *I
Henry IV* on him, and to treat the rest of the play merely as a setting for him. But
despite his predominating imaginative significance, the play is centered on Prince
Hal, developing in such a way as to exhibit in the prince an inclusive, sovereign
nature fitted for kingship. The relation of the prince to Falstaff can be summarized fairly adequately in terms of the relation of holiday to everyday. As the
non-historical material came to Shakespeare in *The Famous Victories of Henry*

From *Shakespeare's Festive Comedy* (Princeton: Princeton University Press, 1959), pp. 192–221.

the Fifth, the prince was cast in the traditional role of the prodigal son, while his disreputable companions functioned as tempters in the same general fashion as the Vice of the morality plays. At one level Shakespeare keeps this pattern, but he shifts the emphasis away from simple moral terms. The issue, in his hands, is not whether Hal will be good or bad but whether he will be noble or degenerate, whether his holiday will become his everyday. The interregnum of a Lord of Misrule, delightful in its moment, might develop into the anarchic reign of a favorite dominating a dissolute king. Hal's secret, which he confides early to the audience, is that for him Falstaff is merely a pastime, to be dismissed in due course:

> If all the year were playing holidays,
> To sport would be as tedious as to work;
> But when they seldom come, they wish'd-for come . . .
>   (I.ii.228–230)

The prince's sports, accordingly, express not dissoluteness but a fine excess of vitality—"as full of spirit as the month of May"—together with a capacity for occasionally looking at the world as though it were upside down. His energy is controlled by an inclusive awareness of the rhythm in which he is living: despite appearances, he will not make the mistake which undid Richard II, who played at saturnalia until it caught up with him in earnest. During the battle of Shrewsbury (when, in Hotspur's phrase, "Doomsday is near"), Hal dismisses Falstaff with "What! is it a time to jest and dally now?" (V.iii.57). This sense of timing, of the relation of holiday to everyday and doomsday, contributes to establishing the prince as a sovereign nature.

But the way Hal sees the relations is not the way other people see them, nor indeed the way the audience sees them until the end. The holiday-everyday antithesis is his resource for control, and in the end he makes it stick. But before that, the only clear-cut definition of relations in these terms is in his single soliloquy, after his first appearance with Falstaff. Indeed, it is remarkable how little satisfactory formulation there is of the relationships which the play explores dramatically. It is essential to the play that the prince should be misconstrued, that the king should see "riot and dishonor stain" (I.i.85) his brow, that Percy should patronize him as a "nimble-footed madcap" (IV.ii.95) who might easily be poisoned with a pot of ale if it were worth the trouble. But the absence of adequate summary also reflects the fact that Shakespeare was doing something which he could not summarize, which only the whole resources of his dramatic art could convey.

It is an open question, throughout *Part One*, as to just who or what Falstaff is. At the very end, when Prince John observes "This is the strangest tale that ever I heard," Hal responds with "This is the strangest fellow, brother John" (V.iv.158– 159). From the beginning, Falstaff is constantly renaming himself:

> Marry, then, sweet wag, when thou art king, let not us that are squires of the night's body be called thieves of the day's beauty. Let us be Diana's For-esters, Gentlemen of the Shade, Minions of the Moon; and let men say we be men of good government . . .
>
> (I.ii.26–31)

Here Misrule is asking to be called Good Government, as it is his role to do—though he does so with a wink which sets real good government at naught, concluding with "steal":

> . . . men of good government, being governed as the sea is, by our noble and chaste mistress the moon, under whose countenance we steal.
>
> (I.ii.31–33)

I have considered in an earlier chapter how the witty equivocation Falstaff prac-tices, like that of Nashe's Bacchus and other apologists for folly and vice, alludes to the very morality it is flouting. Such "damnable iteration" is a sport that implies a rolling-eyed awareness of both sides of the moral medal; the prince summarizes it in saying that Sir John "was never yet a breaker of proverbs. He will give the devil his due" (I.ii.131–133). It is also a game to be played with cards close to the chest. A Lord of Misrule naturally does not call himself Lord of Misrule in setting out to reign, but takes some title with the life of pretense in it. Falstaff's pretensions, moreover, are not limited to one occasion, for he is not properly a holiday lord, but a *de facto* buffoon who makes his way by continually seizing, catch as catch can, on what names and meanings the moment offers. He is not a professed buffoon—few buffoons, in life, are apt to be. In Renaissance courts, the role of buffoon was recognized but not necessarily formalized, not necessarily altogether distinct from the role of favorite. And he is a highwayman: Shakespeare draws on the euphemistic, mock-chivalric cant by which "the pro-fession" grace themselves. Falstaff in *Part One* plays it that he is Hal's friend, a gentleman, a "gentleman of the shade," and a soldier; he even enjoys turning the tables with "Thou hast done much harm upon me, Hal . . . I must give over this life, and I will give it over . . . I'll be damn'd for never a king's son in Christendom" (I.ii.102–109). It is the essence of his character, and his role, in *Part One*, that he never comes to rest where we can see him for what he "is." He is always in motion, always adopting postures, assuming characters.

That he does indeed care for Hal can be conveyed in performance without imposing sentimental tableaux on the action, provided that actors and producer recognize that he cares for the prince after his own fashion. It is from the prince that he chiefly gets his meaning, as it is from real kings that mock kings always get their meaning. We can believe it when we hear in *Henry V* that banishment has "killed his heart" (II.i.92). But to make much of a personal affection for the prince is a misconceived way to find meaning in Falstaff. His extraordinary meaningfulness comes from the way he manages to live "out of all order, out of all compass" by his wit and his wits; and from the way he keeps reflecting on the rest of the action, at first indirectly by the mock roles that he plays, at the end directly by his comments at the battle. Through this burlesque and mockery an intelligence of the highest order is expressed. It is not always clear whether the intelligence is Falstaff's or the dramatist's; often the question need not arise. Romantic criticism went the limit in ascribing a God-like superiority to the character, to the point of insisting that he tells the lies about the multiplying men in buckram merely to amuse, that he knew all the time at Gadshill that it was with Hal and Poins that he fought. To go so far in that direction obviously destroys the drama—spoils the joke in the case of the "incomprehensible lies," a joke which, as E. E. Stoll abundantly demonstrates, must be a joke *on* Falstaff. On the other hand, I see no reason why actor and producer should not do all they can to make us enjoy the intellectual mastery involved in Falstaff's comic resource and power of humorous redefinition. It is crucial that he should not be made so superior that he is never in predicaments, for his genius is expressed in getting out of them. But he does have genius, as Maurice Morgan rightly insisted though in a misconceived way. Through his part Shakespeare expressed attitudes towards experience which, grounded in a saturnalian reversal of values, went beyond that to include a radical challenge to received ideas.

Throughout the first three acts of *Part One*, the Falstaff comedy is continuously responsive to the serious action. There are constant parallels and contrasts with what happens at court or with the rebels. And yet these parallels are not explicitly noticed; the relations are presented, not formulated. So the first scene ends in a mood of urgency, with the tired king urging haste: "come yourself with speed to us again." The second scene opens with Hal asking Falstaff "What a devil hast thou to do with the time of day?" The prose in which he explains why time is nothing to Sir John is wonderfully leisurely and abundant, an elegant sort of talk that has all the time in the world to enjoy the completion of its schematized patterns:

> Unless hours were cups of sack, and minutes capons, and clocks the tongues of bawds, and dials the signs of leaping houses, and the blessed sun himself a fair hot wench in flame-colored taffeta, I see no reason why thou shouldst be so superfluous to demand the time of day.
>
> (I.ii.7–13)

The same difference in the attitude towards time runs throughout and goes with the difference between verse and prose mediums. A similar contrast obtains about lese majesty. Thus at their first appearance Falstaff insults Hal's majesty with casual, off-hand wit which the prince tolerates (while getting his own back by jibing at Falstaff's girth):

> And I prithee, sweet wag, when thou art king, as God save thy Grace—
>   Majesty I should say, for grace thou wilt have none—
> PRINCE. What, none?
> FALSTAFF. No, by my troth; not so much as will serve to be prologue to an egg and butter.
> PRINCE. Well, how then? Come, roundly, roundly.
>
> (I.ii.17–25)

In the next scene, we see Worcester calling into question the grace of Bolingbroke, "that same greatness to which our own hands / Have holp to make so portly" (I.iii.12–13). The King's response is immediate and drastic, and his lines point a moral that Hal seems to be ignoring:

> Worcester, get thee gone; for I do see
> Danger and disobedience in thine eye.
> O, sir, your presence is too bold and peremptory,
> And majesty might never yet endure
> The moody frontier of a servant brow.
>
> (I.iii.15–19)

Similar parallels run between Hotspur's heroics and Falstaff's mockheroics. In the third scene we hear Hotspur talking of "an easy leap / To pluck bright honor from the pale-face'd moon" (I.iii.201–202). Then in the robbery, Falstaff is complaining that "Eight yards of uneven ground is threescore and ten miles afoot for me," and asking "Have you any levers to lift me up again, being down?" (II.ii.25–28, 36) After Hotspur enters exclaiming against the cowardly lord who has written that he will not join the rebellion, we have Falstaff's entrance to the tune of "A plague of all cowards" (II.iv.127). And so on, and so on. Shakespeare's art has reached the point where he makes everything foil to everything else. Hal's imagery, in his soliloquy, shows the dramatist thinking about such relations: "like bright metal on a sullen ground, / My reformation, glitt'ring o'er my fault" (I.ii.236–237).

Now it is not true that Falstaff's impudence about Hal's grace undercuts Bolingbroke's majesty, nor that Sir John's posture as a hero among cowards invalidates the heroic commitment Hotspur expresses when he says "but I tell you, my lord fool, out of this nettle, danger, we pluck this flower, safety" (II.iii.11–12). The relationship is not one of a mocking echo. Instead, there is a certain distance between the comic and serious strains which leaves room for a complex interaction, organized by the crucial role of the prince. . . .

. . . Hotspur's quality is not invalidated; rather, his achievement is *placed*. It is included within a wider field which contains also the drawers, mine host, Mistress Quickly, and by implication, not only "all the good lads of Eastcheap" but all the estates of England. When we saw Hotspur and his Lady, he was not foolish, but delightful in his headlong, spontaneous way. His Lady has a certain pathos in the complaints which serve to convey how all absorbing his battle passion is. But the joke is with him as he mocks her:

> Love? I love thee not;
> I care not for thee, Kate. This is no world
> To play with mammets and to tilt with lips.
> We must have bloody noses and crack'd crowns,
> And pass them current, too. Gods me, my horse!
> (II.iii.93–97)

One could make some very broad fun of Hotspur's preference for his horse over his wife. But there is nothing of the kind in Shakespeare: here and later, his treatment values the conversion of love into war as one of the important human powers. Hotspur has the fullness of life and the unforced integrity of the great aristocrat who has never known what it is to cramp his own style. His style shows it; he speaks the richest, freshest poetry of the play, in lines that take all the scope they need to fulfill feeling and perception. . . .

The whole effect, in the opening acts, when there is little commentary on the spectacle as a whole, is of life overflowing its bounds by sheer vitality. Thieves and rebels and honest men—"one that hath abundance of charge too, God knows what" (II.i.64)—ride up and down on the commonwealth, pray to her and prey on her. Hotspur exults that "That roan shall be my throne" (II.iii.73). Falstaff exclaims, "Shall I? Content. This chair shall be my state" (II.iv.415). Hal summarizes the effect, after Hotspur is dead, with

> When that this body did contain a spirit,
> A kingdom for it was too small a bound.
>   (V.iv.89–90)

The stillness when he says this, at the close of the battle, is the moment when his royalty is made manifest. When he stands poised above the prostrate bodies of Hotspur and Falstaff, his position on the stage and his lines about the two heroes express a nature which includes within a larger order the now subordinated parts of life which are represented in those two: in Hotspur, honor, the social obligation to courage and self-sacrifice, a value which has been isolated in this magnificently anarchical feudal lord to become almost everything; and in Falstaff, the complementary *joie de vivre* which rejects all social obligations with "I like not such grinning honour as Sir Walter hath. Give me life" (V.iii.61). . . .

In valid heroic and majestic action, the bodies of the personages are constantly being elevated by becoming the vehicles of social meanings; in the comedy, such elevation becomes burlesque, and in the repeated failures to achieve a fusion of body and symbol, abstract meanings keep falling back into the physical. "A plague of sighing and grief! it blows a man up like a bladder" (II.iv.365–366). The repetition of such joking about Falstaff's belly makes it meaningful in a very special way, as a symbol of the process of inflation and collapse of meaning. So it represents the power of the individual life to continue despite the collapse of social roles. This continuing on beyond definitions is after all what we call "the body" in one main meaning of the term: Falstaff's belly is thus the essence of body—an essence which can be defined only dynamically, by failures of meaning. The effect of indestructible vitality is reinforced by the association of Falstaff's figure with the gay eating and drinking of Shrove Tuesday and Carnival. Whereas, in the tragedy, the reduction is to a body which can only die, here reduction is to a body which typifies our power to eat and drink our way through a shambles of intellectual and moral contradictions.

So we cannot resist sharing Falstaff's genial self-love when he commends his vision of plump Jack to the prince, just as we share the ingenuous self-love of a little child. But the dramatist is ever on the alert to enforce the ironies that dog the tendency of fantasy to equate the self with "all the world." So a most monstrous watch comes beating at the doors which have been clapped to against care; everyday breaks in on holiday.

The Trial of Carnival in *Part Two*

In *Part One,* Falstaff reigns, within his sphere, as Carnival; *Part Two* is very largely taken up with his trial. To put Carnival on trial, run him out of town, and burn or bury him is in folk custom a way of limiting, by ritual, the attitudes and impulses set loose by ritual. Such a trial, though conducted with gay hoots and jeers, serves to swing the mind round to a new vantage, where it sees misrule no longer as a benign release for the individual, but as a source of destructive consequences for society. This sort of reckoning is what *Part Two* brings to Falstaff.

But Falstaff proves extremely difficult to bring to book—more difficult than an ordinary mummery king—because his burlesque and mockery are developed to a point where the mood of a moment crystallizes as a settled attitude of scepticism. As we have observed before, in a static, monolithic society, a Lord of Misrule can be put back in his place after the revel with relative ease. The festive burlesque of solemn sanctities does not seriously threaten social values in a monolithic culture, because the license depends utterly upon what it mocks: liberty is unable to envisage any alternative to the accepted order except the standing of it on its head. But Shakespeare's culture was not monolithic: though its moralists assumed a single order, scepticism was beginning to have ground to stand on and look about—especially in and around London. So a Lord of Misrule figure, brought up, so to speak, from the country to the city, or from the traditional past into the changing present, could become on the Bankside the mouthpiece not merely for the dependent holiday scepticism which is endemic in a traditional society, but also for a dangerously self-sufficient everyday scepticism. When such a figure is set in an environment of sober-blooded great men behaving as opportunistically as he, the effect is to raise radical questions about social sanctities. At the end of *Part Two,* the expulsion of Falstaff is presented by the dramatist as getting rid of this threat; Shakespeare has recourse to a primitive procedure to meet a modern challenge. We shall find reason to question whether this use of ritual entirely succeeds.

But the main body of *Part Two*, what I am seeing as the trial, as against the expulsion, is wonderfully effective drama. The first step in trying Carnival, the first step in ceasing to be his subjects, would be to stop calling him "My Lord" and call him instead by his right name, Misrule. Now this is just the step which Falstaff himself takes for us at the outset of *Part Two;* when we first see him, he is setting himself up as an institution, congratulating himself on his powers *as* buffoon and wit. . . . In the saturnalian scenes of *Part One*, we saw that it is impossible to say just who he is; but in *Part Two*, Falstaff sets himself up at the outset as Falstaff:

> I am not only witty in myself, but the cause that wit is in other men. . . .
> A pox of this gout! a gout of this pox! for one or the other plays the rogue
> with my great toe. 'Tis no matter if I do halt. I have the wars for my colour,
> and my pension shall seem the more reasonable. A good wit will make use
> of anything. I will turn diseases to commodity.
>
> (I.ii.11–12, 273–278)

In the early portion of *Part One* he never spoke in asides, but now he constantly confides his schemes and his sense of himself to the audience. We do not have to see through him, but watch instead from inside his façades as he imposes them on others. Instead of warm amplifications centered on himself, his talk now consists chiefly of bland impudence or dry, denigrating comments on the way of the world. Much of the comedy is an almost Jonsonian spectacle where we relish a witty knave gulling fools.

It is this self-conscious Falstaff, confident of setting up his holiday license on an everyday basis, who at once encounters, of all awkward people, the Lord Chief Justice. From there on, during the first two acts, he is constantly put in the position of answering for his way of life; in effect he is repeatedly called to trial and keeps eluding it only by a "more than impudent sauciness" (II.i.123) and the privilege of his official employment in the wars. Mistress Quickly's attempt to arrest him is wonderfully ineffectual; but he notably fails to thrust the Lord Chief Justice from a level consideration. Hal and Poins then disguise themselves, not this time for the sake of the incomprehensible lies that Falstaff will tell, but in order to try him, to see him "bestow himself . . . in his true colours" (II.ii.186). So during the first two acts we are again and again put in the position of judging him, although we continue to laugh with him. A vantage is thus established from which we watch him in action in Gloucestershire, where the Justice he has to deal with is so shallow that Falstaff's progress is a triumph. The comedy is still delightful; Falstaff is still the greatest of wits; but we are constantly shown fun that involves fraud. Falstaff himself tells us about his game, with proud relish. Towards the end of the play, Hal's reconciliation with his father and then with the Lord Chief Justice reemphasizes the detached vantage of judgment. So no leading remarks are necessary to assure our noting and marking when we hear Falstaff shouting, "Let us take any man's horses; the laws of England are at my commandment. Blessed are they that have been my friends, and woe unto my lord chief justice!" (V.iii.140–144). The next moment we watch Doll and the Hostess being hauled off by Beadles because "the man is dead that you and Pistol beat among you" (V.iv.18).

Many of the basic structures in this action no doubt were shaped by morality-play encounters between Virtues and Vices, encounters which from my vantage here can be seen as cognate to the festive and scapegoat pattern. The trial of Falstaff is so effective *as drama* because no one conducts it—it happens. Falstaff, being a dramatic character, not a mummery, does not know when he has had his day. And he does not even recognize the authority who will finally sentence him: he mistakes Hal for a bastard son of the king's (II.iv.307). The result of the trial is to make us see perfectly the necessity for the rejection of Falstaff as a man, as a favorite for a king, as the leader of an interest at court.

But I do not think that the dramatist is equally successful in justifying the rejection of Falstaff as a mode of awareness. The problem is not in justifying rejection morally but in making the process cogent *dramatically,* as in *Part One* we reject magical majesty or intransigent chivalry. . . .

We have seen that Shakespeare typically uses ritual patterns of behavior and thought precisely in the course of making clear, by tragic or comic irony, that rituals have no *magical* efficacy. The reason for his failure at the close of *Part Two* is that at this point he himself uses ritual, not ironically transformed into drama, but magically. To do this involves a restriction instead of an extension of awareness. An extension of control and awareness is consummated in the epiphany of Hal's majesty while he is standing over Hotspur and Falstaff at the end of *Part One*. But *Part Two* ends with drastic restriction of awareness which goes with the embracing of magical modes of thought, not humorously but sentimentally.

It is true that the latter half of *Part Two* very effectively builds up to its finale by recurrent expression of a laboring need to be rid of a growth or humor. King Henry talks of the body of his kingdom as foul with rank diseases (III.i.39), and recalls Richard's prophecy that "foul sin gathering head / Shall break into corruption" (III.i.76–77). There are a number of other images of expulsion, such as the striking case where the rebels speak of the need to "purge th' obstructions which begin to stop / Our very veins of life" (IV.i.65–66). Henry himself is sick in the last half of the play, and there are repeated suggestions that his sickness is the consequence both of his sinful usurpation and of the struggle to defend it. Since his usurpation was almost a public duty, and his defense of order clearly for England's sake as well as his own advantage, he becomes in these last scenes almost a sacrificial figure, a king who sins for the sake of society, suffers for society in suffering for his sin, and carries his sin off into death. Hal speaks of the crown having "fed upon the body of my father" (IV.v.160). Henry, in his last long speech, summarizes this pattern in saying:

> God knows, my son,
> By what bypaths and indirect crook'd ways
> I met this crown; and I myself know well
> How troublesome it sat upon my head.
> To thee it shall descend with better quiet,
> Better opinion, better confirmation;
> For all the soil of the achievement goes
> With me into the earth.
> (IV.v.184–191)

The same image of burying sin occurs in some curious lines with which Hal reassures his brothers:

> My father is gone wild into his grave;
> For in his tomb lie my affections . . .
> (V.ii.123–124)

This conceit not only suggests an expulsion of evil, but hints at the patricidal motive which is referred to explicitly elsewhere in these final scenes and is the complement of the father-son atonement.

Now this sacrificial imagery, where used by and about the old king, is effectively dramatic, because it does not ask the audience to abandon any part of the awareness of a human, social situation which the play as a whole has expressed. But the case is altered when Hal turns on "that father ruffian" Falstaff. The new king's whip-lash lines stress Falstaff's age and glance at his death:

> I know thee not, old man. Fall to thy prayers.
> How ill white hairs become a fool and jester!
> I have long dreamt of such a kind of man,
> So surfeit-swell'd, so old, and so profane;

> But being awak'd, I do despise my dream.
> Make less thy body, hence, and more thy grace;
> Leave gormandising. Know the grave doth gape
> For thee thrice wider than for other men.
>
> (V.v.51–58)

The priggish tone, to which so many have objected, can be explained at one level as appropriate to the solemn occasion of a coronation. But it goes with a drastic narrowing of awareness. There are of course occasions in life when people close off parts of their minds—a coronation is a case in point: Shakespeare, it can be argued, is simply putting such an occasion into his play. But even his genius could not get around the fact that to block off awareness of irony is contradictory to the very nature of drama, which has as one of its functions the extension of such awareness. Hal's lines, redefining his holiday with Falstaff as a dream, and then despising the dream, seek to invalidate that holiday pole of life, instead of including it, as his lines on his old acquaintance did at the end of *Part One*. (Elsewhere in Shakespeare, to dismiss dreams categorically is foolhardy.) And those lines about the thrice-wide grave: are they a threat or a joke? We cannot tell, because the sort of consciousness that would confirm a joke is being damped out: "Reply not to me with a fool-born jest" (V.v.59). If ironies about Hal were expressed by the context, we could take the scene as the representation of his becoming a prig. But there is simply a blur in the tone, a blur which results, I think, from a retreat into magic by the *dramatist,* as distinct from his characters. Magically, the line about burying the belly is exactly the appropriate threat. It goes with the other images of burying sin and wildness and conveys the idea that the grave can swallow what Falstaff's belly stands for. To assume that one can cope with a pervasive attitude of mind by dealing physically with its most prominent symbol—what is this but magic-mongering? It is the same sort of juggling which we get in Henry IV's sentimental lines taking literally the name of the Jerusalem chamber in the palace:

> Laud be to God! Even there my life must end.
> It hath been prophesied to me many years,
> I should not die but in Jerusalem . . .
>
> (IV.v.236–238)

One can imagine making a mockery of Henry's pious ejaculation by catcalling a version of his final lines at the close of *Richard II* (V.vi.49–50):

> Is this that voyage to the Holy Land
> To wash the blood from off your guilty hand?

An inhibition of irony goes here with Henry's making the symbol do for the thing, just as it does with Hal's expulsion of Falstaff. A return to an official view of the sanctity of state is achieved by sentimental use of magical relations.

We can now suggest a few tentative conclusions of a general sort about the relation of comedy to ritual. It appears that comedy uses ritual in the process of redefining ritual as the expression of particular personalities in particular circumstances. The heritage of ritual gives universality and depth. The persons of the drama make the customary gestures developed in ritual observance, and, in doing so, they project in a wholehearted way attitudes which are not normally articulated at large. At the same time, the dramatization of such gestures involves being aware of their relation to the whole of experience in a way which is not necessary for the celebrants of a ritual proper. In the actual observance of customary misrule, the control of the disruptive motives which the festivity expresses is achieved by the group's recognition of the place of the whole business within the larger rhythm of their continuing social life. No one need decide, therefore, whether the identifications involved in the ceremony are magically valid or merely expressive. But in the drama, perspective and control depend on presenting, along with the ritual gestures, an expression of a social situation out of which they grow. So the drama must control magic by reunderstanding it as imagination: dramatic irony must constantly dog the wish that the mock king be real, that the self be all the world or set all the world at naught. When, through a failure of irony, the dramatist presents ritual as magically valid, the result is sentimental, since drama lacks the kind of control which in ritual comes from the auditors' being participants. Sentimental "drama," that which succeeds in being neither comedy nor tragedy, can be regarded from this vantage as theater used as a substitute for ritual, without the commitment to participation and discipline proper to ritual nor the commitment to the fullest understanding proper to comedy or tragedy.

Historically, Shakespeare's drama can be seen as part of the process by which our culture has moved from absolutist modes of thought towards a historical and psychological view of man. But though the Renaissance moment made the tension between a magical and an empirical view of man particularly acute, this pull is of course always present: it is the tension between the heart and the world. By incarnating ritual as plot and character, the dramatist finds an embodiment for the heart's drastic gestures while recognizing how the world keeps comically and tragically giving them the lie.

Echoes of Art

Dudley Andrew

"**I** wrote and directed this film; my name is Orson Welles." His voice leaves the most lasting impression even as the image of the microphone swings away from us at the end of *The Magnificent Ambersons*. Welles' voice is resonant and voluminous, satisfyingly thick. It is, as much as possible, the voice of God, confident because omniscient, demanding that we hearken to it and interpret our situation in relation to its message. If this feeling is greatest in *The Magnificent Ambersons,* where paradoxically he hides behind the camera, it emanates just as surely from his other films: the booming voices of Kane, Hank Quinlan, the Advocate, and Gregory Arkadin; the subtly modulated roles which that voice adopts in the Shakespeare films where he would render up to eight different parts. Because of the genius of his own voice and the experience this gift opened up for him first in the theater and then in radio, Welles was able to break decisively with Hollywood sound practice and to give to his films a new tone bearing an unaccustomed feeling.

Welles' sound practice is first perceived as a problem to be overcome. Particularly in his European films, dialogue is so muffled that in many instances it is incomprehensible at first hearing. This has always been attributed to the cheap postsynchronization his budgets required. Yet we find already in the RKO films the first seeds of a conception of sound necessitating increased audience acuity. Dialogue overlaps would seem to be the key to this new method, but more central is Welles' practice of microphone placement in conjunction with the overlaps. *Citizen Kane* and *The Magnificent Ambersons* abound in examples in which a close-up voice will unexpectedly smother a conversation taking place at mid-distance, or where a boisterous exchange will be followed by whispering or sobbing. Altogether these oppositions produce a veritable audio space in which events take place. Obviously adopted from the techniques spawned by dramatic radio production, this spatializing of the sound track is built up through throat-miking for whisper effects, apparent directional sound, reverberation, and high-level ambient noise inclusion. Such extended space is put into play in conjunction

From *Film in the Aura of Art* (Princeton: Princeton University Press, 1984), pp. 164–171.

with a heightened use of the conventional "sound off." In the Amberson mansion voices emanate from unseen rooms (the good-night scene after the ball) and huge doors when pushed closed off-camera. Sound so dominated Welles' conception of this film that most sequences are designed to integrate audio information with the fewest possible camera positions. We have mentioned already the single-take sequences in the kitchen, at the train station, and of the Major before the fire. These are static scenes, readily accessible to the single angle. Welles goes beyond this in certain action scenes where one couple walking in conversation will pass out of view urging the camera to pick up what the sound track is already giving to us, a second conversation of a second couple. It is the flow of conversation that dictates the rhythm of this film and the role of the camera. Doubtless, over the course of ninety minutes a much larger, more atmospheric space is represented than we are accustomed to, thanks to which this comedy of manners, this satire, can affect us with unusual power.

Touted for his expressionist visual sense, Welles' most signal moments come to us from devices realized on the sound track. When placed counter to the image, the voice delivers rhetoric or irony, as in the haughty recitation of the Holinshed Chronicles or in the narrator's judgment toward the end of *Ambersons:* "George Amberson Minafer had got his comeuppance, had got it three times full and running over." On other occasions the sound track, far from smugly commenting on what we see, is the very vehicle of pathos: Welles' most outrageously authoritative voice screaming, "You can't do this to me Gettys. I'm Charles Foster Kane," the murmurs following Isabel Amberson's death, the train whistle calling Jack away after her funeral, the phone call Tania makes prefiguring the downfall of Quinlan, Quinlan's own voice betrayed by a walkie-talkie in the final moments of *Touch of Evil,* Joseph K. pleading for justice to a raucous courtroom in *The Trial* and the pathetic ditty sung as he awaits the blast of the dynamite. Added to all these scripted effects is the continual friction of ambient noise and choral voicing which thicken the image, dragging it toward its slow decline.

Welles' fascination with the possibilities of sound culminates in his *Chimes at Midnight.* Perhaps the greatest adaptation of Shakespeare that the cinema has yet produced, this is also the adaptation most difficult physically to hear. Lines are delivered at lightning speed, often over the shoulder, mixed with the dialogue or laughter of other characters, by quick turns bellowed, then murmured. Some viewers find it maddening to find our greatest poet left to the mercy of Welles with his bizarre sense of sound mixing and of pace. They prefer the Olivier films where every speech is directed to the audience, amplified by the closed shell of its decor, separated from neighboring speeches by studied silences if not actual changes in camera setup. In this way we miss not a line; indeed we might think of *Henry V* or *Hamlet* as films based on Shakespeare's *writing* whereas *Chimes at Midnight* is tied to the actor's *voice*. *Henry V,* especially, with its Duc de Berry sets, is an embellishment of a sacred text, truly a manuscript illuminated by the three-strip Technicolor filmstock and by the bright light of the projection arc. In contrast, Welles violated the sanctity of the manuscript, piecing and patching a single film from the fragments of five different plays. Instead of a *text* which comfortingly remains behind the scenes and outlasts the film, Welles gives us a *voice* disconcertingly disappearing over time. Welles has taken as his model not the immortal Bard but "a poor player that struts and frets his hour upon the stage and then is heard no more."

Shakespeare, even Shakespeare, cannot outlast deterioration in time and diminution in space. Once again Welles has put forth an immense power, here the greatest dramatist the world has known, only to listen to it echo away inconsequentially in an infinitude of natural space and time. The effect is the more disturbing for the simplicity of its means. Whereas the techniques of transition, of embedding, and of parable all depend upon the magician's panoply of tricks, Welles also knows how to devastate through sheer sound recording.

Far from betraying theater, cinema here bestows upon it a most intimate gift, to let its cultured speeches contend with the wind of a truly open space, to test human struggle in the vast stretches of inhuman time. Recall Gielgud as the king in his cold, enormous castle, Hotspur spewing forth heroic epithets on the windy hill, or Falstaff discoursing white-robed in the birch forest . . . the words of all these die out as we hear them, are carried away by the wind they cannot hush. Thus, the nostalgia expressed in the prologue ("Where have they all gone? Dead, all dead") comes through the sound track to haunt every moment of the film. Only the Holinshed Chronicles, read imperiously by Ralph Richardson, pretends to outlast the events it comments on. Yet this is precisely that official view of history and of life satirized by the human life of the Boar's Head, by the flesh of Shakespeare's verse, and by the raspiness of the actors delivering that verse. Despite its victory over impersonal monumentality, such realism pays a price, the price of transition, deterioration, and mortality. Welles' great reverberating laugh is locked within the body of Falstaff borne off in a box at the end to be lowered deep into the earth.

Despite his background in theater and the evident theatricality of his personality, Orson Welles is fully a man of the cinema, if by this we mean someone whose most profound realizations are made possible in this medium. The illusory quality of the image, the magic-trick effects of motion picture technology, the depth of sound, and the shallowness of the screen all contribute to the expression of Welles' meditations on authenticity, mirage, impermanence, and loss.

First Bazin and now Roland Barthes have written evocatively of the relation of photography to death.[1] The image is the trace left by an object gone before us in time. More than representing that object, it expresses its absence. And yet the animating power of motion confers on the cinema a vibrancy missing from the still photograph. Barthes recognized this in his classic formulation: "Film can no longer be seen as animated photographs: the *having-been-there* gives way before a *being-there* of the thing."[2] Popular criticism supports Barthes' distinction. Movies are thought of as the artform that captures life, brings to life, animates our dreams, and so on.

Welles is one of those few directors (Truffaut is another) whose overriding obsession with the past and death goes against the grain of the medium even while it is best expressed in that medium. How does he distort the moving image to make it figure its own demise? We have already encountered his most calculated strategy for this in the embedded story. By consigning his images to a teller, especially when that teller is representing a past event, Welles manages to frame what we see like an expanded still photograph. The images of Kane at the newspaper office or at the opera or at Xanadu may affect us greatly but part of what we feel about them is their distance from us. Unable to break out of the temporal boundary constructed for them, they are the property of the teller who recounts them. Once again Welles plays with the tension between power and debility, this time between the strength of living pictures and our realization that these are of the past.

Doubtless this tension gives to *Chimes at Midnight* a sentiment absent even from the Shakespearean original. Not only is the life at the Boar's Head contrasted with the tomblike empire at the court, that life has already been put into the realm of memory by the rueful preface where two old men reflect upon the days that they have seen, all gone. The film then operates under two time schemes, that of the eternal history of the Plantagenets as chronicled in the heroic language of Holinshed, and that of the mortal history of Falstaff and the common

---

1. André Bazin, "The Ontology of the Photographic Image," *What Is Cinema?* (Berkeley and Los Angeles: University of California Press, 1967), pp. 10–15. Roland Barthes, *Camera Lucida* (New York: Hill and Wang, 1980).

2. Roland Barthes, *Image, Music, Text*, trans. Stephen Heath (New York: Hill and Wang, 1977), p. 44.

folk, livingly expressed in the human verse of Shakespeare. We must add to this that other nostalgia for Shakespeare himself which Welles is able to inject into the film, a regret for a time now gone when life and history could be so completely and satisfyingly represented.

In all his films the images arrange themselves in such a way as to embody the notion of loss and death. They obliterate themselves in the characters' flow away from the camera, in the deep shadows that settle on them, in the contrived quaintness of their presentation, and of course in the architectural structures that dominate the compositions (sepulchral rooms, old castles, timeless and inhuman spaces).

We watch Welles' films not as living artifacts emerging into our present, but as traces of a power that once was. We want to be astounded by the strength of that power even while the greater power of time reduces this strength to dust, to memory. While it is true that Welles indecorously promotes this reading of his films through overt references to death and loss lodged in the dialogue or contributed by the morbid voice of the narrator, the tone of the past and of things passing is constantly maintained by the work of the sound track. For an image is always potentially graspable, sight being, as Walter Ong urges, a most possessive sense as it seizes views like postcards.[3] But sound is the sense of hearkening, of vocation. Its source remains outside us, profoundly in the Other. When, as in Welles, this source retreats from us, we are left with a nostalgia for the full-throated presence left in its echo on the sound track. In short, unlike the simple pastness of the still photograph, Welles' films are simultaneously grand and gone; we are present to their fading.

To characterize this effect critics have called upon a series of spatial metaphors: the cavernous volume of his images, the screen as window onto a vanishing point which swallows up the figures that had loomed so large. Our meditation on sound and on temporality suggests other, potentially corrective metaphors. These films do not dwell on something that once was close and now is far away; instead their source, like some original vibrating chord, is settled deep within them, producing a tone which, through successive borrowings, modulations, usages, and distortions, is transformed into the gaudy surface of the films. But the inauthenticity of this showman's technique still serves as a great volume for the vibrations of life within it. In other words, the very hollowness of Welles' personal world view, the emptiness of his paradoxes, his characters, and his tricky plots, prepares us for the sound of something in its core.

3. Walter Ong, *The Presence of the Word* (New Haven: Yale University Press, 1967), pp. 166–168.

Although unrecoverable in literal fact, it is wrong to suggest that this something (this authentic feeling or formulation) is utterly lost in the past. For the tense of Welles' films is never that of the simple past, but of the historical preterite. No event in his film floats free; all are bound up in an historical account which Heidegger would call "recollection in care." [4] And even when, at his most relentless, as in *Chimes at Midnight* or *The Magnificent Ambersons,* he questions the very histories that hold the past so dear, Welles effectively encloses time in the giant box of his narration. He may no longer feel able to touch the real life of Merrie England, nor that of Shakespeare, but he can allude to them, or rather (to maintain our metaphor) he can permit something of their sound to vibrate the empty space he has fashioned around them.

He has, in both senses of the term, *related* something to us. In this way his films are repetitions of a care about mortality, repetitions to which we can now add our own meditation which is related to and relates his subject. The cultural extension this produces is, Ricoeur would suggest, an artistic compensation for the essentially nontransferable character of death. [5] If our criticism is a mere echo of his films, Welles' corpus itself issues up an echo of art and through art the tremolo of something feeble but authentic by which we sense both feeling and life.

4. Martin Heidegger, *Being and Time,* trans. Macquerrie and Robinson (New York: Harper & Row, 1962), pp. 437, 438.
5. Paul Ricoeur, "Narrative Time," *Critical Inquiry* 7 (Autumn 1980), 188–190.

"Every Third Word a Lie": Rhetoric and History in Orson Welles's *Chimes at Midnight*

Michael Anderegg

Chimes at Midnight has come to be recognized, over the last decade or so, both as one of the most intelligent and imaginative of films adapted from Shakespeare and as one of Orson Welles's finest achievements, a film at least equal in energy and brilliance to *Citizen Kane* and *The Magnificent Ambersons*.[1] The chorus of praise occasionally includes a few sour notes, however; as so often with Welles's post–*Citizen Kane* films, various qualifications temper even highly enthusiastic assessments.[2] Criticism tends to center on the sound track and on the uncertain relationship between sound and image: the recording is technically faulty, Shakespeare's words are frequently unintelligible (Welles's Falstaff, in particular, is difficult to understand much of the time), several sequences are poorly synchronized, and, disconcertingly, a number of the minor actors have been dubbed by Welles himself—all signs that inadequate financing forced artistic compromise. Additionally, critics find fault with Welles for the film's haphazard continuity and for a general inattention to detail, especially in the casting and playing of the secondary roles. In short, *Chimes at Midnight* is often discussed in terms that remind us of Shakespeare's Sir John Falstaff him-

From *Film Quarterly* 40 (Spring 1987): 18–24.

1. See, for example, Joseph McBride, *Orson Welles* (New York: Viking Press, 1972); James Naremore, *The Magic World of Orson Welles* (New York: Oxford University Press, 1978); Samuel Crowl, "The Long Goodbye: Welles and Falstaff," *Shakespeare Quarterly* 31 (Autumn 1980): 369–380; and the comments of David Bordwell ("*Citizen Kane*," *Film Comment* 7 [1971]:6–11); both of these essays have been reprinted in *Movies and Methods*, ed. Bill Nichols (Berkeley and Los Angeles: University of California Press, 1976).

2. Most of the negative points are summarized by Jack Jorgens in *Shakespeare on Film* (Bloomington: Indiana University Press, 1977); Jorgens, however, provides a generally positive analysis. See also Charles Higham, *The Films of Orson Welles* (Berkeley and Los Angeles: University of California Press, 1970); Higham writes of Welles's "impatience with detail and finalization that, combined with [his] tragic perennial lack of funds, have left the work just short of the triumph it should have been" (p. 177).

self: attractive, vibrant, large, complex, but, withal, so deeply flawed as to negate many of its virtues.

In this essay, I would like to place both the unquestioned successes and the supposed defects of *Chimes at Midnight* within the context of what I take to be the film's governing strategy: the rewriting of Shakespeare's text, a rewriting that includes an attempted erasure of writing, a critique of rhetoric, an undermining of language itself. Taking up what is undeniably present in Shakespeare—no writer shows more awareness of the dangerous seductiveness of words—Welles carries the questioning of language much further than Shakespeare, whose primary resource was language, ever could. *Chimes at Midnight* centers squarely on a conflict between rhetoric and history, on the one hand, and the immediacy of a pre-linguistic, pre-lapsarian, timeless physical world, on the other. This conflict comes to us primarily through the actions and character of Falstaff, as we might expect, but it informs as well the texture and style of each moment of Welles's film. With remarkable boldness, Welles has made a Shakespearean film in which poetry itself seems to undergo a rigorous devaluation.

To a certain extent, of course, Welles had to rewrite Shakespeare as part of the process of adaptation: no Shakespearean film reproduces Shakespeare's text in its entirety (nor, for that matter, do most stage productions). But Welles's editorial decisions nevertheless aim at a particular end and have a specific focus. He compresses and reshapes his source material at will, reducing it to a bare minimum of words. Drawing primarily on *Henry IV, Parts I* and *II*, adding a few lines from *Richard II, Henry V,* and *The Merry Wives of Windsor,* Welles gives Shakespeare's story of a prince's coming of age a single plot line and a new emphasis. Critics have often noted that *Henry IV, Part II,* in many ways recapitulates, albeit in a different key, the structure and theme of *Part I:* Shakespeare presents two scenes of reconciliation between Hal and his father, two military engagements (Shrewsbury and Galtree Forest), two moments when Hal realizes his destiny, and so forth. Welles, while doing away with much of this repetition, shifts scenes and parts of scenes around at his convenience, placing Falstaff's recruitment of soldiers in *Part II,* for example, before *Part I's* battle of Shrewsbury. Although Welles's refashioning of Shakespeare's text(s) has a number of consequences, the primary effect is to shift the thematic emphasis away from Hal and towards Falstaff, or, to put it another way, away from history and towards satire.[3]

---

3. Samuel Crowl, cited above, convincingly demonstrates that "Welles's overriding visual and structural emphasis is to signal farewell, to say a long goodbye to Falstaff, rather than to celebrate Hal's homecoming to princely right reason and responsible rule" (p. 373).

The critique of history in *Chimes at Midnight* completes a process already begun by Shakespeare, but Welles's attack is harsher, his conclusion far less optimistic. "History," for the purposes of my argument, includes the whole world of kings and politics, of war and chivalry, as well as the language, the rhetoric, which is that world's chief expressive medium. Shakespeare's Henriad comprehends a set of binary oppositions—Court/Tavern, Honor/Dishonor, Hotspur/Falstaff, Henry IV/Falstaff, Time/Timelessness, Word/Being, Serious/Non-serious—where either the first term is the privileged one or where both terms have been suspended in an uneasy equilibrium, leaving to Hal the task of determining which to choose, or if indeed a choice has to be made at all. In Welles's film, these paired alternatives are unbalanced, diminished, reversed, or exploded. Shakespeare's Hal has always already made the choice, though he appears to be choosing all the time. For Welles's Hal, the choice poses genuine and insoluble problems.[4] The various embodiments of "positive" values, what I have simply termed "History," have little exemplary force in *Chimes at Midnight,* tending at times to degenerate, at the level of language, into the incoherent babbling of poseurs, cynics, and fools. At the same time, any attempt to abolish language, to ignore the power of words, leads inevitably to destruction. Here, Falstaff stands as the cautionary figure, and his desire to abolish language and put sheer physicality in its place becomes the tragic fulcrum upon which Welles's film turns.

Welles's strategy for undermining history and rhetoric only begins with the process of adaptation. His tactics are primarily stylistic. History and (verbal) rhetoric are constantly displaced, replaced by Welles's nervous, erratic, decentered, unstable visual and aural style, a flow of images and sounds that thoroughly dismantle Shakespeare's text, peeling away layers of strategically placed and carefully joined verbal and thematic checks against disintegration. In this context, the supposed problems with the sound track become less a matter of technical flaws (though flaws there are, as Welles has publicly lamented), and more a question of Welles's intentions and methods.[5] In some shots, for example, the actors deliver their lines as they, or the camera, or both, are in rapid motion.

4. For a sensitive discussion of Hal's role in Welles's film, see Leland Poague, "Reading the Prince: Shakespeare, Wells, and Some Aspects of *Chimes at Midnight," Iowa State Journal of Research* 56 (August 1981):57–65.
5. Dudley Andrew's comments on the nature of Welles's sound track in *Chimes at Midnight* and in other films closely parallel my own observations. See *Film in the Aura of Art* (Princeton, N.J.: Princeton University Press, 1984), pp. 164–168.

Or a character will make an important speech from the depth of an extreme long shot, depriving us of lip movement and facial expression, both important cues for the understanding of unfamiliar language and syntax. Furthermore, Welles constructs jarring editing patterns that easily distract from the spoken word. At several points, even what Welles has structured to resemble continuity editing turns into something unexpected. A simple reverse shot, for example, may involve illogical changes in time and/or space. These and other stylistic idiosyncrasies help to explain why we can follow the sound track of *Chimes at Midnight* more easily if we keep our eyes closed. In effect, Welles generates a constant tension between what we see and what we hear, a tension that points to the ambiguous status of language in its relation to action.

Welles further exhibits his ambivalence towards rhetoric in his handling of soliloquies. In his previous Shakespearean films, Welles had already suggested some discomfort with filmed soliloquies, resorting to a variety of voice-over techniques in *Macbeth,* and in *Othello* having some of his actors deliver soliloquies and speeches with their backs to the camera. In *Chimes,* Welles virtually does away with soliloquies as such by not allowing anyone to speak directly to the camera or to be truly alone: Hal's revelation (in Shakespeare, to the audience only) that his madcap humor is primarily for show ("I know you all") is spoken in Falstaff's presence; Falstaff delivers both his catechism on honor and his later dissertation on the virtues of sherris-sack directly to Hal. Even King Henry is not allowed a true soliloquy. His famous meditation on sleep, to choose a notable instance, though filmed in a single, uninterrupted take and in close-up, becomes an address to his courtiers; he is not, as he is in the play, alone. All soliloquies have thus become, at least implicitly, attempts at conversation, at communication within the diegetic universe, and not, as soliloquies can be, privileged moments where language provides a more or less unmediated access to thought.

We can see Welles's strategy ideally realized at that moment when Hotspur— whose bath has been interrupted by the pressing demands of history—cries "That roan shall be my throne" and simultaneously drops the towel in which he has draped himself and turns away from the camera, revealing his bare behind. Hotspur's towel falls in the midst of a highly rhetorical gesture, a wide sweep of the arm that serves as punctuation for his words. Welles comically undermines Hotspur's rhetoric, lays bare his linguistic bravado, and ridicules his historical pretensions, his (partly unconscious) desire for the English throne. Hotspur's words have already been mocked throughout this scene by the trumpeters who echo his belligerent posings with elaborate, comic fanfares. The trumpets say as much as he does, and are equally meaningful as rational statement. Hotspur's dropped towel suggests an additional meaning as well, one contiguous with that just described: for a moment, Hotspur reveals the physical he tries to deny or push aside in the semi-playful, semi-serious exchange with his wife, Kate, that follows this scene. The dropped towel signifies the return of the repressed, cancelling Hotspur's attempt to replace sensuality with rhetoric (war, history, etc.), to deny the body by asserting the word.

In what is perhaps the most remarkable sequence in *Chimes at Midnight*, the battle of Shrewsbury, Welles presents us with another kind of history—a history stripped of all rhetoric, denuded of language, and at the same time supremely eloquent. Here, the rhetorical dismemberment of the body politic, the scenes of accusation and counter-accusation between the royal party and the highborn conspirators, becomes displaced and mocked by the literal dismemberment of the body physical. Welles's style forcefully underlines the brutal, unheroic character of hand-to-hand combat in a nervously edited mosaic of varied shots, some photographed with a handheld camera, some filmed with wide-angle lenses, some in slow motion, some speeded up, some shots static and others that employ swish pans or other kinds of rapid movement, together with a complex, many-layered sound track of shouts and screams, of the clash of sword against sword, armor against armor, of grunts and cries and cracking bones. Welles conjures up Armegeddon, a nightmare vision of destruction which points up the futility of this or any other war. By the end, both armies have become one huge, awkward, disintegrating war machine, a grotesque robot whose power source slowly begins to fail and finally comes to a frozen halt. Verbal rhetoric—language itself—seems, for the moment, both irrelevant and obscene.

In this context, the highly verbal King Henry IV, the only character in the film whose words and speeches are allowed their full Shakespearean weight and style, stands in ironic counterpoint to the carnage of Shrewsbury. As John Gielgud plays him, and as Welles directs his scenes, King Henry is reduced to a nearly disembodied voice. The most "poetic" and rhetorical figure in Welles's film, he is also the most ethereal. Cold, pinched, ascetic, photographed sitting on or standing near his throne set on a high stone platform, his face illuminated by a harsh, white light, he is an isolated, distant figure of overbearing but brittle authority. As Falstaff seems to be all flesh, Henry seems all words. But even the king's voice fails him: he can neither govern his son with it nor tame the rebels, who refuse to credit his verbal promises. Henry's highly rhetorical manner, meant to gloss over his insecurities and fears, finally serves to reveal them. His voice becomes an object of parody: at various points in the film, Hotspur, Hal, and Falstaff all imitate Gielgud's immediately recognizable vocal characteristics. The "beauty" of Henry's speech only serves to place in an even harsher light his asceticism, coldness, and largely self-imposed isolation; a supreme poseur, he cannot see beyond his role. Although never really alone, Henry seems to speak only to himself.

King Henry's dependence on words becomes ideally focused in a scene Welles has totally refashioned from Shakespeare. After the battle of Shrewsbury, Falstaff takes credit for killing Hotspur, spinning another one of his outrageous lies for Hal's benefit. Welles gives the scene a special emphasis by having King Henry present as Falstaff tells his tale. The king, for once, says nothing, and Hal, too, is silent, but their faces tell a clear enough story. Earlier, Hal had told his father that he would redeem himself for his bad behavior "on Percy's head / And in the closing of some glorious day, / Be bold to tell you that I am your son." Now is the moment when this prophecy should come true, when the moving rhetoric should be realized in action. But Hal fails to make good on his promise. Unwilling to expose Falstaff, he refuses to say the words his father so much wants to hear, and the moment slips by. The silence, emphasized by a series of static closeups, takes on precise thematic significance. We can tell, from Henry's expression, that he knows very well who killed Hotspur, but the knowledge, without the words, is not enough. We see, too, the conflict within Hal. And, finally, we can read in Falstaff's face his understanding of what the other two are thinking. For all three as well as for us, silence acquires a rhetorical force ordinarily reserved to speech.[6]

If the world of kings overvalues words, the tavern world fatally undervalues them. In the tavern world, which for my purposes includes the Justice Shallow scenes, words are acknowledged to mean very little. Falstaff's notorious lies, and the ease with which everyone sees through them, are symptomatic, but many of his cohorts share his linguistic deviance. Shallow constantly reminisces about the old days, but "every third word" he speaks, according to Falstaff, is "a lie." Falstaff's hanger-on, Ancient Pistol, is perhaps the most unintelligible character in the film. In Shakespeare, he is already rhetorically tedious; his primary function is to cast in ironic light, through high-flown speeches and outrageous behav-

---

6. John Gielgud later recalled that "we never did the scene at all. On the last day Orson said, 'There's a close-up I have to do of you, just look down there, that's Hotspur's body, now look up at me'" (Gyles Brandreth, *John Gielgud: A Celebration* [Boston: Little, Brown and Company, 1984], p. 152).

ior, the chivalric code. But in a world where rhetoric and history are so constantly and thoroughly brought into question, Welles takes the extreme course of reducing Pistol to little more than noise. Against Pistol's meaningless bombast, we have Silence's inability to say anything at all. Welles afflicts him with a stutter so severe that he cannot complete his sentences. Shallow must speak for him, must become in effect his voice (a nice joke in a film where so many characters are clearly dubbed). Words are interchangeable, attach themselves to no one in particular, have no individual meaning. Speech, in short, appears to be as debased through undervaluing in the tavern world as it is debased through overvaluing in the court world.

The difficulty of penetrating language, of determining the truth and weight of words, of reading history, comes to be, in especial, Falstaff's dilemma. Falstaff distrusts words; in a sense, he himself has nothing to say, certainly nothing with which to answer King Henry, who is all speech, all words, the very incarnation of *logos*. Falstaff's own words are frequently unintelligible, or nearly so, because he wants to deny the efficacy of language. (Welles the actor here exaggerates his post–*Citizen Kane* tendency to downplay the orotund and avuncular qualities of his vocal delivery by deliberately "throwing away" words and lines and even entire speeches.) But, though words may be questioned, subverted, and parodied, they cannot be abolished. Falstaff's refusal to credit words at all leads to his undoing. Even Hal's words—especially Hal's words—mean little to Falstaff, though Hal is at great pains throughout to make his motives clear. Welles's presentation of Hal, an attractive, appealing prince as played by Keith Baxter, runs counter to some modern, especially theatrical, views of the Henriad which condemn Hal as a cold, hypocritical careerist who cynically uses Falstaff for his own ends. Instead, Welles deliberately distorts Shakespeare's text at several points in order to stress Hal's straightforwardness. I've already noted that Hal's revealing "I know you all" meditation is no longer a soliloquy in the film; it is delivered in Falstaff's hearing, the second half of it spoken directly to him. Similarly, when Hal, speaking as his father at the end of the famous play scene, tells Falstaff that he will indeed banish him ("I do; I will"), he gives the words a moving, elegiac tone that renders their meaning unmistakable to anyone not as bent on self-deception as Falstaff is.

Against language, Falstaff posits being, presence, physicality. We are made aware, throughout Welles's film, of Falstaff as sheer physical mass. His huge figure—sometimes just his face alone—often dominates the frame. Although he enters the film in the depth of an extreme long shot, a small, round object on the horizon, he gradually moves toward the camera until his head alone fills over three-fourths of the image, leaving what remains to his companion, Shallow. In the play scene, two men and a boy must help Falstaff onto his makeshift "throne." Before the battle of Shrewsbury, his followers valiantly attempt to raise him to his saddle with block and tackle, only to drop his armor-encased body to the ground. At the Boar's Head tavern, stairways and corridors seem too narrow for his passage. The point is made most strikingly in the Gadshill episode, where Falstaff's monk's robe transforms him into a huge white tent which sharply contrasts with the thin, black trees that surround him. Falstaff's girth is, of course, a running joke in Shakespeare, but Welles goes out of his way to elaborate on the theme; he seems intent on suggesting the extent to which Falstaff's world is physical, corporeal, of the flesh. Falstaff's relationships are expressed in predominently tactile ways, his rotund figure giving others, especially Hal and Doll Tearsheet, something to grasp, to hold on to, or—in Doll's case—to climb on.

Although Welles has said that, for him, Falstaff was "the greatest conception of a good man, the most completely good man, in all drama," [7] *Chimes at Midnight* presents a far more ambivalent portrait of Falstaff than these words suggest. We cannot doubt that Welles sympathizes, both as director and as actor, with Falstaff's desire to bypass language and thereby gain access to an unmediated reality. At the same time, we know, and Welles knows, that in a fallen world, such a desire is folly. And we know as well that, like many Wellesian heroes, Falstaff longs for an Edenic world only because he has long since forfeited it. Welles's Falstaff is far from the jolly knight seen in various theatrical interpretations of the role. Rather, he seems more the corrupt, gross "misleader of youth" that Hal and others claim he is. Some readers have seen two Falstaffs emerging from the two parts of *Henry IV*, the second considerably less pleasant than the first. But whether the Falstaff of *Part II* is really a different character from the Falstaff of *Part I*, or whether he evolves naturally in the course of the two plays, Welles chose to combine both Falstaffs in his performance. Welles's Falstaff is, in Beverle Houston's felicitous phrase, a "Power Baby," an "eating, sucking, foetus-like creature" [8] whose benignity is an illusion. Pre-linguistic, he is forever locked in the imaginary world of infancy. Like Kane, like Arkadin, like Quinlan, like Clay, Falstaff is fundamentally, irredeemably corrupt. A larger-than-life figure flawed by hubris, he tragically collaborates in his own destruction.

Falstaff's defeat has a specifically linguistic dimension: Hal's rejection of him

---

7. Juan Cobos and Miguel Rubio, "Welles and Falstaff," *Sight and Sound* 35 (Autumn 1966):159.
8. "Power and Dis-Integration in the Films of Orson Welles," *Film Quarterly* 35 (Summer 1982):2.

is a rhetorical act, the new king of England's maiden speech, the son's entrance into the symbolic world of his father. (By staging this scene in the midst of the coronation ceremony, Welles puts the emphasis as much on Hal's humiliation as on Falstaff's.) Falstaff's response to Hal's elaborate, majestic, and witty rebuke is nonverbal: we must read it in Welles's expression. What we see are emotions in conflict: awe, perhaps pride (this is *his* king, after all), and a wistfulness not unmixed with cunning (is he already thinking of a "starting hole," a way out?). The dominant emotion, however, is disbelief: Hal's words cannot be meaningful, they are rhetoric only; Falstaff sees through and beyond them. Shakespeare's Falstaff, we feel, indulges himself in sheer bravado when he tells Shallow "This that you heard was but a color . . . I shall be sent for soon at night." For Welles's Falstaff, these words suggest not bravado so much as a deeply felt hope, a nearly desperate attempt to render words meaningless. But Hal not only means what he says, he now has the power to turn words into deeds, and his words and deeds kill Falstaff.

In keeping with his method throughout the film, Welles strips even Falstaff's death of easy sentiment. Mistress Quickly's description of Falstaff's last moments functions as a piece of information for a clearly unmoved Poins; spoken with Falstaff already in his coffin, her words lack the immediacy they have in Shakespeare's *Henry V.* Welles barely prepares us for this crucial finale: one moment Falstaff is alive, if crushed; the next moment he is dead. No illness, no tears, no bedside scene as in Laurence Olivier's film of *Henry V.* Only a final irony: words continue to fail Falstaff, even after death. In a complete departure from Shakespeare's text, Welles concludes his film with the image of Falstaff's coffin passing away in the distance while on the sound track Ralph Richardson recites a passage from Holinshed's *Chronicles of England, Scotland, and Ireland,* a passage in praise of King Henry V, who, we are told, "was so humane withal that he left no offense unpunished or friendship unrewarded." [9] Whatever we may think of the truth or justice of Holinshed's words, one irony, at least, is certain: in *Chimes at Midnight,* a film that thoroughly reveals the hollowness of kings and their fine words, language and history stubbornly abide when all else is gone. [10]

9. Stanley S. Rubin discusses Welles's use of Holinshed as a narrative device in "Welles/Falstaff/Shakespeare/Welles: The Narrative Structure of *Chimes at Midnight," Film Criticism* 2 (Winter/Spring 1978):66–71.

10. By the end of Welles's film, Andrew McLean notes, "An epoch has passed, a world view has altered, and a new historical consciousness has been born" ("Orson Welles and Shakespeare: History and Consciousness in *Chimes at Midnight," Literature/Film Quarterly* 11 [1983]:202).

Filmography and Bibliography

Welles Filmography, 1941–1978

This filmography lists only feature films of Orson Welles that have actually been released. For each of those films, script sources and scriptwriters are cited. The most detailed account of unreleased works and unrealized projects, a substantial category in Welles's career, can be found in Jonathan Rosenbaum's article, "The Invisible Orson Welles" (*Sight and Sound* 55, Summer 1986). Listings of Welles's projects in theater, radio, and television, as well as a record of his film appearances as an actor or narrator, can be found in the works by Peter Cowie, Joseph McBride, and James Naremore listed in the Bibliography.

1941 *Citizen Kane*
Original screenplay by Welles and Herman J. Mankiewicz, with the assistance of John Houseman. For a full account of the authorship of the film, see Robert Carringer, *The Making of Citizen Kane* (Berkeley and Los Angeles: University of California Press, 1985).

1942 *The Magnificent Ambersons*
Screenplay by Welles, based on the novel by Booth Tarkington (New York, 1918; reprint, New York: Arbor House, 1986).

1943 *Journey into Fear,* directed with Norman Foster, Welles uncredited.
Screenplay by Welles and Joseph Cotton, based on the novel by Eric Ambler (New York: Knopf, 1940).

1946 *The Stranger*
Screenplay by Anthony Veiller, with the assistance of Welles and John

Huston, based on a story by Victor Trivas and Decla Dunning.

1946   *The Lady from Shanghai*
Screenplay by Welles, based on *If I Should Die before I Wake*, a novel by Sherwood King (New York: Simon & Schuster, 1938).

1948   *Macbeth*
Screenplay by Welles, adapted from the play by Shakespeare.

1952   *Othello*
Screenplay by Welles, adapted from the play by Shakespeare.

1955   *Mr. Arkadin* (British title: *Confidential Report*)
Screenplay by Welles, based on his own novel, *Mr. Arkadin* (Paris: Gallimard, 1954; London: W. H. Allen, 1956; New York: Crowell, 1959).

1958   *Touch of Evil*
Screenplay by Welles, adapted from an earlier script by Paul Monash, based on *Badge of Evil*, a novel by Whit Masterson, a pseudonym for Robert A. Wade and H. Billy Miller (New York: Dodd, Mead, 1956).

1962   *The Trial*
Screenplay by Welles, based on the novel by Franz Kafka.

1966   *Chimes at Midnight* (later U.S. title: *Falstaff*)
Screenplay by Welles, adapted from Shakespeare's *Henry IV, Parts 1 and 2*, with additional material from *Richard II, Henry V*, and *The Merry Wives of Windsor*. Additional narrative commentary from Raphael Holinshed's *Chronicles* (1577, 1587).

1968   *The Immortal Story*
Screenplay by Welles, based on a story in *Anecdotes of Destiny* by Isak Dinesen, a pseudonym for Karen Blixen (New York, 1958; reprint, New York: Vintage Books, 1985).

1973   *F for Fake*
Screenplay by Welles, employing material from an earlier film by François Reichenbach.

1978   *Filming Othello*
Documentary conceived by Welles, with Welles as participant and commentator.

Selected Bibliography

Anderegg, Michael. " 'Every Third Word A Lie': Rhetoric and History in Orson Welles's *Chimes at Midnight.*" *Film Quarterly* 40 (Spring 1987): 18–24.

Andrew, Dudley. "Echoes of Art." In *Film in the Aura of Art.* Princeton: Princeton University Press, 1984.

Barber, C. L. "Rule and Misrule in *Henry IV.*" In *Shakespeare's Festive Comedy.* Princeton: Princeton University Press, 1959.

Cahiers du Cinéma, n.s., no. 12 (1982): special issue on Orson Welles.

Cobos, Juan, and Miguel Rubio. "Welles and Falstaff." *Sight and Sound* 35 (Autumn 1966): 158–163.

Cowie, Peter. *A Ribbon of Dreams: The Cinema of Orson Welles.* New York, 1973; reprint, New York: Da Capo, 1983.

Crowl, Samuel. "The Long Goodbye: Welles and Falstaff." *Shakespeare Quarterly* 31 (Autumn 1980): 369–380.

Hapgood, Robert. " 'Chimes at Midnight' from Stage to Screen: The Art of Adaptation." *Shakespeare Survey* 39 (1987): 39–52.

Higham, Charles. *The Films of Orson Welles.* Berkeley and Los Angeles: University of California Press, 1970.

———. *Orson Welles: The Rise and Fall of an American Genius.* New York: St. Martin's Press, 1985.

Johnson, William. "Orson Welles: Of Time and Loss." *Film Quarterly* 21 (Fall 1967): 13–24.

Jorgens, Jack J. *Shakespeare on Film.* Bloomington: Indiana University Press, 1977.

Leaming, Barbara. *Orson Welles.* New York: Viking Press, 1985.

McBride, Joseph. *Orson Welles.* New York: Viking Press, 1972.

Mercury Shakespeare, The. Edited for reading and arranged for staging by Orson Welles and Roger Hill. New York and London: Harper and Brothers, 1939.

McLean, Andrew. "Orson Welles and Shakespeare: History and Conciousness in *Chimes at Midnight.*" *Literature/Film Quarterly* 11 (1983):197–202.

Naremore, James. *The Magic World of Orson Welles.* New York: Oxford University Press, 1978.

Poague, Leland. " 'Reading' the Prince: Shakespeare, Welles, and Some Aspects of *Chimes at Midnight.*" *Iowa State Journal of Research* 56 (August 1981):57–65.

Prior, Moody E. *The Drama of Power: Studies in Shakespeare's History Plays.* Evanston, Ill.: Northwestern University Press, 1973.

Rosenbaum, Jonathan. "The Invisible Orson Welles: A First Inventory." *Sight and Sound* 55 (Summer 1986):164–171.

Wilson, J. Dover. *The Fortunes of Falstaff.* Cambridge: Cambridge University Press, 1945.

Breinigsville, PA USA
17 January 2011
253478BV00002B/114/A